NOTES

I

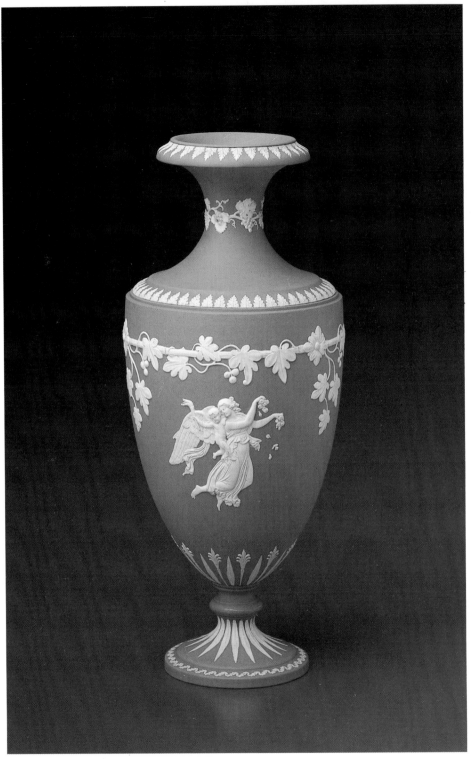

Frontispiece. A brown solid body jasperware urn "Night and Morning" showing Morning Night is on the reverse side. 12″ Incised 1500. Impressed -⫯- 1850/60.

We make our pots of
what we potters are.

(Origin unknown)

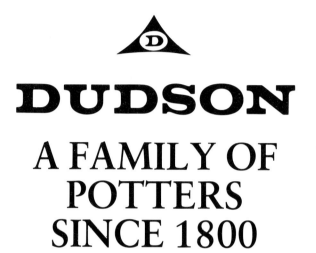

DUDSON

A FAMILY OF POTTERS SINCE 1800

by

AUDREY M. DUDSON B.Sc.

Published by DUDSON PUBLICATIONS
Dudson Brothers Ltd.,
Hope Street,
Hanley,
Stoke-on-Trent,
Staffordshire.

First Published 1985
First Edition Limited to 2000 Copies
© Copyright Audrey Dudson

Photography:

Colour by Gary Leggett. Hanley, Stoke-on-Trent, Staffordshire.

Black and White by Kenneth Edwards. Leek, Staffordshire.

Sprig Moulds by William Lucy. Blakenhall, Nantwich, Cheshire.

Illustrations by Helen Cooper

ISBN 0-9510126-0-6

Printed and Produced in Great Britain
by Rushton and Turner Ltd, Hanley, Stoke-on-Trent, Staffordshire

ACKNOWLEDGMENTS

Help, interest and wonderful support has been received from many organisations and individuals during the years of research work. I must, however, especially acknowledge my indebtedness to the following people. First to my late husband, Derek, whose original idea started the whole project, to my late mother-in-law, May, who patiently sorted, classified and, above all, cleaned the early sooty documents; to Mr. Brian Page who devised with me a way for the two of us to clean all the equally sooty jug and sprig moulds and for his help in many other ways, to the late Mr. Tom Graham whose expert advice and encouragement persuaded me to produce this book. Without their able assistance the work would probably have remained a hobby.

My most grateful thanks are also extended to the following organisations for their assistance in a variety of ways. Mr. A.R. Mountford, Mrs. Pat Halfpenny, Mrs. Kathy Niblett and Mr. A. Townsend of the City Museum and Art Gallery, Hanley; Mr. F.B. Stitt and staff of the William Salt Library, Stafford; the staff of the Staffordshire Record Office; the staff of the Lichfield Joint Record Office; Mr. D. Beard and staff of the Horace Barks Reference Library, Hanley; Mr. Martin Phillips and staff of the Local Collection, Keele University; Dr. Celoria and staff of the Gladstone Pottery Museum; the officers of the Wedgwood Museum, Barlaston; Mr. D. Barker and members of the Hanley Museum Archeological Society; Mrs. E.D. Graham of the Wesleyan Historical Society; Dr. David Murfin and Mr. Wilfred Roberts of the British Ceramic Research Association; members of the North Staffordshire Society of Genealogy.

I am very grateful to the following who have generously given their time and expertise, Mr. M. Berthoud, Mr. P. Bowcock, Mr. C.B. Dudson, Mr. T. Dudson, Mr. G. Elliott, Mr. G. Godden, Mr. R. Haggar, Mr. R. Halson, Mr. R. Hampson, Mr. I. Henderson, Dr. R.K. Henrywood, Mrs. Kathleen Hughes, Mr. J. Kiff, Mr. W. Mayer, Mrs. C. Oxborrow, Mr. William Podmore, Mr. J. Robertson (Canada), Mr. J. Shorter and Mr. R. Thomas (Australia), Mr. R.A. Smith, Dr. Hugh Torrens.

I owe very special thanks to the following, Brian and Margaret Page, Max and Carol Dudson and Russell and Vera Taylor for without their tireless and inspired searching for pieces of Dudson ware the work would not have been possible; to my sister-in-law Helen Cooper for her beautiful art work; to Mrs. Beryl Steele for typing the manuscript, to Dr. G.M. Urquhart for undertaking a considerable proportion of the necessary research work in London and to Mr. W. Lucy for photographing all the sprig moulds so clearly.

Finally, I would like to gratefully thank all the family, directors and staff (present and past) of the Company for their patience, help and support, and all my friends who kindly read the manuscripts.

We gratefully acknowledge that the prosperity and continued existence of the Company, especially during difficult times, also largely depends on the loyalty, skill and efforts of all in the Company's employment.

NOTES

FOREWORD

Turn to any standard work of reference relating to the history and development of the Staffordshire Potteries and you will of course find details of the larger and long-established factories particularly those where records have been wisely preserved. For the vast majority of the smaller firms however (and there were hundreds in the locality during the 19th Century) their story is often limited to a mention in an encyclopaedia of ceramics or perhaps a single entry in a book of marks and countless enterprises disappeared without trace. The overall picture of the Staffordshire Pottery industry is all the poorer for the lack of documentation relating to its smaller "pot-banks" and this absence of the written word has inevitably acted as a deterrent to many a would-be researcher. Fortunately from time to time there emerges a dedicated investigator who has a compelling reason for embarking on an in-depth study of a particular factory. In the case of Audrey Dudson it was the family connection which stimulated the long and patient search for facts and figures. The results of her diligent probings and accumulation of fresh information present us with an enlightening and comprehensive appraisal of a factory which is quickly approaching its second century of continuous manufacture. This carefully researched history of the Dudson factory and its products is a welcome addition to the ceramic library.

2/10/1984

A.R. Mountford, C.B.E.,M.A.,F.M.A.,F.S.A.
Director of Museums
CITY MUSEUM AND ART GALLERY
HANLEY
STOKE-ON-TRENT

CONTENTS

		Page
Foreword by A.R. Mountford		VII
List of illustrations: a) colour plates		X
b) monochrome plates		XII
List of plans and maps		XIII

CHAPTERS

1.	Introduction	1
2.	Richard Dudson 1768 — 1833	3
3.	Richard Dudson Junior 1794 —	12
4.	Thomas Dudson 1786 — 1845. Family History	24
5.	Thomas Dudson The factory site at Hope Street	25
6.	Thomas Dudson. Production	33
7.	Thomas Dudson. Body and colour recipes	47
8.	Thomas Dudson. Conclusion	59
9.	James Dudson 1812 — 1882. Family history	62
10.	James Dudson. Early management — A turbulent start	68
11.	James Dudson. Production	71
12.	James Dudson. Extension to Hope Street factory and conclusion	102
13.	James Thomas Dudson 1841 — 1917 Family History	104
14.	James Thomas Dudson. Production	110
15.	James Thomas Dudson. Conclusion	123
16.	James Robert and Harry Dudson 1898 — 1918. Family History — A tragic period	124
17.	Production 1898 — 1918	126
18.	Dudson, Wilcox & Till Ltd., 1902 — 1926	135
19.	Hubert Dudson 1899 — 1964	141
20.	Post war to present day	150

CONTENTS

	APPENDIX	Page
Appendix A.	The archeological dig	161
Appendix B.	Some notes on the Keeling & Dimmock families	167
Appendix C.	Pottery production 1819 — 25, 1834	171
Appendix D.	Pottery production 1842 — 44	174
Appendix E.	Figure and animal production 1850 s	185
Appendix F.	Basalt, Parian, Lustre and other wares	187
Appendix G.	Mosaic ware 1840 — 1960 s	192
	Leadless patterns 1900 — 1930	193
Appendix H.	Plain coloured body stoneware	195
Appendix I.	Badged ware	198
Appendix J.	Relief moulded stoneware	201
Appendix K.	Jasperware	208
Shapes		215
Marks		222
Photographs of Sprig moulds		225
Bibliography		265
Complete family tree		266
Glossary		268
Index		278

COLOUR PLATES

		Page
Frontispiece, Urn "Night and Morning"		II
1.	Richard Dudson Inkwell	19
2.	Turk's Head Tobacco Jar	20
3a.	Tulip Jugs	21
3b.	Copper Lustre Tulip Jug	21
4.	Relief-Moulded Stoneware Jugs	22
5.	Jasperware Jugs 1850 s	63
6.	Terracotta Tobacco Jar, Enamelled Stoneware Jug and Pink Jasperware Jug	64
7.	Jasperware Kettle, Sucrier and Wheatsheaf Jug	65
8.	Jasperware Jugs Mid 19th Century	66
9.	Jasperware Mid 19th Century	105
10.	Jasperware 1870 s — 1880 s	106
11.	Jasperware Coffee Pot with Widow Finial	107
12.	Turquoise Urn, Coffee Can and Cream Jug	108
13.	Group of Jasperware	115
14.	Mosaic Ware	116
15.	Enamelled Coral Jug and Sprigged Stoneware Jug	117
16.	Majolica Jug and Jasperware 1900 — 1920	118
17.	Jasperware 1900 — 1920	137
18.	Jasperware 1950 — 1965	138
19.	Jasperware 1950 — 1965	139
20.	Hotelware 1950 s	140
21.	Hotelware 1960 s	153
22.	Hotelware 1970 s	154
23.	Dudson Fine China	155
24.	Dudson Fine China Custom Specials	156
25.	A selection of sherds from the Archeological excavation	166

MONOCHROME PLATES

1.	Rear of Hope Street Factory Showing Original Back Lane	36
2.	Black Basalt Jug	38
3.	A Double Faced Tobacco Jar	44
4.	Flower Jug	44
5.	James Dudson	62
6.	James Dudson's Office	69

7.	Jasperware Jug "Wheatsheaf and Hops"	73
8.	China Jug "Pansy"	76
9.	China Cheese Dish	76
10.	Relief-Moulded Stoneware	81
11.	Relief-Moulded Stoneware Jugs	81
12.	Relief-Moulded Stoneware Jugs	82
13.	Relief-Moulded Stoneware	82
14.	Relief-Moulded Jugs	83
15.	Relief-Moulded Jugs	83
16.	Relief-Moulded Jugs	83
17.	Relief-Moulded Stoneware	84
18.	Stoneware Jug 1850 s	84
19.	Master Model For Tulip Jug	85
20.	Master Mould And Case For Tulip Jug	85
21.	A Tulip Jug	85
22.	Original Drawing For Pineapple Registration	86
23.	Night — "Night And Morning" Jug	87
24.	"New Pineapple" Jug — Enamelled	88
25.	"Vine Border" Jug — Enamelled	88
26.	Two Pages Of Relief — Moulded	89
26a.	Stoneware Designs	90
27.	"Chinese Figures" Jasperware Jug	91
28.	Three Jugs mid 19th Century	91
29.	Jasperware Jugs 1840/50 s	92
30.	"Hunting" Jug	94
31.	"Bird and Butterfly" Jug	96
32.	"Bird and Butterfly" Jug — Reverse	96
33.	"Fern Wreath" Jug	96
34.	"Wheatsheaf and Hops" Jug 1850 s	96
35.	"Wheatsheaf and Hops" Jug 1860 s	96
36.	"Tropical Bird" Jug 1871	96
37.	"Sacrifices" Jug	96
38.	"Acanthus and Bluebell" Jug — late 1850 s	96
39.	An 1860 s — 70 s Group	97
40.	A Mosaicware Candlestick	98
41.	A Mosaicware Jug 1860 s	98
42.	"Hen On The Nest" (Hen Box)	98
43.	Jasperware Stilton Cheese Dish	99
44.	"Festoon" Biscuit Barrel on Stand	99
45.	A Group of Wall Plaques	100
46.	Biscuit Barrels and Flowerpot	100
47.	James Thomas Dudson	104
47 a.	William Henry Dudson	104
48.	Jasperware Vase Introduced 1897	111
49.	"Blind Man's Buff" Jug 1891 — 1900	112
50.	"Festoon and Muses" Tobacco Jar	112
51.	Queen Victoria Golden Jubilee Stoneware Jug	113
52.	Queen Victoria Golden Jubilee Jasperware Jug	113

		Page
53.	1899 Commemorative Jug	113
54.	Blue Jug with Brown Neck	119
55.	Pepper and Mustard Pots 1880 s	122
56.	James Robert Dudson	124
57.	Harry Dudson	124
58.	Pressed Ware Master Models	127
59.	Master Models Blancmange Moulds	128
60.	1890 s Jasperware	129
61.	1880 — 1913 Jasperware	130
62.	Glazed Jasperware Jug 1900 — 1939	133
63.	Jasperware Vases	134
64.	Douglas Dudson	135
65.	Joan Dudson Figure 1922	136
66.	Rex Dudson	141
67.	Hubert Dudson	141
68.	Jasperware Teapots 1920 s	145
69.	Jasperware 1900 — 1939	145
70.	Early Electric Kettle & Double Spouted Teapot	149
71.	Derek Dudson	150
72.	Bruce Dudson	150
73.	Ian Dudson	159
74.	Max Dudson	159
75.	1980 s Vitrified Hotelware	158
76.	Master Model for Relief-moulded Jug	206
77.	Master Model for Relief-moulded Jug	206
78.	Master Model for Relief-moulded Jug	206
79.	Master Model for Relief-moulded Jug	206
80.	Master Model "Gladioli" Modelling Slightly Changed	206
81.	Master Model "Floral"	207
82.	Master Model "Cane"	207
83.	Master Models for two more	207
84.	Variations of Fern Jugs	207
85.	1870 s Wine Cooler on Stand	214
86.	1850 s Jasperware Mustard Pot	272
87.	Jasperware Vase	273
88.	Relief-moulded Stoneware Jug	274
89.	The Hope Street Factory c. 1975	275
90.	The J.E. Heath Factory in 1985	276
91.	The Duraline factory in 1985	277

LIST OF PLANS

	Page
Plan 1. Mill Field	26
Plan 2. Shelton in 1825	27
Plan 3. First Factory Purchase	33
Plan 4. Second Factory Purchase	33
Plan 5. Third Factory Purchase	35
Plan 6. Fourth Factory Purchase	35
Plan 7. Factory Site in 1845	61
Plan 8. Plan of factory in 1882	103

LIST OF MAPS

Map 1. Map of Hanley in 1800	4
Map 2. Shelton Hall In 1779	29
Map 3. Map with the Indenture 1811	31

FAMILY TREES

Dudson Potters	2
Dudson — Keeling Relationship	8
Keeling — Dimmock Relationship	9
Dudson — Mare Relationship	13
Dudson Family Tree	266-7

DUDSON POTTERS

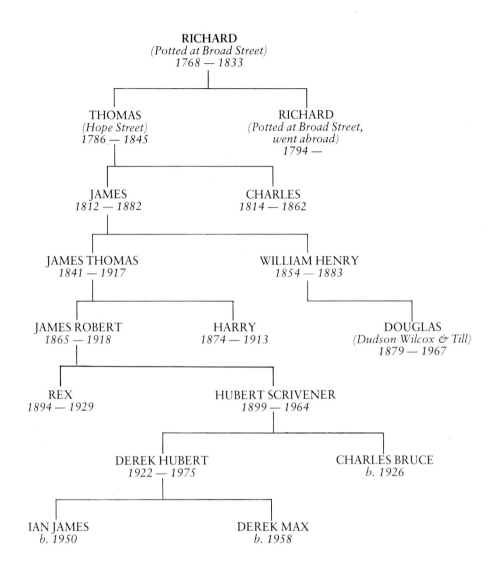

RICHARD
(Potted at Broad Street)
1768 — 1833

THOMAS
(Hope Street)
1786 — 1845

RICHARD
*(Potted at Broad Street,
went abroad)*
1794 —

JAMES
1812 — 1882

CHARLES
1814 — 1862

JAMES THOMAS
1841 — 1917

WILLIAM HENRY
1854 — 1883

JAMES ROBERT
1865 — 1918

HARRY
1874 — 1913

DOUGLAS
(Dudson Wilcox & Till)
1879 — 1967

REX
1894 — 1929

HUBERT SCRIVENER
1899 — 1964

DEREK HUBERT
1922 — 1975

CHARLES BRUCE
b. 1926

IAN JAMES
b. 1950

DEREK MAX
b. 1958

1

INTRODUCTION

The art of potting has been developed to a very high standard in Staffordshire over some 300 years, and many famous names have contributed to this development. Indeed, these well-known names are constantly to be found in the industry today although many of the early family businesses have been absorbed into larger groups. Nevertheless, several independent family firms are still operating today and there is one family firm that is in an unusual, if not unique, position. This firm, Dudsons, has survived from the turn of the nineteenth century, not only with the same family name but in an unbroken direct line from the founder, and is still in production today with the seventh and eighth generations in control. This appears to be longer than any other family pottery has been in existence as the same independent firm. This book attempts to set down all that is known of the Dudson family and pottery.

Although the line is unbroken unfortunately records remaining on the factory are not and very many documents were destroyed some 50 years ago to provide space. Not only factory records but some of the local records which would have yielded valuable information were also destroyed by one cause or another, Chartist Riots, floods etc. This applied to other potteries too, but does not make the job of the researcher any easier.

NOTES

2

RICHARD DUDSON

1768 — 1833

When Richard Dudson was born, in 1768, the area we now know as the Staffordshire Potteries was just coming into existence. The small towns and villages, each a few miles apart, were expanding as the pottery industry grew and gradually the gaps between them were narrowing. Thus Tunstall, Burslem, Cobridge, Hanley, Etruria, Stoke, Fenton, Longton and a few more villages were eventually to merge and together form "The Potteries".

In the early 18th century the country potters had their workshops and hovel ovens scattered around these villages, the majority concentrating around Burslem. Hanley, at this time, consisted of two small villages about half a mile apart. These were known as Upper Hanley Green and Lower Hanley Green [1]. There were a few small potteries scattered around them, between the farms and cottages.

After 1750, due to the expansion of the pottery industry during the Industrial Revolution, the built up area of Hanley spread, especially south westwards into Shelton where a new township was being created. The main part of Shelton developed along the slope from Stoke, which was in the valley, up Snow Hill and Broad Street to Hanley on the hill top. This slope was described in 1763 as being "in a ruinous condition, narrow and incommodious" [2]. Broad Street was where Richard Dudson came to live.

There is very little to be found of Richard's early life, but it seems probable that his family came to find work in this flourishing pottery industry. Very possibly they came from one of the farming villages lying to the north of Stafford. Several Dudsons are recorded, from the 16th century onwards, in many of these villages but especially Seighford, Bradley-by-Stafford and Gnosall. The fact that there are no Dudson entries at all, in any of the Potteries parish registers, before a burial in 1781 points, fairly evidently, to the family moving into the area in the latter part of the 18th century. This view is strengthened by the fact that from this date and throughout the first half of the 19th century all Dudson records in Potteries registers have proved to be members of this same family.

(1) *Victoria County History Vol. 8. p.142.*
(2) *Victoria County History Vol. 8. p.145.*

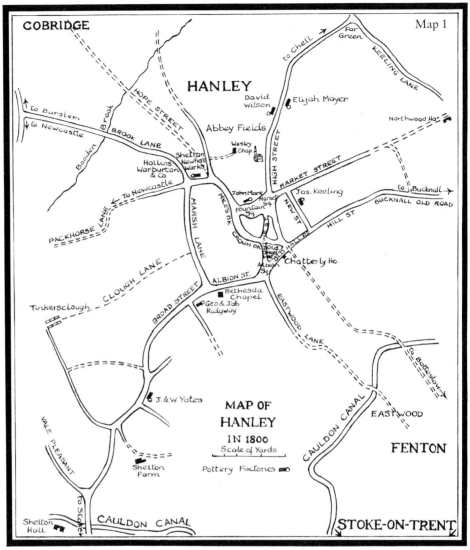

COBRIDGE

HANLEY

Map 1

to Chell
Far Green
KEELING LANE
to Burslem
to Newcastle
HOPE STREET
Brook
BROOK LANE
Booden
To Newcastle
PACKHORSE LANE
MARSH LANE
CLOUGH LANE
Tinkersclough
BROAD STREET
Shelton Newhall Works
Hollins Warburton & Co
John Maro
Market Sq
Fountain Sq
ALBION ST.
Bethesda Chapel
Geo & Job Ridgway
Abbey Fields
Wesley Chap.
David Wilson
Elijah Mayer
HIGH STREET
MARKET STREET
NEW ST
Northwood Ho.
Jos. Keeling
to Bucknall
BUCKNALL OLD ROAD
HILL ST
CROWN BRIDGE
Chatterly Ho.
Albion Sq.
EASTWOOD LANE
to Botteslow
J. & W. Yates

MAP OF
HANLEY
IN 1800
Scale of Yards
Pottery Factories

VALE PLEASANT
to Stoke
Shelton Farm
CAULDON CANAL
EASTWOOD
FENTON
Shelton Hall
CAULDON CANAL
STOKE-ON-TRENT

Adapted from map by G W. Bacon & Co. Ltd., 127 Strand, London.

However, as no record of Richard Dudson's baptism can be found, we can only speculate from whence the family came. Similarly his parentage cannot be proved. The first three entries in the Potteries parish registers do suggest that his father was Joseph and his mother either Ann or Elizabeth Dudson — Elizabeth Dudson buried Stoke 27th January. 1781; Ann Dudson buried Stoke 7th October, 1796; and Joseph Dudson buried Stoke 25th December, 1800.

During Richard's childhood improvements were made in both factory buildings and pottery techniques. One of the most outstanding technical achievements was the perfecting of creamware by Wedgwood in the 1760 s. New forms of stoneware were developed between 1767-1785, notably black basalt, jasperware, caneware and pearl white ware.

4

Creamware became the standard earthenware of the Staffordshire pottery industry by the late 18th century and various durable forms were produced, e.g. stone china, ironstone china, opaque china and granite china.

As the industry developed markets at home and abroad expanded. Transport became quicker and cheaper because of the building of canals and turnpike roads. The Trent and Mersey Canal was opened in 1777.

There were several large, flourishing pottery factories established in the area by this time. Josiah Wedgwood had started production at Etruria in 1769. Ephraim and Charles Chatterley and Samuel Hollins had factories in Shelton and in Broad Street itself there were John Yates and the Baddeleys — Ralph, John and Edward. Humphrey Palmer had converted the Shelton New Hall estate into a pottery factory which was being run, from 1773, by his son Thomas Palmer, [3] and this factory was later taken over by the New Hall Porcelain Co. These factories were largely supplying the wealthier sections of the population.

At the same time the number of labourers increased due to the movement from the country into the towns during the Industrial Revolution. There resulted a demand for cheaper ware which the workers could afford and to meet this many new, small and often ramshackle pot-works sprang up.

It would have been extremely helpful if some light could have been thrown on Richard Dudson's early working life, for whom he worked and what he did. The vast majority of children at that time started work at a very early age, nine years old being quite usual, and there is no reason to think Richard did any other (c. 1777). He probably worked in a larger factory, for one of the manufacturers in Shelton where he lived. During this time he obviously learnt much about the different pottery bodies and colours being used by the industry to enable him, eventually, to specialise as a colour maker[4].

Potters were beginning to specialise in several sections of the industry, including engravers, enamellers, crate makers. Why was it an advantage that colour makers should specialise? The production of pottery bodies needed knowledge of the different clays, the proportions in which they should be mixed and how to adjust the plasticity. Similarly a fairly comprehensive knowledge of chemistry was needed to produce a glaze that would adhere to the particular body being used. The production of colours for staining the body, or decorating the pot, called for knowledge of the chemistry of metals. These metallic compounds had to resist high temperatures during firing so that the article was produced in the intended colour. The large potteries produced their own bodies and colours but the numerous small potters did not always have the facilities, or skills, to produce for themselves. They therefore had to place some processes with specialists.

(3) *Duchy of Lancaster Manorial roll 14th July, 1773.*
(4) *1822/23 Newcastle and Potteries Directory.*

This gives some picture of the local Shelton community in which Richard spent his youth. Growing up at the same time, although in Hanley not Shelton, was another family with whom the Dudsons were to be closely involved for many decades to come. This was a branch of the Keeling family — in particular three of the children of Samuel Keeling who moved from Newcastle-under-Lyme to Hanley about 1760. His eldest son Robert was baptised at Newcastle parish church on 24th December, 1758. Later records show that Samuel's son James and daughter Jane were members of St. John's Church, Hanley and it seems possible they were baptised there in the 1760s. That James Keeling was born in 1762 is shown by his obituary notice but Jane's date of birth is unknown.

Unfortunately these registers were destroyed on the night of the 15th/16th August 1842 during the Chartist Riots. It appears, from notes entered in the registers, that the curate of St. John's took the registers from 1754 (the earliest) to 1789 home with him. They were still in his house on the night the rioters burned it down and only the registers which remained in the Church safe are available[5].

This destruction greatly increases the difficulty of proving the relationship between Robert, James and Jane, but Llewellyn Jewitt, fortunately, confirms that Robert and James were brothers[6]. He refers to Robert's grandson Samuel Keeling (who took over John Glass' factory in Market Street) as James' great nephew. (See Dudson/Keeling relationship).

Dudson factory and family records give strong circumstantial evidence that Jane was their sister.

Richard Dudson married Jane Keeling on the 24th December, 1786 at the parish church of Norton-le-Moors. This church was called "The Gretna Green of the Potteries" because, according to the notes at the beginning of the parish register, a remarkable number of marriages were carried out there. There were four churches which were popular for fashionable weddings at this time. The other three were Whitmore, Newcastle and Bucknall. Many members of the major pottery families married at one or other of these country churches, even though they were non-parishioners.

Richard was only 18 when he married Jane. Although early marriages were not unusual at that time (nor indeed today) there was a reason for this one. Their son, Thomas, had been born earlier in 1786, which is confirmed by his death certificate. No record of Thomas' baptism is available as the St. John's register for 1786 was one of those destroyed. The preserved registers show that Richard and Jane had another son born on 2nd December 1789 and baptised four days later. Obviously an ailing child, he died during that winter and was buried at

(5) *Bishops transcripts for St. John's, Hanley are not available at Lichfield J.R.O. before 1791.*
(6) *Ceramic Art of Great Britain, 1878. Virtue & Co. p.310.*

Stoke on 23rd February 1790. Their next son was born on the 7th November 1794 and baptised on 2nd August 1795 at St. John's Hanley. His name was also Richard.

Inter-marriages between the early pottery families were very common and it will occasion no surprise that Dudsons were also involved. Through this marriage into the Keeling family Dudsons became further associated with the Dimmocks since James Keeling married twice, his second wife being Sarah Dimmock, (See table p.9).

James Keeling, Richard Dudson's brother-in-law, was the highly respected earthenware manufacturer in New Street, Hanley, from about 1790-1832. He patented improvements in the pottery industry (see Appendix B). In addition to New Street he owned one third of a factory in Hanley which was occupied by William Hackwood, (junior) and was also a senior partner in the firm of Keeling, Toft & Co.

The occupation of Robert Keeling, Richard Dudson's other brother-in-law, is referred to as a potter, but where is not indicated. It was his family, especially his grandsons, that became most closely involved with the Dudsons.

Establishing these relationships (and the later relationships to the Baddeleys, Mares and Hollins) has involved considerable research, made difficult not only by the destruction of relevant records but also by frequent use of the same baptismal names. Greater detail relating to the Keeling and Dimmock families has been included in Appendix B. The other families are referred to in the next chapter.

Jane Dudson died in 1801[7] and four years later Richard married Ann Clark[8] by whom he had a daughter Mary Ann[9].

Richard started his own business in 1800, when he was 32 years of age, in Broad Street, Shelton. Contemporary documents relating to this no longer exist but there is plenty of evidence to the fact.

In 1878 Llewellyn Jewitt recorded in his *Ceramic Art of Great Britain* (Page 73) that James Dudson was at the "Hope Street Works in Shelton (now Hanley), these works having been established in 1800". (This is slightly inaccurate as the second works at Hope Street were not begun until c. 1809). However, James Dudson was the grandson of the founder Richard and had either provided the information for Jewitt or at least had not contradicted it. As he had worked with his grandfather at Broad Street, before moving to Hope Street, he could be

(7) *22nd January, 1801 Stoke parish register.*
(8) *18th December, 1804 St. Giles, Newcastle-under-Lyme.*
(9) *26th July, 1807 Stoke parish register. She married George Elkin in October 1832 at St. Peter Ad Vincula, Stoke.*

DUDSON/KEELING RELATIONSHIP

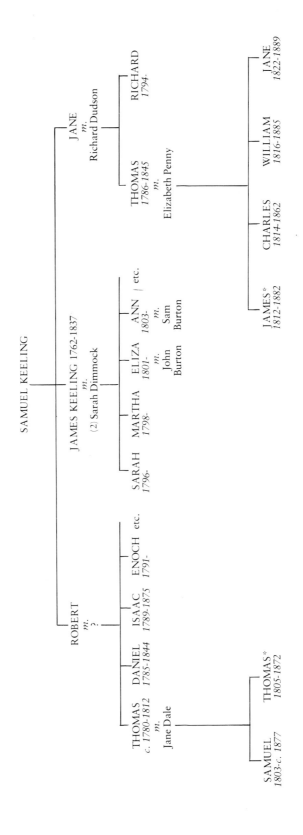

SAMUEL KEELING

ROBERT
m.
?

JAMES KEELING 1762-1837
m.
(2) Sarah Dimmock

JANE
m.
Richard Dudson

THOMAS
c. 1780-1812
m.
Jane Dale

DANIEL
1785-1844

ISAAC
1789-1875

ENOCH
1791-

etc.

SARAH
1796-

MARTHA
1798-

ELIZA
1801-
m.
John
Burton

ANN
1803-
m.
Sam
Burton

etc.

THOMAS
1786-1845
m.
Elizabeth Penny

RICHARD
1794-

SAMUEL
1803-c. 1877

THOMAS*
1805-1872

JAMES*
1812-1882

CHARLES
1814-1862

WILLIAM
1816-1885

JANE
1822-1889

*Co-executors of Thomas Dudson's will.
All references for the Keeling's are given in the Appendix, together with further information.

8

KEELING/DIMMOCK RELATIONSHIP

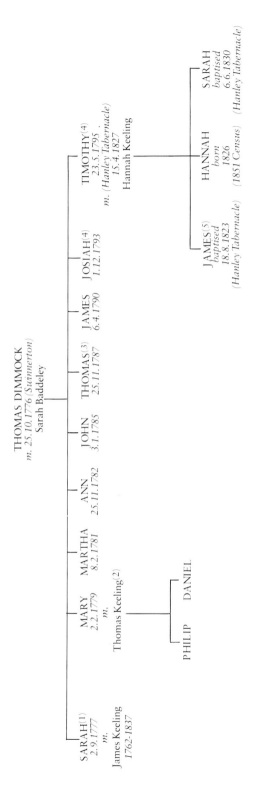

THOMAS DIMMOCK
m. 25.10.1776 (Swinnerton)
Sarah Baddeley

SARAH[1]
2.9.1777
m.
James Keeling
1762-1837

MARY
2.2.1779
m.
Thomas Keeling[2]

PHILIP   DANIEL

MARTHA
8.2.1781

ANN
25.11.1782

JOHN
3.1.1785

THOMAS[3]
25.11.1787

JAMES
6.4.1790

JOSIAH[4]
1.12.1793

TIMOTHY[4]
23.5.1795
m. (Hanley Tabernacle)
15.4.1827
Hannah Keeling

JAMES[5]
baptised
18.8.1823
(Hanley Tabernacle)

HANNAH
born
1826
(1851 Census)

SARAH
baptised
6.6.1830
(Hanley Tabernacle)

(1) All births are recorded (with the baptisms) at the Congregational Chapel Newcastle.
(2) From Thomas' will proved 10.7.1810.
(3) Potter in Albion and Tontine Streets.
(4) Partners with Thomas Keeling in Timber and Boat Building business at Etruria.
(5) Timothy Dimmock died in 1870. (document filed in Dudson Deeds)
    His son James went to Darwen in Lancashire. (same document).

expected to know and indeed the heading on James' notepaper includes ''Established 1800''.

There are references by other members of the family too.

In a *Descriptive Account of the Potteries Illustrated 1893*[10] with reference to James T. Dudson, there appears.... ''Among the houses that, in Hanley and its vicinity, have risen to enviable distinction in this line of industry, a firm of particular noteworthiness is that controlled by Mr. James T. Dudson of Hope Street works.... this business is by no means of mushroom growth for its history dates back to the beginning of the present century, in the first year of which it was founded by a progenitor of the present proprietor''.

A letter from this same James T. Dudson, great grandson of the founder, to J. F. Blacker, author of *Nineteenth Century Ceramic Art 1911* speaking of his firm, now renamed Dudson Brothers, says.... ''This business was established in 1800 and has descended in a direct line ever since''.

We have no knowledge of the size of Richard's factory in Broad Street. There were at this time several large potteries in the same area. James Keeling has already been mentioned but in addition there were Hollins, Warburton & Co., of New Hall, Job and George Ridgway, the Baddeleys, Elijah Mayer, John Mare and several more. Certainly, in comparison with these, Richard's concern was small.

There is no indication that he belonged to a wealthy family and it seems that his business was built by his own efforts which must have been considerable.

All potters obviously faced many difficulties but these would present greater problems to the small men, without capital to solve and ease them. Many of these small potters in business at the beginning of the 19th century went bankrupt. It can be assumed, therefore, that Richard was reasonably efficient and possessed business acumen not only to have survived these difficult years but to have prospered. Indeed, he prospered enough to own his property, at

(10) *Published by Robinson, Son and Pike, Duke Street, Brighton, Hanley Section p.23.*

least by 1807 when he is noted in the rates book as owning his property in Broad Street, and also to have started another small factory in Hope Street (c. 1809) with Thomas (his son) in charge. As will be seen later, Thomas built this up and, as it became more successful, assumed complete responsibility for it.

Richard continued working at Broad Street as both colour maker and potter. Directories of the time refer to him sometimes as one, sometimes the other [11]. This combination of two sides to the business is characteristic of all Dudson factories up to the end of the 19th century. Richard junior worked with his father, as a pottery presser[11], at least until 1822, but shortly afterwards began his own business, leaving James (Thomas' eldest son) who was being trained by his grandfather, working at Broad Street. James remained until Richard died, in 1833, then a few months later, in the early part of 1834, joined his father at Hope Street. Notices of Richard's death were inserted in both the Staffordshire Advertiser and the Staffordshire Sentinel[12] when he died at Broad Street aged 65. Unfortunately he left no will.

Richard junior and his wife took control of the Broad Street premises and were still there in 1841 according to the Census, but presumably it was sold or pulled down shortly after this.

(11) *Staffordshire Directory 1818. p.63. Parsons & Bradshaw*
  ''Richard Dudson Potter — Broad Street''.
  Newcastle & Pottery Directory 1822/23.
  Richard Dudson — colour maker — Broad Street.
  Richard Dudson — pottery presser — Broad Street.
  Thomas Dudson — colour maker — Hope Street.
(12) *Both papers dated 12th October, 1833.*

3

RICHARD DUDSON JUNIOR

1794 —

It was the Hope Street factory that developed into the present firm and Richard Dudson's first son Thomas was responsible for its beginning. His second son, Richard, born in 1794, did not work at Hope Street but nevertheless contributed to the family history.

He lived and worked with his father in Broad Street, Shelton. On 2nd August 1818 he married Hannah Mare* at Norton-le-Moors[11].

There are three births of Hannah Mare recorded which could possibly apply to Richard's wife.

1. Hannah, daughter of Thomas Moore Mayer and Mary, baptised at Hanley Tabernacle 3rd September, 1798.

2. Hannah, daughter of William and Charlotte Mayer baptised 28th April, 1793 at Burslem.

3. Hannah, daughter of John Mare and Hannah, baptised 19th April, 1801 at Stoke.

   (John Mare married Hannah Baddeley 23rd October, 1796 at Norton-le-Moors)[12].

Absolutely nothing has been found to link Richard Dudson, or any other member of the Dudson family, with either of the first two families, nor with Burslem, whereas two or three facts indicate connection with the third, this relationship has, therefore, been accepted. By this marriage Dudsons became associated with the Baddeleys also, Richard's mother in law having been Hannah Baddeley.

---

(11) *Parish register.*

 * *The spelling of the Mayer family name varies considerably between Mare and Mayer (and others), the two even appearing on one document involving close relations.*

(12) *John Mayer, the proprietor of The Swan Inn, Hanley, also had a wife called Hannah, but Hannah could not be their daughter for John died in 1799. (Staffs. Advertiser 27th April, 1799). Their children were born between 1788 and 1798.*

DUDSON — MARE RELATIONSHIP

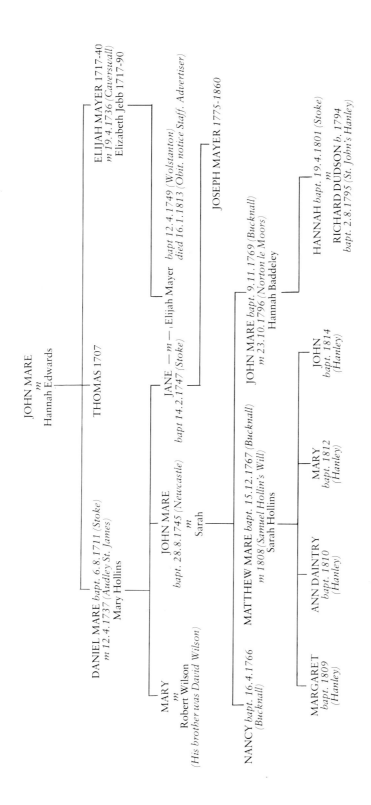

JOHN MARE
m
Hannah Edwards

ELIJAH MAYER 1717-40
m 19.4.1736 (Caverswall)
Elizabeth Jebb 1717-90

THOMAS 1707

DANIEL MARE bapt. 6.8.1711 (Stoke)
m 12.4.1737 (Audley St. James)
Mary Hollins

JANE — m — Elijah Mayer bapt 12.4.1749 (Wolstanton)
bapt 14.2.1747 (Stoke)   died 16.1.1813 (Obit. notice Staff. Advertiser)

JOSEPH MAYER 1775-1860

JOHN MARE
bapt. 28.8.1745 (Newcastle)
m
Sarah

MARY
m
Robert Wilson
(His brother was David Wilson)

JOHN MARE bapt. 9.11.1769 (Bucknall)
m 23.10.1796 (Norton le Moors)
Hannah Baddeley

MATTHEW MARE bapt. 15.12.1767 (Bucknall)
m 1808 (Samuel Hollin's Will)
Sarah Hollins

HANNAH bapt. 19.4.1801 (Stoke)
m
RICHARD DUDSON b. 1794
bapt. 2.8.1795 (St. John's Hanley)

NANCY bapt. 16.4.1766
(Bucknall)

MARGARET 1809
bapt. 1809
(Hanley)

ANN DAINTRY
bapt. 1810
(Hanley)

MARY
bapt. 1812
(Hanley)

JOHN
bapt. 1814
(Hanley)

The majority of this pedigree is reproduced by kind permission of Mr. W. E. Mayer. His collaboration in establishing the Mare/Dudson relationship is very much appreciated.

13

Hannah Baddeley was the sister of Ralph, John and Edward Baddeley who potted in Broad Street. Their father was John Baddeley. His will, which is filed in the Manorial Rolls (DL30/507/21), shows his family to have been as follows:

JOHN BADDELEY
Married (29.4.1754)
ANN GODWIN
RALPH "eldest son" JOHN, THOMAS, EDWARD,
ANN, SARAH, HANNAH

There is no indication given as to the ages so the order of their births may be different from the above. (John is not actually mentioned in the will but other evidence shows there is no doubt as to his parentage)[13].

The Baddeleys potted at two factories in Broad Street. Ralph in control of one (later Ashworths) and John and Edward in control of the factory adjoining. The latter was held by John and Edward until 1807[13] and later by George Taylor and Hicks and Meigh before John Mare took it over in the early 1820 s until he went bankrupt in 1826[14]. It has been previously assumed that this was the John Mare who potted in Fountain Square, but as he died in 1819[15] this is not possible.

It seems more likely that it was Hannah's husband John Mare (born 1769). See Mare/Dudson "tree" on Page 13. In 1820 he was 51 years old and may already have known something of the factory when it was run by his brothers-in-law. That this John Mare was already an experienced potter is known because the rates books[16] show him to be, with his brother Matthew, in control of Samuel Hollins factory at Vale Pleasant from 1817-1821. Matthew Mare was Samuel Hollins' son-in-law, having married his daughter Sarah in 1808. According to Meigh the Hollins' factory was unoccupied until Matthew went to join Samuel. The rates from 1809-1816 show owner S. Hollins — occupied by Mare and Hollins. In 1817 the occupancy changes to Messrs. Mare and from 1818 is stated as Matthew and John Mare. John left Matthew a few months after Samuel Hollins died (5th November, 1820) for the ownership changed to Thomas Hollins (Samuel's son) and occupancy to Matthew only, until 1826. As the dates coincide it seems likely that John left Matthew to move into the Baddeley factory early in 1821.

After Richard Dudson and Hannah Mare were married in 1818, they lived in Broad Street with Richard senior, and worked with him in his pottery — Richard as a presser and Hannah as a pottery paintress[17].

(13) *Victoria County History Vol. 8 p.168 Note 72.*
(14) *Staffordshire Advertiser 15th April, 1826.*
(15) *Death notice in Staffordshire Advertiser 27th March, 1819.*
(16) *Meighs List of Potters.*
(17) *1841 Census.*

14

Shortly after Hannah had borne her two children, Charles in 1819[18] and Jane in 1821[19], Richard rented a plot of land from Hannah's uncle, Matthew Mare, and built himself a dwelling house on it. The plot was in the Zachary — a close which fronted onto a new street called Wheatsheaf Street.

After moving to his new home, he completed any other necessary buildings and began colour making there,[20] although it appears that he was still potting, possibly part time, with his father. Certainly Hannah appears to have continued working at Broad Street when not too involved with her family.

By 1825 Richard had made enough money to purchase the land from Matthew Mare[21] and he became a copyhold tenant of the Duchy of Lancaster for the first time. The purchase price was £33.6.8d. Frontage to Wheatsheaf Street was "1,200 yards, depth 22 yards, whole 280 square yards".

It should be noted here that part of Shelton was in the Manor of Newcastle-under-Lyme where everyone owning land, or property, was a copyhold tenant of the Duchy of Lancaster. Any purchases, sales, mortgages, transfer of property under a will etc., had to be undertaken at a Manorial Court where the resulting change in the copyhold tenancy was recorded. The Duchy granted power to their tenants to build houses, kilns and other buildings with the lease. Many of the copyhold tenants had "under-tenants", i.e. they sub-let the land and passed on this power to build to the sub-tenants. It was therefore a normal and common practice for under-tenants to build themselves houses and/or workshops on land which they did not own, and then to purchase the land when they could afford it. Wheatsheaf Street and Hope Street were among the areas in the Manor of Newcastle and in the Duchy, but Broad Street was not.

After his father's death in 1833, Richard took control of the pottery and colour making business in Broad Street[22] whilst still keeping his house and business in Wheatsheaf Street. For a period, he was also the proprietor of the appropriately named Jug Inn, which was in Bedford Row off Broad Street[23]. The Jug Inn was obviously one of the most interesting buildings in the area.

W. Scaratt writing in 1906 in Old Times in the Potteries says "Perhaps the oldest inn of the district is the 'Jug'.... and, as it bears the date of 1620 on a mural tablet in the new structure, we may fairly infer that it was a hostelry in that remote day". Exactly how long Richard had it is not known, but certainly Matthew Booth was proprietor by 1846. The Staffordshire Advertiser (1st May, 1847) tells us that "the Jug Inn is partly converted to a Museum of animated nature".

(18) *St. Johns, Hanley — baptism 13th June, 1819.*
(19) *St. Peter Ad Vincula Stoke - baptism 4th January, 1821.*
(20) *Pigot & Co. National Commercial Directory 1830.*
(21) *Manorial Roll 5th May, 1825.*
(22) *White's History, Gazetteer & Directory of Staffordshire, 1834.*
(23) *White's ditto 1834 (under 'Inns & Taverns')*
     Pigot & Co. National Commercial Directory, 1835.

At a Manorial Court in November, 1838[24] Richard is described as "within this Manor China Manufacturer" when he surrendered his house and adjoining buildings in Wheatsheaf Street, by way of a mortgage for £1,000 to John Keeling, a commission agent and partner of Mayer and Keeling in Charles Street, commission dealers[25]. The property was then occupied by Ralph Keeling. Ralph was the grandson of Moses Keeling, and a member of the family of potters and engravers in Shelton, obviously also related to James Keeling of New Street, Hanley, but how is not clear.

Richard used this money to buy a China manufactory in Cannon Street, (a street leading off Broad Street) previously occupied by William Rivers & Co., and commenced potting there in 1839[26]. According to the Poll books of the time, Richard owned and lived in a house in Captains Lane, but still owned a colour business in Broad Street. The 1841 Census lists Hannah, his wife, as a "pottery paintress" at Broad Street and Richard as an earthenware manufacturer at Cannon Street. It seems likely that Captains Lane and Cannon Street were the same street and that the name was changed, Cannon Street was called after Cannon House with its two cannons at the entrance, which had been placed there by the owner, a retired naval officer, Captain Simpson. *Nomenclature of the Old Streets of Hanley* by DORAN (Manuscript at City Museum and Art Gallery, Hanley). An interesting sidelight on the conditions at the time comes from the Report on the Employment of Children in Manufactories, 1842 (Scriven) "Mr. Richard Dudson's China factory, Shelton — Cannon Street;

No. 145 Amy Walker, aged 12.
"I am a painter — have been at work two years, am apprenticed for seven years to Mr. Dudson. I receive 1s 6d a week per year. I can read and write. I went to a private school some years. I now go to Sunday School at the National. I come to work at seven in the morning in winter and at six in the summer. Go home at six in the evening. I never work overtime. Mary Bradshaw looks over us — there are eight of us girls in one room — all can read — some can write. Mary Bradshaw is very good to us. She gives us a slap with her hand sometimes when we work carelessly. She rewards us sometimes by taking half a dozen pieces from us. We get holidays at times".

No. 146 David Smith, aged 11.
"I am sifting flint, washing cranks and helping father at the dipping tub. I can read and write. Went to school Sundays at Primitive Methodists. I have been to day school. I have been to work two years — the work never hurt me yet. I get 3s 6d a week. When my father is in regular work, he gets £2.12s, if in full work that is with two ovens he gets £3.10s. I go home to breakfast and dinner and get tatees and beef, sometimes bacon for dinner and milk meat[27] for breakfast. I come to work at half past seven and work till six".

(24) *Manorial Court 29th November, 1838.* (25) *Parsons and Bradshaw, 1818.*

(26) *John Ward History of Stoke-on-Trent, 1843. p.375.*
 Michael Berthoud in his book H & R DANIEL 1822-46 p.48 records that this factory was worked by Henry Daniel 1832-34.

(27) *Milk meat is a milky porridge (Chambers and Oxford Dictionaires), but also a local name for cow's udder.*

If these childrens' statements are taken at face value, Amy Walker seems badly underpaid compared with young David. As a painter, Amy was employed in decorating the biscuit before the final glaze was applied — and it is well established that in every factory most of this work was done by young children for distressingly low returns. The difference between these two children probably is that whilst David was possibly classed as a worker or 'hand', Amy was 'apprenticed' and after her term might rise to better things. The 'cranks' that David washed are the pottery pieces used to support the ware during firing. From the same report comes Richard Dudson's evidence to the enquiry.

No. 147 Mr. Richard Dudson.

"I have been a manufacturer for two years and a half years, * *but was brought up to the trade commencing with 1s 4d per week for wages. I employ between 30 and 40 hands of all ages. The people are now at play* * *in consequence of the depression of trade and in some measure from the extreme coldness of the weather. They come at seven in the winter and leave at six. I pay them their week's wages on Saturdays in cash. I can seldom get them to work on Saturdays or Mondays, even if they had ever so much work to do. Think this is a bad habit of the people, and from my experience have reason to think it so. If I had been a provident man, when a workman, and worked when I could, I should have been better off than I am now, and so would many others. The consequence of this neglect of time, we have been obliged to work overhours on other days to make up for it, and as our work depends on the boys who work for us, we have unneccessarily taxed their health and strength, and have lost sight of their education. I often regret the hours I have lost. As a manufacturer I have not the least doubt that I should prosper greatly if I could depend on the working hours of men. They come about the premises, but will not buckle to. If I give them a day or so at Easter they take a week, if at Christmas they take another week. Indeed they are not to be depended on.*
RICHARD DUDSON".

Reading this somewhat melancholy statement, it nevertheless appears that Richard's manufactory in Cannon Street was quite sizeable, especially compared with the Wheatsheaf Street site for which he only paid £30 or so. Presumably, some of the £1,000 he mortgaged it for would go in improvements to the newer site. It is obvious he had no intention of letting the officers of the enquiry know any more about his business than he needed to do and, in fact, almost went out of his way to make it appear that he was not doing too well. Of course the evidence was being collected to assess the condition of children working in the industry, so Richard was sometimes speaking for the general business and trade situation as much for his own when he speaks of the results of this 'neglect of time', the admission that the boys' health, strength and education had been unnecessarily sacrificed.

Perhaps there was some cause for Richard to feel less than happy about his business in Cannon Street, though what it was does not appear, for he sells both his house and his factory at an auction sale held on 30th October, 1843 at the Kings Head, Shelton[28].

(28) *Staffordshire Advertiser 21st October, 1843.*
* *This is at Cannon Street.* * *"At play" — i.e. not working.*

Lot 1. The house is described as "a very substantial dwelling house, temporarily divided into two tenants, with lawn and drive in front, very good walled garden, stable, piggeries and detached brewhouse. Also a croft adjoining". Richard Dudson was occupying one half.

The factory was Lot 3 :—

"A large and very complete China manufactory with fixtures and every other convenience suitable for carrying on every department of the business and containing, including the reservoir and adjacent land, 5,119 square yards. This manufactory has an excellent supply of water, there is ample room for the storage of materials in the rough, and no expense has been spared by the proprietor in putting same into substantial repair".

Afterwards there is no further mention of any of his activities other than witnessing his brother Thomas's will during the latter's fatal illness in 1845. It seems fairly evident that Richard and his family went abroad, for none of their deaths are recorded at St. Catherine's House, Kingsway, London. Probably he sold up everything to make plans for their departure — for it was a popular thing for potters to do at this time. A small mystery, where did they go? There are two possibilities although, of course, neither may be correct.

Several potters were going to America at this time. In 1884 the Hanley Operatives Emigration Society was formed aimed at purchasing land in the U.S.A. — especially Wisconsin — and William Evans, who was its agent and also editor of the Potters Examiner, began using this paper to encourage potters to emigrate to Wisconsin — printing letters from individuals who had already emigrated as further enticement. More details of this emigration company are given in *A History of the Potters Union* by Frank Burchill and Richard Ross. (p.84).

Some years earlier there had been a similar move to persuade people to emigrate to Australia. The Staffordshire Advertiser of 29th September, 1837 carried a long article headed "South Australia" which gave information presenting the new colony of South Australia in very glowing terms and included a description of the building of Adelaide.

In 1838 several of James Keeling's family decided to go out there. His daughter Martha married the Reverend R.W. Newland in 1827. He was minister of Hanley Tabernacle Independent Chapel, and Martha was his second wife. At the church meeting in October, 1838 he handed in his resignation as he was going to emigrate to Australia "with his family and friends" to pioneer the settlement of Victor Harber near Adelaide in South Australia. They duly set sail in 1839 — and as James Keeling had died in 1837[29] his widow and several other members of her family, as well as Martha, decided to join the party of whom five were less than 10 years old. In Victor Harber the Rev. Newland

(29) *Staffs. Mercury 12th August. 1837.*

18

1. China inkwell, probably from a desk set, hand painted in enamel colours. Marked by an applied blue pad in the form of a scroll bearing the impressed mark R. DUDSON c. 1840.

2. A Turk's head tobacco jar, earthenware, unmarked. 6¼". c. 1850. Surrounded by some sherds uncovered in the archeological dig.

3 a. A group of Tulip jugs showing different treatments. From left to right:
a) A cheap 1880 s form 6″.
b) Pink and copper lustre with green enamel. Stoneware 7½″. c. 1850.
c) Pale blue relief moulded stoneware. Unmarked. 7½″. Mid. 19th century.
d) Flo-blue and copper lustre. Earthenware. 135 painted on base. 6″. 1840 s.

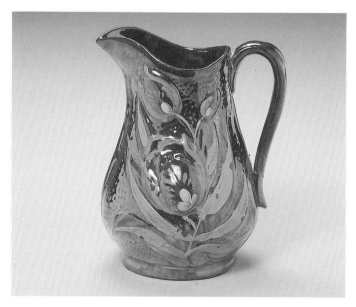

3 b. Copper lustred and
enamelled jug.
Stoneware. 6″.
1845-55.

4. Relief moulded stoneware jugs. From left to right:
a) Sage. "Rose". Impressed DUDSON. 4". 1850 s.
b) Sage. Britannia metal lid. "Lily." Unmarked. 8". 1850 s.
c) White. Britannia metal lid. "Gladioli" Impressed 0.7¾". 1850 s.
d) Blue panelled. Britannia metal lid. Pattern name unknown. Impressed DUDSON. 7½". 1850 s.
e) Blue. "Coral". Impressed curved ENGLAND. 11". 1870 s.
f) Drab, "Fuschia" Impressed DUDSON. 7½". 1850 s.

established the Newland Memorial Congregational Church[30]. As his aunt Sarah, several of his cousins and possibly some of his friends too, had started this settlement it is possible that Richard and his family left to join them in South Australia. Perhaps somewhere there are descendants of Richard and Hannah who may have knowledge of where they went and might one day share it.

Very little is known about production at this Cannon Street factory as all records would, presumably, be destroyed or at any rate scattered at its closure in 1843.

An accurate drawing of Richard's business card.

One of Richard's business cards still exists in such a worn condition that it is barely decipherable. Written on the back of the card is a recipe for a pottery body mixture, so faded that only certain words can be read, but it is dated 1842, and with it is a paper with a recipe for:

> *White figure body from Mr. R. Dudson*
>
> *360 flint*
>
> *360 stone*
>
> *480 china clay*
>
> *1 oz. calk to the cut*

These he obviously sent to his brother Thomas for they were found at Hope Street. From this we can deduce that, like Thomas, he was producing figures and "toys", and probably their products were similar in most respects.

The only known example of R. Dudson ware is shown in colour plate I but, as it is marked, it is to be hoped that more will come to light eventually.

(39) *Tabernacle Records*

4

THOMAS DUDSON

1786 — 1845

FAMILY HISTORY

Thomas Dudson, elder son of Richard Dudson, the founder, was responsible for the beginning of the Hope Street factory. It was this factory that developed into the present firm.

DISCOVERY OF EARLY FACTORY DOCUMENTS

Many of the early documents relating to the Hope Street factory were destroyed in later years during factory and office re-organisation. Information regarding early production at Hope Street could easily, therefore, have been as sparse as is the case at the Broad Street and Cannon Street factories. Fortunately there was at Hope Street an old safe for which the key had been lost. In 1975, during the search for an important, personal family document, it was decided that this safe should be broken open and a professional was called in for this purpose. The safe did not yield the missing document but did reveal the existence of a few early records. These included an early "Day" book dated 1819 which is a mixture of body and colour recipes, orders, and accounts. There were recipe books for pottery bodies and colours for the years 1823, 1825 and 1834, and also a large comprehensive ledger listing all the sales for the years 1842/44. A few pages at the back of this ledger give the prices paid for making and decorating figures in 1850. Finally there was an 1872 book containing a comprehensive collection of colour and body recipes, firing instructions and prices for making the detailed list of articles produced.

Whilst this was not a great deal of information it nevertheless formed a basis from which to start research and was invaluable for the early years (1800 — 1850) when no ware was marked. The present knowledge for these early years is still very far from complete but nevertheless is vastly more than has previously been known. Maybe other collectors or ceramic experts will be able to add to this knowledge now.

THE 1819 and 1825 BOOKS

There is no record as to where Thomas Dudson was educated but his early record books throw a little light on his character. One begins with several pages of questions and answers involving the Bible, for example "What are Christians to layaside and what are they to desire?" Thomas answers himself by quoting 1 Peter Chapter 2:—

1. *"Wherefore, laying aside all malice and all guile, and all hypocrasies, and envies and all evil-speakings".*

2. *"As new born babes desire the sincere milk of the word, that ye may grow thereby".*

These biblical entries are followed by a long poem and orders are interspersed by other verses. This presents a picture of Thomas as a religious person with a romantic nature, although his will shows him to have been very hard-headed too.

One of the poems is entitled "Good night, All's well",

> Deserted by the waning moon
> When sky's grow dim, night's churlish moon
> On tower or fort or tended grounds
> The sentry makes his hourly rounds.
> And should a footstep happly stray
> When caution marks the guarded way
> Who gives this stranger quickly tell
> The word, a friend, good night, all's well.
>
> Sailing on the midnight deep
> When nearby messmates soundly sleep
> The careful watch patrols the deck
> To guard the ship from foes or wreck
> And while his thoughts of home wend near
> Some friendly voice salutes his ear
> What cheer Brother — quickly tell
> All those below — Goodnight — all's well.

This raises two possible explanations as to the inspiration for this poem although it may be, also, that he just felt like writing it.

These were not peaceful times and the streets were not safe after dark. Indeed in 1808/09, just after Thomas married, a gang of reckless young men, some of them respectably connected, carried out a campaign of nocturnal outrage in Hanley and Shelton, rather more for mischief than for plunder it seems, and terrified the community. They were called the Rough Fleet, (John Ward p.369). Several were ultimately prosecuted, thus breaking up the gang. The poem is undated so this, or some other later unrest, may have inspired it.

There are other verses too, all Thomas' own work, for not only are they in his hand but are complete with crossings out and 'improvements'.

They are not unlike the verses found on Sunderland type lustre (splash lustre) which was produced in Staffordshire too. Thomas may have been just a compulsive versifier, or was he perhaps contemplating edging into this type of ware? He certainly produced lustre wares.

Thomas married Elizabeth Penny (known as Betty except in formal documents) at Norton-le-Moors on 12th September, 1808. Betty was the daughter of James and Elizabeth Penny of Burslem and the second youngest of eight children[13]. The eldest, one of only two sons, was her brother Charles, who was also a potter in Hope Street for a time[32].

Thomas and Betty's first child, James, was born on 14th March, 1812[33] Two more sons were born in the next few years, Charles in 1814[34] and William in 1816[35] and they were to have one more child that lived, a daughter Jane, born in 1822[36].

After his marriage, Thomas built two houses in Hope Street and let one of them to William Pointon[37] who probably worked at colour mixing with Thomas as this was his trade. Thomas lived in the other house[37] and worked as a colour maker, producing a wide range of colours, and also as a potter using several different pottery bodies.

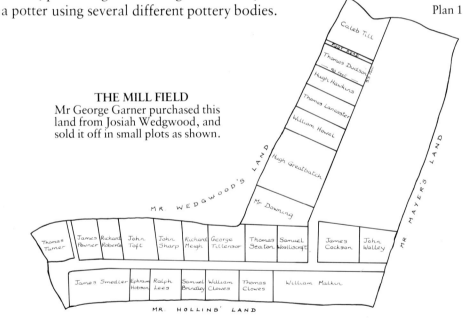

Plan 1

THE MILL FIELD
Mr George Garner purchased this land from Josiah Wedgwood, and sold it off in small plots as shown.

(31) *St. Johns Burslem register. Betty was baptised March 13th, 1791.*

(32) *Manorial Court, 21st November, 1815.*

(33) *Baptised St. Johns, Hanley, 5th April, 1812.*

(34) *Baptised St. Johns, Hanley, 21st May, 1814.*
   as "Charles Penny".

(35) *Baptised St. Johns, Hanley, 11th August, 1816.*

(36) *Baptised St. Johns, Hanley, 25th August, 1822.*
   Jane married Samuel Yates, 28th January, 1854 at Holy Trinity Church, Shelton.

(37) *Manorial Court, 27th January, 1813.*

26

To begin with he seems to have augmented his income, in the way so many of the small potters did at this time, by having a small holding. In 1813, he bought a piece of land in the Mill Field "to use as a garden"[38] (345 square yards). George Garner, a shoemaker in Hanley, had bought quite a large strip of land from Mr. Wedgwood and was selling this off in plots (plan 1). Thomas Dudson was one of the earliest to buy a plot from him. Part of Mill Field eventually became Mill Street and plan 2, below, shows its relationship to Hope Street. Presumably, Thomas sold most of his produce as his family was small. There is no record of what he produced but some of the journeymen potters rented allotments and rotated crops of potatoes, wheat and oats, the straw being in demand for packing pottery.

SHELTON 1825

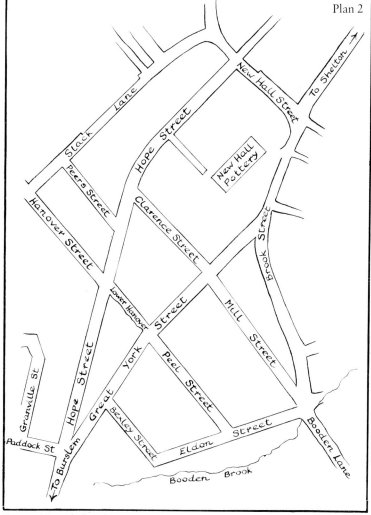

From 1825 sale brochure in Dudson deeds.

(38) *Manorial Court, 27th January, 1813.*

Thomas prospered, sold his garden in 1819 to use the[39] money for expansion and eventually outgrew this small house/potworks. He built a second house farther down the road away from Hanley, at the corner of Hope Street and Lower Hanover Street, and so began the present factory site (121½ square yards), (Plan 3 on p.33).

Confusion has arisen as to whether there were two Dudson factories — one in each of these streets, but in fact they are one and the same factory. Rates books add to the confusion by listing the factory sometimes in one street, sometimes in the other, and the numbering of the houses increases the problem. This house became No. 88 Hope Street and later 105 Hanover Street. Simeon Shaw in 1829[40] records that streets commonly carried their names on the corner but few houses were numbered.

James and Charles, eventually, both worked at Hope Street with their father until his death in 1845 but whilst Charles only worked at this factory James went first to Broad Street. It is believed that he went to his grandfather when he was about nine years old, this being much the same period that his uncle Richard moved from Broad Street to Wheatsheaf Street. Grandfather Richard died in October 1833 and a few months later, James, by now 21 years old, went to join his father at Hope Street. Charles was the "writing clerk" and also seems to have done some modelling, whilst James was more involved with colour making and was, obviously, the more talented potter and better business man of the two.

William was a pottery printer[41] but where he worked is not known, although he may well have been involved with his father's business. He was the first of the sons to marry. Leah Colclough, born in Hanley, a daughter of Thomas Colclough, also a potter, was married to William at Wolstanton on 19th September, 1836. She was a pottery tranferrer[41]. After both his parents had died, William and Leah went to live in Shropshire for a time. They are not involved any further in this account, although their son, Thomas, is at a later date. William and Leah subsequently returned to the Potteries and started a greengrocery business.

William's marriage was quickly followed by Charles' wedding on 25th December, 1836 [42] but this was to prove the first tragedy in what was to turn out to be a very tragic life, for he buried his new bride only four months later on 25th April, 1837[43]. He married Eliza Lees.

James married Jane Spilsbury — the daughter of yet another potter, James Spilsbury, in March 1838[44].

(39) *Manorial Court, June 9th, 1819.*
(40) *History of the Staffordshire Potteries.*
(41) *1841 Census.*
(42) *St. Peter Ad Vincula, Stoke.*
(43) *St. Mark's, Shelton.*
(44) *St. Catherines House, London, Index XVII — 150.*

5

THE FACTORY SITE AT HOPE STREET

Thomas Dudson 1786 — 1845

It was mentioned briefly in the previous chapter that Thomas built a house at the corner of Hope Street and Lower Hanover Street and thus began the principal factory site in Hope Street.

An account of how the factory was gradually built up is interesting for two reasons. Firstly, not much has been recorded as to how a small potter, without a lot of capital behind him, nevertheless persevered and slowly built up the site

Reproduced by kind permission of Art Trade Press Ltd. 9 Rock Hampton Road, Havant, Hampshire.

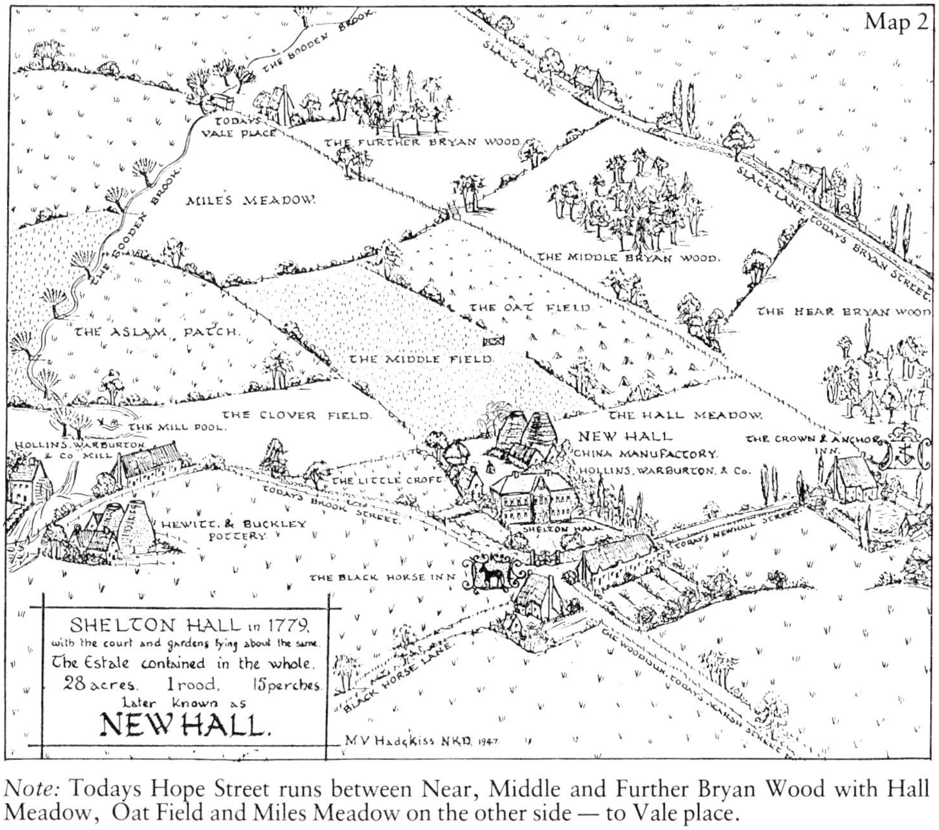

Map 2

Note: Todays Hope Street runs between Near, Middle and Further Bryan Wood with Hall Meadow, Oat Field and Miles Meadow on the other side — to Vale place.

and the business. Secondly, an understanding of this gives a clearer background to his working life and the development of the firm.

For this it is necessary to look very briefly at some of the history of the New Hall Porcelain Company.

The land upon which the Dudson factory now stands was at one time land around Shelton New Hall and was purchased from that estate when it was owned by the New Hall partnership.

The Shelton Hall referred to is that which stood on what is called New Hall Street in modern Hanley, and was called New Hall because there was already an Old Hall in Shelton when the second one was built. Job Meigh manufactured at the Old Hall.

In 1773 the New Hall Estate consisted of the Hall,[45] "with its gardens, yards, stables, outbuildings and all those pieces of land belonging thereto: Hall Meadow, Little Croft, Middle Field, The Aslam Patch, Clover Field, Miles Meadow, Nearer Bryans Wood, Middle and Farther Bryans Wood including the Oat Piece had altogether more than 28 acres", (Map 2).

At a later date some of the meadows were renamed and Little Croft, Hall Meadow and Middle Field became two Brickkiln Fields part of which was to be purchased by Dudson.

When in 1773 the New Hall was no longer required as a private estate, Humphrey Palmer bought it and converted the Hall and outbuildings into a pottery factory which his son worked for some years. After Humphrey Palmer's death in 1789, the estate passed to his daughter Mary,[46] who lived in Birmingham. Mary let the estate to a group of potters who had formed a partnership to manufacture porcelain and in 1803 granted a 14 year lease to the partners who were trading as Hollins, Warburton, Daniel & Co[47]. When Mary died in 1805 all the property and land was sold outright to the partnership.

Originally seven partners had come to New Hall,[48] but the sale was delayed by legal formalities and when it was completed in 1810 the number of partners, due to deaths, was down to four. At a special Court Baron on 26th April, 1810 Samuel Hollins, Peter Warburton, John Daniel and William Clowes bought the estate for £6,800 and became copyhold tenants in common. The estate was shared in four equal parts, each partner having one part. John Daniel was the manager and they manufactured porcelain under Cookworthy's patent which

(45) *Duchy of Lancaster Manorial Court, 14th July, 1773.*
(46) *Duchy of Lancaster Manorial Court 30th September, 1789.*
(47) *Duchy of Lancaster Manorial Court 5th November, 1802 and 1st March, 1803.*
(48) *Duchy of Lancaster Manorial Court 14th February, 1790.*

they had bought some years before (1786), made and sold glazes and pottery bodies to other potters' specifications, and also milled potters materials.

Court Rolls from this time show the partners sub-letting, or selling, small parts of their land, probably to recoup some of their capital outlay, and in fact the Duchy produced a map of the Brickkiln Fields in 1813 which they "filed among the Court Rolls for the benefit of purchasers of plots".

In 1811 the four partners of New Hall, together with William Adams of Cobridge, Robert Bucknall and James Stephenson, who between them owned the land between New Hall and Cobridge, decided it would be "a great convenience and accommodation" to both groups and the public if a road of sufficient width was laid out through their lands from Shelton to Cobridge. A four part indenture was drawn up on 30th December, 1811[49].

They all agreed that:

1. Within two years of the date of the agreement that they would construct a road of thirty feet wide excluding footpaths using refuse from Potworks called shards and schraff following a line shown on the plan.

2. If any party should build, or sell for building purposes, or in lots, any land lying along the line of the said road the same should be laid out with hard fired bricks and lined with a stone kerb on the outside — or laid wholly with durable flags, this to be thereafter kept in repair by the respective owners or occupiers after the sale and to bind them to this.

Nothing appears to have happened until 4th July, 1814 when the original indenture had an addition appended. It was then agreed also[50] that a diversion should be made in the direction of the road insofar as it went through the New Hall Estate to make the road shorter and more commodious (Map 3). An additional road should be immediately opened and deemed a public road, owners having the same provisos applied as before. Eventually the diverted road became Hope Street and the additional road Great York Street.

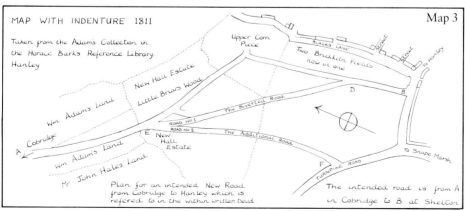

(49) *Part of the Adams collection of documents relating to the Adams family of potters held at the Horace Barks Reference Library in Hanley.*

(50) *Peter Warburton and James Stevenson had both died prior to this date.*

In August, 1814[51] the partners of Hollins, Warburton, Daniel and Company surrendered to John Daniel. He became the sole copyhold tenant and the name of the pottery was changed to the New Hall Porcelain Company. This move would seem to have been very largely a matter of convenience. Instead of each partner having to go to the Manorial Court for every transaction in which they were involved, John Daniel could now handle the sale or letting of much of the land with, one presumes, some internal arrangement for the allocation of moneys received. From then on John Daniel is very actively concerned in the Duchy of Lancaster Rolls as he sells off plots of land. There is no direct evidence or reference, either in the Adams collection or in the Rolls, to the road being made, but every sale of a piece of land contained the proviso that the new owner would give up one yard along his frontage to widen the road. Surrenders by 1816[52] refer to plots being divided by the new road intended to lead from Hanley to Cobridge, and on 10th May, 1816 also to two houses which are farthest from the turnpike road Shelton to Cobridge[53].

At this time many of the plots had under-tenants as it was quite common for copyhold tenants to sub-let, though there are no references to be found of either Richard or Thomas named as under-tenants. This is not too surprising as only a few of the under-tenants were named until such time as they purchased — the presence of such evidence however would have helped in establishing dates. Thomas' purchase of the 'garden' plot in Mill Field in 1813, however, when he is described in the Court Roll as a potter does confirm that he was operating earlier than that date, undoubtedly as an under-tenant to John Daniel, but on the part of the estate owned by Samuel Hollins. He sold this land in 1819 using the money for further expansion.

When Thomas did buy the land in Hope Street it was from William Clowes. John Daniel died on 18th January, 1821, leaving everything to his sister, Alice, as sole heir. This meant that the copyhold tenancy passed to her, but she immediately handed it over to William Clowes who, by this time was the last of the partners still alive[54]. He was to sell for her, on trust, and to surrender the tenancies to the purchasers. Thus the first purchase of 'factory' land which Thomas Dudson made was from William Clowes, in 1821 — a site in Hope Street but nearer to Hanley than the corner site he later bought in the same street. (Plan 3). The land was part of the Brickkiln Field fronting onto Hope Street, and Thomas paid £18 1s. 6d. for it. The two dwelling houses on it had been built by Thomas and he occupied one, having let the other to William Pointon[55]. Like everyone else, Thomas was required to provide "one yard of his frontage to widen the road". At the same court at which he made his

(51) *Manorial Court, 4th August, 1814.*

(52) *Manorial Court, 27th January, 1816.*

(53) *Sales by William Clowes at the Court 6th March, 1821 state: "fronting onto the new road leading from Cobridge to New Hall in Shelton intended to be called Hope Street".*

(54) *Samuel Hollins died in 1820. Peter Warburton in 1813 and Jacob Warburton in 1826 at 86 years of age, having retired some years earlier.*

(55) *Manorial Court 29th November, 1821.*

purchase, he immediately mortgaged both the houses for £50 each to James Bagnall,[55] the son of Sampson Bagnall, using the money to expand the business and set on more employees[56].

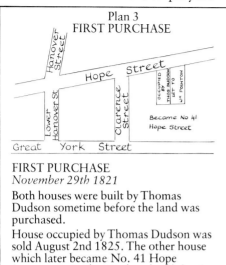

Plan 3
FIRST PURCHASE

FIRST PURCHASE
November 29th 1821

Both houses were built by Thomas Dudson sometime before the land was purchased.
House occupied by Thomas Dudson was sold August 2nd 1825. The other house which later became No. 41 Hope Street, remained in Dudson hands but let to under tenants.

Plan 4
SECOND PURCHASE

SECOND PURCHASE
Land purchased November 3rd 1836
House sub-tenanted from c 1824
This house became 88 Hope Street, later changed to 105 Hanover Street.

The last of the New Hall partners, William Clowes, died in 1823, the remaining parts of the estate being left for disposal by all the heirs of the partners. In Clowes' case the heir was his son-in-law, Hugh Henshall Williamson, and the heirs of Samuel Hollins were his children, Thomas and Catherine Hollins and Elizabeth Russell. Dudsons were only concerned with these two parts of the estate.

The entire New Hall estate was advertised as being for sale on 6th and 7th October, 1825, the advertisement appearing each week during the month of September in The Staffordshire Advertiser. The complete brochure and map for this proposed sale is deposited with the Dudson Deeds in the custody of their Bank. Plan 2 on p.27 is taken from this map omitting the "lots". There is no notice, subsequently, of the cancellation of the sale, nor, for that matter, any report of the sale having taken place, nor did Dudson purchase any lots at this sale. On the other hand, for several years afterwards, plots continued to be sold by the heirs of the original partners through the Manorial Courts. The strong evidence is that the sale did not take place, and it is a matter of some surprise that care was taken to preserve the sale brochure with the Dudson Deeds.

By 1825 Thomas Dudson had moved from his original premises in Hope Street and become an under-tenant on land at the corner of Hope Street and Lower Hanover Street, (See plan 4 above). He built a dwelling house on the corner

(56) *From a factory note book in Thomas' hand comes:—*
   "George from Keel came Feb. 12, 1822 and is to have £4. 10s. for this year out".
   "Thomas Williams sometime in February 1822 to have 8½ guineas for this year out.
   John Stones 1 April, 1822".
   "Elizabeth 1 April, 1822, £6 a year" (his wife).

where the two roads joined, on land owned by William Outrim and Thomas Hindle. William Outrim was an accountant in Stoke[57]. On 2nd August, 1825 it is recorded that Thomas sold "a dwelling house in Hope Street, Shelton, late in the occupation of Thomas Dudson", (See plan 3 p.33). Thomas had raised a mortgage of £50 on this house and it was entered "this £50 and the interest is still owing". A druggist in Hanley, Thomas Hawthorn, bought the house for £71 and also took over the mortgage and interest. "Thomas Dudson being exonerated therefrom" by the Manorial Court[58]. It is reasonable to conclude therefore that Thomas Dudson had once again built his house whilst he was an under-tenant.

This new corner site cost him £52. 12s. 4d. when he subsequently bought it in 1836, the site already had buildings on it "erected and occupied by Thomas Dudson" [59]. Family folklore has it that the privy at this new house was across the yard. Thomas had a goat tethered there which ignored everyone except Betty. For some reason, known only to the goat, whenever Betty went to the privy the goat kept her immured, butting the door whenever she tried to get out.

In May 1837 he mortgaged the plot to William Hopwood and Isaac Legge for £200[60]. This plot on this occasion was described as "adjoining John Bedson's plot, fronting onto Hope Street and also fronting onto Lower Hanover Street...... together with house, workshop, hovel oven and kiln used for colour making...... to which Thomas Dudson was admitted tenant on 3rd November, 1836". William Hopwood (china manufacturer) and Isaac Legge (coarse ware manufacturer) both of Lane End were acting as executors for the estate of William Hilditch (junior) earthenware manufacturer of Lane Delph. Thomas was to "repay £200 plus £10 interest plus expenses when the executors would surrender to him". In fact the mortgage and interest were not repaid until 30th June, 1842.

Thomas seems to have had a piece of luck with regard to the house and land which was let to William Pointon. It will be recalled that he had mortgaged this to James Bagnall for £50, but Bagnall died in 1831 and his executors discharged Thomas from any mortgage liabilities and surrendered the property back to him[61]. William Pointon was still occupying the house. The house was one of those ultimately left to Thomas' son Charles when Thomas died.

The factory site was further extended in 1839 when Thomas bought 1072 square yards[62] at the corner of Lower Hanover Street and Great York Street which already had on it his sliphouse and five houses. He paid the heirs of the New Hall Estate £114. 12s. 8d., (See plan 5 p.35).

(57) *Manorial Court 8th June, 1825.*
(58) *Manorial Court 2nd August, 1825.*
(59) *Manorial Court 3rd November, 1836.*
(60) *Manorial Court 4th May, 1837.*
(61) *Manorial Court 1st March, 1831.*
(62) *Manorial Court 27th March 1839.*

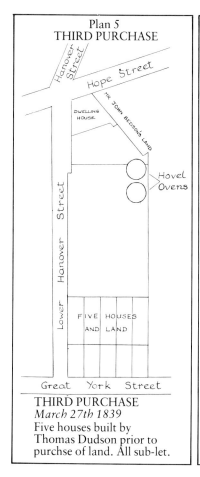

Plan 5
THIRD PURCHASE

THIRD PURCHASE
March 27th 1839
Five houses built by
Thomas Dudson prior to
purchse of land. All sub-let.

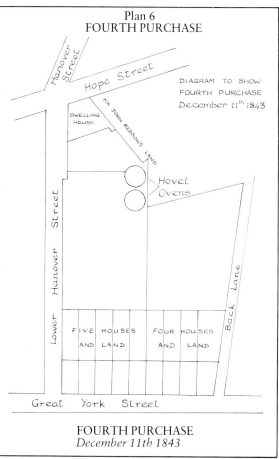

Plan 6
FOURTH PURCHASE

DIAGRAM TO SHOW
FOURTH PURCHASE
December 11th 1843

FOURTH PURCHASE
December 11th 1843

His final purchase was in 1843[63] when he bought the opposite corner of Great York Street which was separated from the back of Clarence Street by Back Lane. This was, and still is, a public right of way, (See plan 6). He had already built four houses and outbuildings and obviously made use of the rest of the land in his business. It would seem very likely that he built these houses as a business proposition as they were fenced off from the factory and all were sub-let. It is possible that he was letting them to some of his employees as many of the tenants were pottery operatives of one kind or another.

The photograph on page 36 shows the back of the factory in January, 1982 the side of one of the Great York Street houses is to the left. Back Lane shows clearly and the grass at the right would have been the back of Clarence Street in 1843.

By 1844 Thomas was sufficiently affluent to change roles, granting a mortgage of £1,000[64] to his nephew Samuel Keeling of Hanley, earthenware

(63) *Manorial Court 11th December, 1843.*
(64) *Manorial Court 1st November, 1844.*

manufacturer, Thomas Adams of Shelton, agent, and John Shirley of Hanley, earthenware manufacturer, on a silk mill, engine house office, etc., at Eastwood in Hanley near to Albion Bridge which had been erected in 1824 by James Baddeley deceased. They were to pay interest at the rate of £5 per £100 per annum. This mortgage was repaid to James Dudson after his fathers death, in quite a complicated manner[65]. Samuel Keeling and Thomas Adams bought John Shirley's share of the mill from him for £760 plus £333. 6s. 8d. which was his portion of the mortgage owed to Thomas Dudson. They paid the latter direct to James Dudson. John Shirley then granted Keeling and Adams a mortgage of £1,000 on the whole of the Eastwood mill, and, out of this cash they received, Keeling and Adams repaid £666. 13s. 4d. plus interest (i.e. the rest of the mortgage due) to James Dudson.

Plate 1. Rear of Hope Street factory showing the original Back Lane — the extreme right side of the photograph would have been Clarence Street in the 19th century.

(65) *Manorial Court 29th March, 1849.*

6

THOMAS DUDSON

1786 — 1845

PRODUCTION

As indicated earlier, it is most likely that Thomas learned his skill and knowledge of colour making and potting from his father Richard. Certainly in his early books (1819, 1823) are to be found the recipes for all types of ware popular throughout the industry in the last quarter of the 18th century and first quarter of the 19th century. Various stoneware bodies including Egyptian black, caneware, pearlware, opaque china, granite china and several china recipes — many containing bone-ash are listed. These will be referred to in greater detail in the next chapter.

Dipped (dipt) ware was a speciality at this period and several colours of dip are given. Wedgwood had developed Jasper, either with a surface colouring (Jasper dip) or the body stained with metallic oxides (solid Jasper). The best known of course being the blue ware with white relief decoration. Many other factories produced jasperware including William Adams, John Turner, Edmund Birch, John Glass, Joseph and Edward Keeling, John Lockett, Nehemiah Massey, Elijah Mayer, James Neale, Humphrey Palmer, John and Richard Riley and John Shorthouse. Dudson early records show that they too were producing blue and white jasper in 1819, as orders were being supplied for jugs at that date. Thomas Dudson also had the knowledge to produce the other coloured jasper bodies, or jasper dips, in this period but sales records are "skimpy" and do not show whether he did or not. Jasper ware may well have been made earlier than 1819, but this is the earliest record book available. This 1819 book, together with a few other early record books and documents, were found about ten years ago in an old factory safe. Most of the early record books were destroyed long ago in factory and office changes.

1819 — 23. TYPES OF POTTERY PRODUCED
Two early books (1819 and 1823) show that Thomas was producing, in addition to colours and pottery bodies, quite a wide range of wares — mainly tablewares — for such a small factory. In addition to customers in England there were several he supplied in Ireland, in Limerick, Cork, Waterford and several in Dublin. The goods were shipped by James Brough, Salters Lane, Liverpool. Messrs. Randles, Old Dock, Liverpool, or by John Bibbough also of Liverpool.

The following selection of types of ware made during this period is taken from the above factory books, but a more detailed list is given in Appendix C.

In this short list are included tea and coffee pots of various shapes, sugar bowls, cream jugs, dinner plates, cups and saucers, muffins, toothmugs and a variety of other mugs and jugs of different sizes. There is mention of six different sizes of blue and white jasper ware jugs, of 'dipt' ware (mugs, jugs and bowls) as well as ewers and basins.

In addition there are china tea services, e.g.

1. China and gilt tea sets, purple and gold pattern, Grecian shape cups, saucers, coffee cups (cans) cake plates, slop bowls, sugar and creams.
2. Black gilt oval and round 'capt' teapots, sugar and creams, (See plate 2).
3. Plain white china with gold edge and line, described as 'vitrified', tea sets, coffee sets, teapots, sugar boxes, jugs, breakfast bowls and egg cups. Some of these were ordered as "the same in cheaper pattern — gilt".

Plate 2. Black basalt jug 4″ — unmarked but identified by sherds from archaelogical dig.

There are orders received from John Daniel, New Hall Porcelain Co., in the 1819 book. One of these was for a Mr. Brammer in Waterford, presumably one of New Hall's customers. The next entry is for *"Grecian shape handle teas, Evening, 2 saucers 2 creams N1600"*. This number and the numbers on the other entries, i.e. N 1696 N 1699 and N 984 are not Dudson numbers, but almost certainly refer to New Hall pattern numbers. Mr. David Holgate has kindly identified two of them (the other two numbers have not as yet been recorded) and has provided the following interesting information. No. 1699 is a very simple polychrome hand painted design found only on bone china. Pattern N 984 was introduced first, about 1810, on hard paste porcelain but it was popular and since the change over to bone china was imminent it is found almost as often on bone china as hard paste. These were bat prints in black painted over with covered enamels, a large number of different scenes being used. Some were just typical countryside scenes but others were of named country houses taken from contemporary engravings. A tea set would probably have a different scene on different pieces. No. 984 also has a simple gold band.

It has been considered that these might have been orders from Dudson to New Hall and not orders from New Hall to Dudson, but this is primarily an order book, although not a formal one. It is difficult to see why, in that case, it should have been recorded in this book, especially as there is no other entry relating to Dudson purchasing anything. The other entries, apart from orders, are for cash received — in some cases from other potters, i.e. Mr. Minton, Mr. Hamilton, Charles Meigh, Joseph Poulson, and also a few recipes for pottery bodies and colours.

Perhaps Dudsons did not make these patterns regularly for New Hall but, more probably, only under certain special conditions. As is shown in later sections of this history it was not unusual for Dudson to make items for other factories, even sometimes applying the other factories' back stamps.

Throughout this 1819 book the customer's name and address was put at the top of the page, as is the case of the first New Hall order and Bentley & Ware. On the order N. 984 it seems that the name had been forgotten at the top and added at the bottom, although of course other interpretations are possible.

Another order of some interest is that for Bentley & Ware (Wear) of Shelton. This is "3 complete tea sets at 35/- each nett money. Each to contain 12 cups and saucers, 12 coffee, 1 slop and 2 cake plates, 1 teapot and stand, and sugar and cream". All three sets were to be in "pink landscape — burnished gold and line — Bute shape",* and a repeat order later was for "1 teapot stand, 1 cream, 3 slops, 1 sugar box, 12 coffee, 2 cake plates, 30 cups and 30 saucers". Bentley & Wear were in Vine Street Shelton. They were engravers, printers and enamellers and presumably printed the design for the landscape. The firm also had a gallery where they displayed paintings by famous and local artists[66].

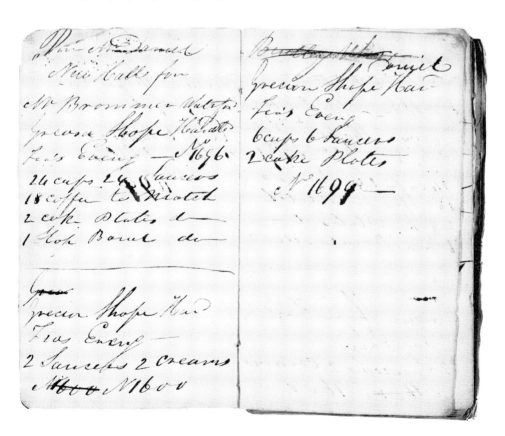

(66) *Simeon Shaw History of the Staffordshire Potteries. 1829 Davis and Charles reprint p. 46.*
  * *Some of the sherds recovered in the archeological dig are pink under-glaze transfer ware.*

Bute Shape Vine Leaf
Even.
6 cups 6 Saucers
6 coffee cans flat Botom
2 cake Plates No 84
from D and
New Hall

Bentley & Ware
Shelton
Pink Landscipe
Bermida Gold & Line
3 Setts compleat
£35 Nett money
Each to contain ——
12 cups 12 Saucers
12 coffee 1 Slop
1 cake Plate 1 Teapot
& Stand 1 Sugar & cr
1 Cream ——

Pink continued
1 Teapot Stand
1 Cream 3 Slops
1 Sugar Box ——
1 coffee 2 cake Plate
30 cups 30 Saucers
all Bute Shape
Evening

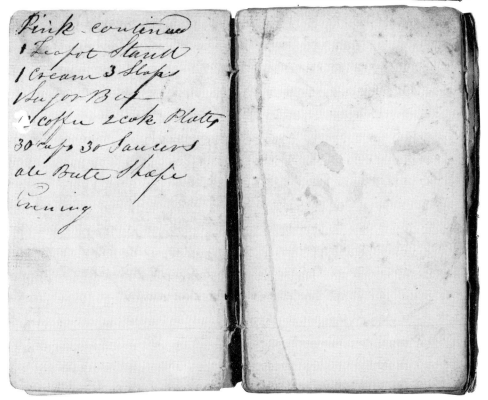

Some orders from other parts of England include Mr. Edward Peters, 16 Summerend Square, Bristol, for Frederick Weston "The Rensar's Whome"! Mr. Lingford at the Sun Tavern, Ludgate Hill, London appears to have been a regular customer. There is also an order from .... (unreadable) at Stone for :

6 white chamber pots, 6 dozen dinner plates

3 evening cups and saucers

6 dozen breakfast plates

6 muffins

Are these three very early examples of Dudsons supplying people engaged in catering?

Customers in Worcester had their goods sent by Waytes boats.

Not many of the orders are entered as being delivered with the accounts settled later, so it seems that most of the transactions were of a cash-and-carry nature and not entered. Prices are not always shown very clearly but the following gives some indication :

Mr. John Faulkener, Chesterton

Black gilt.

Round Capt teapots 12, 18, 24 at 14/- per doz	
Round Capt teapots 30, 36	*15/- per doz*
Sugars 24	*20/- per doz*
Creams 30	*18/- per doz*
Oval teapots 12, 18, 24	*20/- per doz*

Mr. Charles Davenport, Brown Street, Cork

4 crates cups

Teapots 12, 18, 24, 30, 36 at 5/-

7 dozen oval teapots 2/12, 2/18, 2/24, 1/30 at 12/-

1 dozen coffee pots 4 at 4/-

1 dozen coffee pots 6

1 dozen coffee pots 9

1 dozen coffee pots 12

To fill up 12, 24 jugs Dutch shape 3/-

5 dozen salts 1/6

2 dozen oval coffee pots

1 dozen oval sugars

1 dozen oval ewers

2 dozen bowls 24 at 4/-

Old Capt teapots 12, 18, 24 at 5/-

*Crate off care of James Brough Liverpool —
money when goods arrive*

Mr James Barry, Kyrles Quay, Cork
2 crates cut cups

3	6	3	2	1
12	18	24	30	36	*at 4/6*

8 dozen 6 — 12 mugs 1/3

4 dozen 36 salts on feet — 1 crate 1/8

Teapots 12, 18, 24, 30 at 4/-

1 crate oval teapots 12, 18, 24, 30 at 12/-

2 crates Dipt mugs, jugs and bowls at 2/6

and 15/- — crate of bowls 12, 18, 24, 30, 36

Other prices :

*Pink landscaped, burnished gold and line china tea sets
complete sets — 35/- each*

Purple and gold pattern china tea sets — 8 complete sets for £5. 5s 0d

Brown milk jugs 12   18   24   30
5/-   5/-   5/6 5/6 per dozen

Dutch jugs 3/- per dozen

Roman jugs 2/6 per dozen

Blue figured jugs 6   12   18   6/- per dozen
24   30   36   8/- per dozen

Records show that the firm continued to make these types of goods for many years, even later when the main production was of "toys" (Chimney ornaments).

Colour making was always an important side of Dudson's work, and probably the main part of the business for the first half of the 19th century. Although the balance swung later in favour of potting, colour making remained important throughout most of the second half of that century too — which accounts for the fact that, in comparison with some other factories, Dudson pottery orders were small.

Some of the cash entries are very formal, the pages drawn in faint red lines and columns, the entries properly dated and the opposite page to the receipts headed 'Contra'.

For various dates in 1819 there are receipts such as the following :
1819 Mr. Hamilton

Jan. 12th 1819	£60.0.0
Jan. 20th 1819	£20.0.0
Feb. 19th	£40.0.0
Mar. 26th	£30.0.0

This is probably Robert or James Hamilton who were potters in Shelton at this period[67].

Mr. Hamilton	£150.0.0
Edward Poulson	£350.0.0
S. Steel	£5.0.0
Joseph Poulson	£52.0.0

Other cash entries are less formally made, one of particular interest :

1822 Jan 20th	*To Cash £79. 12s. 6d*
	Rec'd of Mr. Minton

It is interesting that the ledger for this year which is in the Minton Archives, shows that Mr. Minton drew out over £100 in cash the previous day.

Although it is understood that Minton had his own colour mill it may well be that Thomas was producing some colour which was worth buying to save a firm like Minton making it specially. Some other cash entries:

Rec'd from S. Steel	*Cash £20.0.0*	
	His a/c	*£21.35½. (presumably £21. 3s. 5½d)*

Ref. He was a slip maker in Hope Street.

---

(67) *Manorial Court 10th June, 1807.*

An interesting entry in the 1823 book in pencil in different handwriting to other entries :

Rayner & Co.,

Tobacco Manufacturers,

Neil Street,

Liverpool.

Call when in Liverpool .

This seems to indicate that Thomas Dudson sometimes travelled himself at least to Liverpool.

No order books are available between 1825 and 1834 and then another gap occurs until 1842, but during this period (1825-42) production had gradually swung over to making "toys" and other ornaments. The 1834 recipe book shows that figures and animals were certainly being made then (see next chapter).

Fortunately, there is a comprehensive order book for 1842/43 so it is possible to give a very detailed list of items produced (see Appendix D. p. 174). Sadly no pieces of this ware remain on the factory, nor any drawings, and it seems unlikely that many, if any, of them were ever marked.* Identification therefore, is a matter for research. Fortunately the archeological dig (see Appendix A) has yielded some clues and a small start has been made. Other people may be able to add to the knowledge in due course. One other proof of Dudson production in this field comes in the Government report on the employment of children in manufactures in 1842 referring to the factory in Hope Street "Thomas Dudson — an ornamental Figure Factory — inspected several girls under 13, but playing Christmas week. Premises very good".

Plate 3. A double faced tobacco jar. Earthenware unmarked 4¾". 1850 s. (See colour plate 2, p.20).

Plate 4. Glazed earthenware jug, gilded and hand painted on glaze in enamels. "Flower Jug." Rope handle. Incised ⁻⸍⁻ 703 painted on base 1840 s. A spray of blue flowers and leaves is on the reverse side.

*Some of the sherds uncovered in the dig have ⁻⸍⁻ impressed on the base which may assist in future identification of pieces, (See marks p.222).

A Mr. Stokes of London appears to have been a good customer in this period. He took a comprehensive range of items but dogs were obviously what he could sell best. In the six months from April to September, 1842 he bought 942 dozen of the 9d. per dozen dogs and 75 dozen of the 1/6d. per dozen dogs plus orders for the better quality poodles and spaniels such as Blue Spaniels, Rough Spaniels — corner dogs. He also bought cans, jugs and bowls each month.

A letter found in the factory safe which has had the stamp removed but which is franked April 27th, 1842, is addressed simply to "Mr. Thomas Dudson, Shelton, Staffordshire Potteries" giving some indication that Thomas' business was well known. The letter is an order for various dogs, eagles and other figures to be delivered as soon as possible to Henry Soloman & Co., again regular customers in London.

A complete list has been compiled from the orders for 1842 — 1844 of the articles manufactured in this period and is to be found in Appendix D.

This order book includes orders for export across the Atlantic, especially to Baltimore and Boston. Ireland was an important market in addition to all parts of Britain.

Orders are also recorded from other local manufacturers — most notably Davenports of Longport, who order dogs from time to time. The order shown below was not recorded in the order book as usual — but the loose paper was inserted.

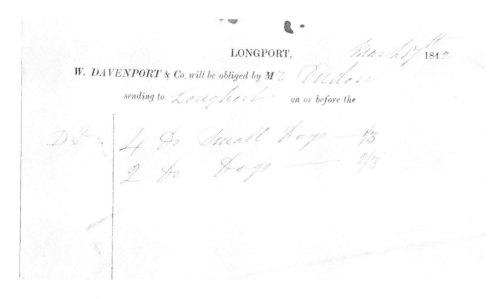

Hilditch and Hopwood had a comprehensive range of samples sent to them and orders followed in June 1842 for:

1 set of seasons, 1 custard cup middle size

1 dozen Inks, 1 dozen boxes, 12 cottages

6 figures, assorted, and 6 cheaper figures assorted

2 white and gold Toby jugs

4 greyhounds and 6 eagle Inks (Inkwells)

One is left wondering whatever they did with such a strange assortment.

In 1843 Samuel Keeling & Co. ordered:

19 dozen tea sets printed

2 dozen teapots round and pressed in turquoise

2 dozen teapots in drab

1 dinner set - printed

Several orders were supplied to Mr. John Gerrard of Hanley. These were large, and included a wide range of the Dudson products. It is presumed that this was John Gerrard, the Hanley potter, for the orders often included large quantities of common clay.

7

BODY AND COLOUR RECIPES

Thomas Dudson 1819 — 1834

Thomas Dudson mixed a fairly extensive range of bodies, but he appears to have had the milling done for him by either the New Hall Mill, owned by Hollins, Warburton & Daniel, or by Hackwoods. There is a note in 1826 ...... "Send marl to mill at Hackwoods". The New Hall mill supplied many potters with their materials and Thomas possibly bought some of his clays and other materials direct from them.

1819 — 1823 BODY RECIPES

The body recipes listed in these years appear to be Thomas' own and not made to other people specifications, i.e. he was using them for his own manufacture and not to sell them. The list is as follows :

Stone body	*White stone*	*Brown stone*
Chalk body	*Flat body*	*Common white body*
Jasper body (2)	*Pearl body*	*China body (several)*
White opaque body (2)		

There were also two bodies for printed ware, one containing china clay and the other without.

Colour Bodies

Blue, green, brown, cane, Egyptian black and drab.

Orders appear for "blue figured jugs" in this period, so Thomas was obviously making jasper from either, or possibly both, of his jasper body recipes, and coloured dip recipes. Orders also show that some of the other body recipes were in use. For example, Thomas was selling brown-necked jugs, brown milk jugs, also 'round', 'Dutch' and 'Roman' jugs, some of these presumably being made in stone or coloured bodies, pearl, cane, and black basalt may well have been in production. Pink transfer printed ware was made for Bentley and Wear, and as two recipes for "printed bodies" were available — plus the underglaze colours blue, green and brown, perhaps he was able to print ware in all these colours. (See colour plate 35 p.166).

China Bodies

Turning to the china bodies produced, Thomas was selling variously decorated china tea services, including some form of body which was acceptable to New Hall Porcelain Company, and several recipes are given for china bodies.

Josiah Spode (1754 — 1827) developed the following bone china recipe :

Bone ash	52 parts/weight	52%
Cornish stone	24 parts/weight	24%
China clay	24 parts/weight	24%

This contains no ball clay but bone ash provides some plasticity, so ball clay may be dispensed with in manufacturing bone china. The first of Thomas Dudson's recipes for china body in 1819 does contain some ball clay :

Bone ash	51.85%
Stone	25.92%
China clay	14.81%
Ball clay	7.4%

Ball clay was presumably added at the expense of china clay in an attempt to improve plasticity.

China body recipe No. 3 was quite different in that it had much less bone and stone with more Ball clay and China clay.

Bone ash	39.59%
Stone	17.59%
China clay	19.06%
Ball clay	23.76%

(Bone china recipes in 1980 are usually in the range of 50 — 22 per cent bone).

Yet another bone china recipe of this period was :

		1980 recipe for comparison
Bone	33.33%	50.00%
Cornwallstone	27.77%	21.43%
China clay	27.77%	25.00%
Ball clay	4.16%	3.57%
Fritt	7.00%	—

The recipe for this china frit is :

> *100 parts of Lyme sand*
>
> *4 parts of Pearl ash*
>
> *To be fired in the Biscuit oven .*

The china glaze for these recipes is as follows :

> *50 parts Borax*
>
> *40 parts Stone*
>
> *20 parts Flint*
>
> *20 parts best Paris White*
>
> *10 parts Pearl Ash*
>
> *15 parts best china clay*

Fritted in glost oven. Then add 20 parts of white lead and 10 parts of stone. Calcine the stone before grinding as this makes the glaze whiter .

(The OED described 'Paris White' as 'fine kind of whiting used in polishing'. More properly it is ground limestone, chalk or marble as a source of calcium oxide)[68]. Plaster was used in some of the bodies, possibly foreshadowing the use of lime in certain bodies for technical reasons.

From this it does appear that bone china was produced. Sales of various china tea sets and coffee sets were made at this period (see notes on production) and during the 1840 s and 1850 s Dudson's advertised both earthenware and china figures and, in documents, described themselves sometimes as earthenware manufacturers, sometimes as china manufacturers.

One of the recipes for White Stone body is interesting in that it contains salt :

Stone	55.55%
China clay	30.55%
Ball clay	11.11%
Salt	2.77%

One explanation for this is that it was an attempt to produce a glost article in one firing by producing a dense surface skin on the ware similar to glaze. Because salt is soluble in water it would migrate to the outer surface of the clay ware during drying and firing and would then melt to produce the denser layer.

(68) *Pottery & Porcelain: A Glossary of Terms. Bernard H. Charles.*

Alternatively it may have been included with the idea of helping to vitrify the body more easily. This was obviously an experiment but, as it would be difficult to fire, may not have been a success.

By 1834 the following had been added to the list of recipes used in the production of pottery.

Figure body (several)   *Good drab body*

Ironstone body   *Stone body (several)*

Casting body   *Pitcher mould clay*

Bisquit blue for grounds   *Mortar body*

Best bisquit blue   *Chalk body*

Blue for grounds   *Stilt clay body*

Lomoss body   *Stone china body*

Coloured bodies:

Blue, Turquoise, Sage, Lilac

Drab, Buff, Cane, Green

Brown, Chocolate

Blue Jasper and Blue dip for Jasper jugs

THOMAS DUDSON AS A COLOURMAKER (1819 — 25)

One of the main lines of business of this factory, which was at least as important as potting at this period, was the mixing of colours and glazes for supply to other manufacturers. There was the extensive range of pottery bodies referred to above but just how widely these were for sale is not so clear. Undoubtedly some would be sold to small potters in the area but existing accounts show that some of the bigger potters were also supplied with special lines from time to time — quite often this was colour or glazes but among the recipes are those used by other manufacturers.

Why, is a matter of speculation. They may have been 'acquired' for comparison, or perhaps supplied because the larger factories required a relatively small amount for a special order and found it easier to buy than to prepare themselves.

In general, the majority of recipes appear to be very much those typical of the period. The comprehensive range indicates that the Dudsons were competent and knowledgeable ceramic chemists, especially as there was little printed information available in this early part of the 19th century. Because of the lack of printed information colour recipes were guarded carefully and sometimes recipes were offered for sale — at a high price if they were well tested and approved. However, colour recipes which did not work were also sold, so care had to be taken as to what was bought.

There is an interesting example of this among Thomas Dudson's papers. He bought three recipes for enamels from James Glassbrook in Birmingham in 1823. At this time Birmingham was the centre for enamels for 'toys' — especially for enamelling on copper.

On the back of the recipes there is the following guarantee :

I hereby certify the annexed receipts to be correctly stated according to my agreement with Thomas Dudson as witnefs.

My Hand   *James Glassbrook*
Witnefs Present   *Wm. Folyfield, Major*

The recipes Thomas was buying were all enamels, and are recipes containing tin :

RECIPES FOR TIN

1 oz of water

2 oz of tin

3 oz of Sault (? Spirits of)

1 oz of Nitre

1½ oz of Nitre

2 oz of Tin

RECIPE FOR FLUX No. 1

4 lb of Glass

2 lb 4 of Red Led

RECIPE FOR PURPLE 1 CHARGE

10 peney weets of gould

2 blocks of tin

7 books of silver

6 oz of Rose colour

3 oz of flux No. 1

RECIPE FOR FLUX No. 4

10 oz of flint

1 lb 13 oz of borax

2 lb 4 oz of red led

3 lb glass

RECIPE FOR ROSE COLOUR 1 CHARGE

1 book of tin 5 peney weets of gould

2 lb 13 ½ oz flux No. 1

7 lb ½ oz of flux No. 4

Colours Thomas Dudson mixed either for his own use or which were offered for sale are as follows: (1819 — 1825)

BROWNS :	Queen's brown, Devonshire brown, purple brown, red brown and several simply 'brown'. Dip for brown necked jugs.
GREENS :	Burbon green, pea green, coburg green, grass green, Wright green, green base, blue green, dark green, yellow green, green underglaze, and green for printing. Also blue green for underglaze printing. Green glaze.
PINKS & REDS :	Pink underglaze, 8 different recipes for rose colour, pink, red, mulberry.
PURPLES :	Purple underglaze. Violet
YELLOWS :	Yellow body colours, several different recipes, cane colour, brown gold.
BLACKS :	Egyptian black, black underglaze, shining black (doubtless for 'Jackfield' ware) and a recipe to precipitate chrome to make black.
ENAMELS :	Blue, red, yellow, white, brown, orange.
BLUE :	Blue edge glaze, blue dip for jugs, blue body.

In this period there are also a total of 27 recipes for glazes including : White, flint, red lead, cream, china, printed, flat, chalk, blue edge, 'The Glaze' (a Dudson speciality), cane colour, china glaze, 'The Gloss' (another Thomas Speciality), with several lead glazes.

THOMAS DUDSON'S SPECIAL GLAZE

THE GLAZE

Frit

30 lbs loden

60 lbs stone

To 50 lbs of the above fritt add

50 lbs stone

22 lbs whiting

25 lbs flint

80 lbs lead

5 oz stone

Williamson's 10/- Blue

Different smear glazes are given for the various coloured bodies and also for a painted glaze. In the 1850-60 Dudson jasperware was normally painted with glaze on the exterior. It looks as if this process was in operation earlier.

Bone is used in some of these glazes which appears noteworthy at this time. Lustres recorded include: tin, blue, yellow green, silver, gold and copper.

For 'dipt' ware the following colours are noted: blue dip, brown dip, French gray dip, olive green dip, cain (cane) dip, drab dip and for coloured bodies there are recipes for blue, green, brown, cane, Egyptian black and drab. There are many various recipes for different fluxes. It is difficult to decide which specific recipes might be picked out but the following points emerge:

An interest in gold and gold colours is very evident from the number of different recipes, and a working knowledge of chemical methods was obviously known in that gold colours were being produced by the co-precipation of tin and gold. For example, Dudson was mixing the famous 'Purple of Cassius'.

There was also a great interest, and Thomas appeared to have specialised in, shades of pink, especially rose. In 1823 there are seven different recipes of rose colour listed, some using silver, some gold, some both. In the recipe book dated 1834 these recipes are all repeated and several more variations are included.

A FEW EXAMPLES: (1823)

BEST PINK :	75 lb tin ash
	58 lb Witne (whiting)
	3/2 lb crome potash
	6 lb Allume (alum)
No. 1 PINK:	10 lb tin ash
	5 lb Witne
	2 lb Allum
	3 ¼ oz crome potash
No. 2 PINK:	1 lb tin ash
	½ lb Witne
	6 oz Allume
	6 drams crome potash
	1 oz Barittas (barytes)
FEB, 9TH, 1836	
PINK No. 20:	6 lb tin
	3 lb Witne
	1 lb glass
	½ lb Allume
	3 ¼ oz crome potash .

Dudson seems to have been early in the field of pink underglaze transfer printing, (See colour plate 25). Recipes are given in 1819 — 1823 for two different recipes for "printed bodies" — one with china clay, one without, a recipe for pink underglaze colour and the special recipe for the glaze for printed ware. That these were 'working' recipes is evident in that in 1819/20 Thomas made 'Pink Landscape' tea and coffee services for Bentley & Ware (Wear). Bentley, Wear & Bourne were engravers who between 1810 and 1820 produced superbly engraved designs which they sold to potters nationwide. When they ordered these tea and coffee sets from Thomas Dudson they presumably supplied the transfers from their own engravers. Blue transfer printing had been in vogue for many years, but printing in pink, green and brown was only just coming about this period. In the 1830 s Dudson also had recipes for green, brown and black underglaze printing colours.

An amusing recipe in this 1823 book is :

How to deal with Bones for China. Buy your bones at 5/- per hundred. Boy has meat bones — beef — sheep trotters and bones fresh out of the horse.

The bones are to be washed clean before being put in the furnace 6 inches from the top.

Fill the container with clean water and boil for 6 hours.

Skim the fat off.

Run through a No. 8 lawn. Put in your furnace again —

Boil till it becomes 22 ounces to the pint to every hundred weight. When boiled to the abof menshund weight put the fire out and to every ...... hundred ......

Unfortunately, the page is torn here and there is nothing further. Dudson obviously went on preparing bone ash for many years because sales to Charles Meigh at Old Hall are recorded in 1842.

Mr. C. Meigh, Old Hall

½ *cwt Bone*	*Feby 18th*
1 *cwt Bone*	*April 29th 1842*
½ *cwt Bone*	*May 12th Bill delivered*
½ *cwt Bone*	*May 12th Bill delivered*
½ *cwt Bone*	*July 29th*

Settled August 2nd £1. 16s. 9d

1834

The 1834 recipe book collected together and tidied up the record of the earlier recipes, but also includes many new colours. The additional colours noted in this 1834 book are :

Pink (several)	*Rose colour (several)*	*Best Rose colour*
Rose colour flux	*Dark purple*	*Tin for purple*
Light purple	*Crimson flux*	*Chrome red*
Underglaze purple	*Flowing blue*	*Blue green (2)*
Green underglaze	*Chrome green base (several, for ground)*	
Matt blue base	*Best blue*	*Wrights green*
Bailey's print green	*Yellow green*	*Grass green*
Underglaze printing, Olive green and Edging green		*yellows (several)*
Fawn colour	*Salmon colour*	*Underglaze orange*
Underglaze yellow	*Printing black*	*Printing brown(2)*
Underglaze black	*Red Egyptian black*	*Black*
Brown	*Shining black glaze*	*Queen's brown*
Auburn brown	*Stain for blue teapots and blue jugs*	

There were also various dipt colours and dipt glaze recipes.

Among recipes for other preparations is one to prepare silver, one to make burnished gold from green gold and several tin and gold solutions. Additions to enamels include hard white, soft white and red. Glazes which are new include three 'Rockingham' glazes, smear, 'shiny' and a smear glaze for black body. There are many flux recipes. The fluxes used for enamels in all the recipes (more than thirty are listed) are basically very similar to those used until quite recently. In recent times flux receipts have been modified to reduce lead contamination in food. The system is the $PbO-SiO_2-Na_2O-B_2O_3$ range of compositions. From the early glaze recipes it is clear that there was little concern about lead poisoning. Although frits were used none had lead introduced into the frits. All the glaze formations contained raw lead !

The numbers of body recipes have considerably increased as will be seen by referring to the list of this period, and this gives some interesting pointers to production in 1834 (Appendix C p.173). Although the moulds found on the factory for stoneware jugs are of a later period (1850 — 1900) as several recipes are labelled 'Stone Jug Body' they would appear to have been made very much earlier — especially as a recipe for smear glaze is now specified also. Coloured body recipes are much in evidence too; drab, turquoise, lilac, sage, buff, brown and chocolate (with a special glaze for it). Jasper is apparently still one of the main productions — both solid jasper and dipt jasper, and the manufacture of pottery figures — such a feature of the 1840 s, 1850 s and 1860 s — were already well in production because of the following recipes being listed :

Recipes For Figure Bodies (several)

Recipe for figure wash

Recipe for stump colour

Recipe for hare colour

Recipe for ground colour

Recipe for figures and animals to stand

Recipe for No. 2 figure body and its glaze

Recipe for white figure body

Glazes specified for different figure bodies

Recipe for flesh colour

Recipe for blue figures

Recipe for colour for horses

In all the recipe books there are loose scraps of paper giving recipes, not in the usual handwriting of the book entries. There is no indication in many cases why the recipes are there and certainly no indication they were ever used or even from whence they came. In some cases, however, the recipe is given and an offer is made to let Mr. Dudson have the ingredients very cheaply as the vendor "is short of cash at the present".

It is probable that many of these early recipes, especially where there are duplications, were experimental. In later recipe books (1854 and 1872) many of the early recipes are again recorded but not as many duplicates. Presumably only the trustworthy ones were carried forward.

Quite apart from an interest in recipes used in the daily work the Dudsons were obviously also interested in some culinary recipes and some home cures for medical conditions. Among the former are recipes for rhubarb wine, ginger beer and lemonade. Among the latter are recipes for troublesome coughs, opening medicine for summer and autumn, and opening medicine for spring and winter.

The most amusing of all is

A CURE FOR SCURVY

1 lb treacle	*½ oz flower of brimstone*
½ oz cream of tartar	*¼ oz mineral earth*

Mix together and take 1 teaspoon each night and morning

56

One feels tempted to add "the best of luck" for obviously this concoction would do nothing at all for scurvy. Perhaps they were misled by drinking the homemade lemonade at the same time, obtaining the necessary vitamin C from the lemons and misunderstanding which concoction had cured them.

The following is a list of special recipes supplied to other potters — for colours, glazes, etc., in the period 1834 — 1845.

1.	Bailey	Print green. Blue green
2.	N. Simpson	White stone body also turquoise and drab for jugs
3.	John Walley	A blue stain
4.	Wm. Stubbs	Glaze
5.	C. Malkin	Enamel yellow
6.	E. Malkin	Two bone china bodies with details of frit for them
7.	Worthington & Green	Gold. Saggar wash. Bisquit blue
8.	Ridgways	China glaze
9.	Thomas Keeling	Fritt and glaze
10.	S. Keeling & Co.	Common body
11.	Williamson	Blue
12.	William Stubbs	Glaze
13.	W.G. Sargeant	Blue flux
14.	M. Turner & Co.	Granite body
15.	Turton	Jug body
16.	James Wardle	White stone jug body
17.	Morten	Body - earthenware
18.	Wright	Green body
19.	W. Harrison	Sage stain and body (see below)
20.	Elijah Taylor	Turquoise stain; drab stain
		Pearl body; white stone body
21.	Thomas Mayer	Earthenware body

A SPECIAL SAGE STAIN FOR W. HARRISON

5 lbs oxide of chrome green

7 lbs oxide of zinc

7 lbs Cornwall stone

1½ lbs blue about 8/-

This to be fired in the hardest place in the biscuit oven and then ground. The above to weigh 32 ounces to the pint.

Mixing slip for the above

288 lbs sifted dry ball slip

176 lbs china clay

180 lbs flint

124 lbs stone

50 lbs shavins

10 lbs of the above stain

The book from which these extracts is taken is not an order book and is, therefore, by no means a comprehensive list of Dudson customers. By and large most of these customers were local potters.

8

CONCLUSION

Thomas Dudson 1819 — 1834

Thomas Dudson continued to live in his house on the factory site, with his wife Elizabeth, until his death. During the latter part of his life he suffered a kind of heart disease and some time before he died he gave up potting, his sons James and Charles carrying on the business as a co-partnership. They had both worked for many years with their father.

Being seriously ill, Thomas made his will on 2nd June, 1845. His brother Richard was there with him and, as he was not a beneficiary, he witnessed the will. Thomas died on 17th July, 1845 in the presence of his son William[69] and probably other members of his family. Thomas' will was very detailed and caused several changes in the family circumstances. Briefly, he appointed his eldest son James and his nephew Thomas Keeling, a timber merchant in Etruria, as his executors and left his house and its contents to his wife during her life time. His manufactory he left to James with special conditions. Quoting from the will these were :

Now it is my express wish and desire that the said co-partnership (between James and Charles) *shall, within ten days of my decease, be dissolved and no longer continue, and that a proper legal dissolution shall be signed by them and inserted in the London Gazette*[70] *and that my said son Charles shall thereupon assign over by a proper deed all his estate and interest in the said partnership and business, stock in trade, debts, capital and effects to my said son James and in consideration of his so doing, I do, by this my will, make other provision.* (for him).

This was done[70] and Charles received "four manufacturages or dwelling houses and premises in Great York Street, and other manufacturage or dwelling house and premises in Hope Street". (See plan I on p. 26).

This Hope Street house was No. 41 built by Thomas Dudson and next door to where he commenced potting. At this date it was left to Samuel Johnson.

---

(69) *Referred to on death certificate.*
(70) *London Gazette 25th July, 1845 also Staffordshire Mercury 2nd August, 1845.*

Charles was living in one of the four houses in Great York Street having moved there in 1844. Up until this time Charles had always lived with his parents, with the possible exception of the four months of his tragically short first marriage to Eliza Lees when they were both just 21.[71] There is no record as to how or why Eliza died so soon but this was the first tragedy in what was to be a very sad life for Charles. However, Charles married again in 1844, to Mary Wardle of Leek,[72] and moved from his parents' home to one of his father's houses in Great York Street where they set up home. Having to break up the partnership and change his occupation must have been another cruel blow to Charles, but he does not appear to have been a very strong character nor to have made a conspicuous success of any of his undertakings. Possibly Thomas was wise, for the sake of the pottery, to put everything into James' considerably more capable hands. Charles appears to have continued working for his brother for a few years as clerk and as a modeller,[73] but between 1845 to 1853 or 1854 he obtained a mortgage from James[74] upon one of his Great York Street houses and used the money to convert another two of these four houses into "The York Tavern". Here he brewed his own beer, as most of the innkeepers of that time did, and completely severed any connection with the pottery industry. Charles and Mary had four children but only two survived beyond infancy. Charles, their second child was born in 1846 but died in 1853[75] when he was only seven. Mary gave birth to their fourth child, Richard, two months later[76]. In 1853, when Richard was only 3, Mary died of tuberculosis after just under twelve years of marriage. This left Charles, whilst working as a beer seller, with the responsibility of bringing up his little son Richard. Obviously saddened by all his misfortunes Charles committed suicide in 1862[77]. Richard lived as a ward of his uncle James until 1869 when he died aged fifteen[78] and all of Charles' property, which he had left in trust to Richard, reverted as decreed in Thomas' will to James.

Thomas had also bequeathed in his will "three manufacturages, tenements and appurtenances" to his daughter, Jane, and two houses to his grandson Thomas (plus £200 for his education), all those properties being adjacent in Great York Street to those which had been left to Charles. These properties were all let, (See plan 7).

(71) *Married 25th December, 1836 at Stoke. Eliza was buried on 25th April, 1837 at St. Marks, Shelton.*

(72) *1st May, 1844 at St. Peters, Stoke.*

(73) *1851 Census and so described at the baptism of his son Richard at St. Johns, Hanley on 26th September, 1853.*

(74) *Factory documents.*

(75) *Buried at St. Marks, Shelton, 1st July, 1853.*

(76) *Baptised at St. Johns, Hanley 26th September, 1853.*

(77) *Staffordshire Advertiser 9th August, 1862.*

(78) *16th June 1869 — death certificate.*

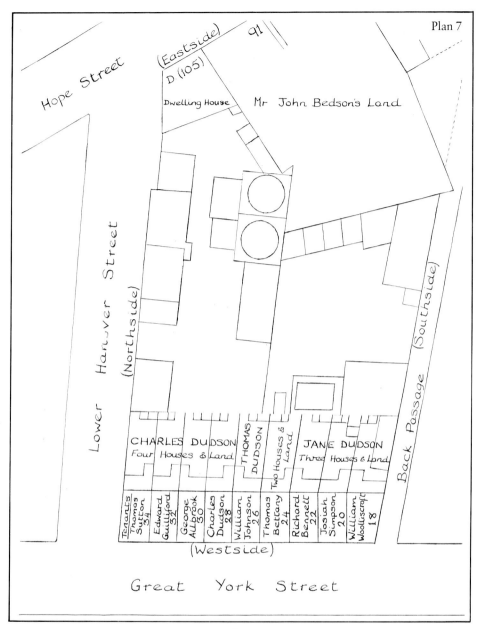

Factory Site in 1845

This plan was attached to Thomas Dudson's will.

9

JAMES DUDSON

1812 — 1882

FAMILY HISTORY

Throughout his working life James was to augment his income by dealing in property and renting houses and shops — a fairly common practice amongst the potters. He began by renting part of the New Hall estate in Clarence Street, from the Hollins family, upon which he built two houses. One he sub-let and, on his marriage to Jane Spilsbury in 1838, went to live in the other one (No. 30)[79] finally purchasing them in 1843 at the same Court at which his father purchased the last portion of the factory site[80]. The rear of his house opened onto Back Lane behind the factory (Plate I p.36).

Plate 5. James Dudson.

Only two of his other property deals have any interest here. In 1854 Meigh's list of potters states Dudson J., Broom Street. This was not a manufactory, James and his family lived there for a few years. It is also quite interesting that he bought, in 1864, some property which was part of the estate of Joseph Mayer, including his pew in St. John's Church, Hanley. Joseph Mayer was Elijah Mayer's son and a distant relative, by marriage, to James. James and Jane had two sons: James Thomas, born 1841 and William Henry, born 1845[81], both of whom, eventually, joined him in the factory.

In September 1864 James Thomas married Elizabeth Scrivener. She was the eldest daughter of Robert Scrivener, the architect and civil engineer, and her brother was Robert George Scrivener, the potter of Norfolk Street works, who

(79) *1841 Census.*
(80) *Manorial Court 11th December, 1843.*
(81) *Family records.*

5. Jasperware jugs, late 1850 s. From left to right:

a) "Claret brown" solid body, "Patent Lift" metal lid. Twisted branch handle.
"Acanthus and Bluebell." Incised 595. Impressed 30. 6½".

b) Brown solid body, Britannia metal lid. Twisted branch handle. Incised 802 on
base. Impressed 0 on foot. 8¼".

c) Slate-blue solid body. Metal lid missing. Twisted branch handle "Acanthus and Bluebell."
Geometric border. Incised 815. Impressed 0 on foot. 7½".

d) Brown solid body tankard shape. "Patent Lift" metal lid. Rope handle. "Vine, blackberry
and wheatsheaves." Incised 996. Impressed 30 L. 6½". (probably modelled by J. Dudson as
sprig moulds are signed).

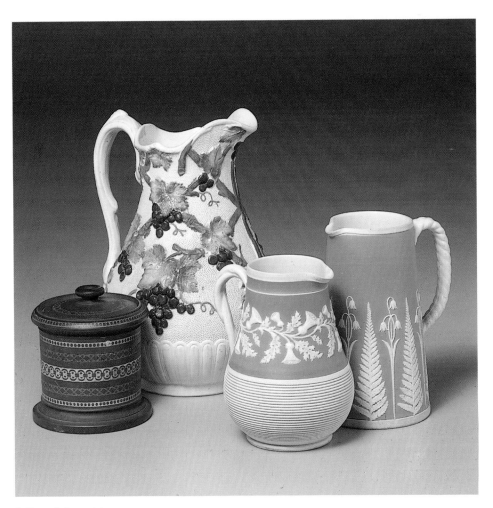

6. From left to right:

a) Early Mosaic tobacco jar. Terracotta. Impressed 2 ozs. PATENT MOSAIC 120. 4¼."

b) Moulded stoneware jug. Twisted branch handle "Vine border." First produced in 1860 s. This enamel decorated example is 1870 s 8¼."

c) Pale grey solid body, pink slip dipped band. Turned grooves. Twisted branch handle. "Thistle Wreath." 'incised 854. Impressed 36 W. 5." 1850 s.

d) Pale grey solid body, pink slip dipped. Tankard shape. Rope handle. "Fern and Bluebell." Incised 1064. Impressed 30 W. 6." 1850-60 s

7. From left to right:
a) Pale blue solid body kettle. Cane handle. "Muses and Trees." Impressed W. B and curved
ENGLAND 6." 1860-1890.
b) White relief-moulded stoneware jug. Twisted branch handle. "Wheatsheaf." Gilded.
Unmarked. 8." 1870-1890.
c) Sage green solid sucrier. "Muses and Trees." Impressed S. 5½." 1860-80

8. From left to right:
a) Brown solid body jug. Rope handle. Turned band 1¼″ below rim. "Fern wreath." Incised 998. Impressed 0 12 H. 7¼″. 1860-1890.
b) Dark green slip dipped on white. Rope handle "cherubs" Incised 13. 6½″. c. 1850.
c) Light brown four sided jug on four small feet. Stylised dragon handle. Incised 1679. 7½″. 1860 s.
d) Blue slip dipped on white. "Patent Lift" metal lid. Moulded foliage handle. Incised 1152. Impressed 12 ✣ 5″. 1870 s. This designs was registered 21st November, 1870 (247901) by Joseph Parker of 19 Ely Place, London, believed to be a retailer.

is probably best known for patenting, in 1872, a jug wholly in the shape of a barrel. Elizabeth's sister, Sarah, married Boyce Adams who started the high class grocery business in Piccadilly, Hanley.

William Henry married Maria Williamson. Maria's sister, who unfortunately died from cancer in her thirties, married Louis Taylor, founder of the firm of auctioneers and estate agents in Hanley.

In 1866, James and Jane moved to Alsager, just over the Cheshire border and about ten miles from Hanley, where he had purchased a house, "Hope Villa". Thus began the family's association with Alsager which was to last for 100 years. "Hope Villa" was near the station and they were able to travel to the factory by train. It must still have been considered rather hazardous for they took out insurance policies for £500 each. Indeed they were involved in a minor accident in 1881 for which they received compensation of £100.

During James' lifetime he was much involved with the Keelings, especially Thomas Keeling who was co-executor with him of Thomas Dudson's will, and also some of the Dimmocks. This relationship has already been described, (p.7).

10

EARLY MANAGEMENT — A TURBULENT START

James Dudson 1812 — 1882

By 1840 managers had emerged in the larger firms, the smaller firms still being owned and managed by the master. Both masters and managers were usually called bailiffs and records refer to Bailiff Thomas and Bailiff James. After the partnership was broken bailiff James took over the management and his brother Charles continued to work with him for some years as a modeller.

This was a period when relationships in the industry between employers and employees were often strained and difficult with faults on both sides.

Working conditions were very hard, the hours long, and the workforce had various just grievances about their methods of payment and terms of employment. In addition they were feeling insecure over the introduction of new machinery. It was during the first half of the 19th century that the tentative beginnings of the Trade Union movement in the Potteries were seen, the first Potters Union being formed in 1824. The membership was very small but gradually the Union increased in power and influence.

The management had grievances too. Richard Dudson's statement to the Children's Employment Commission of 1842, which has already been quoted (Page 17), points out some of the difficulties experienced by management. Richard is certainly not alone in complaining that potters preferred to "play" on certain days instead of working — and even when at work did not "buckle to." Excessive drinking was also a problem. Many factories found it necessary to establish rules of conduct and imposed a system of fines and penalties if their rules were broken. Wedgwood attempted to establish a basis of discipline by maintaining regular hours and had rules which fined employees for coming late to work, carrying ale onto the premises, playing fives near the windows and so on[82].

(82) *A History of the Potters Union by Frank Burchill and Richard Ross. p.43.*

In 1834 there was a successful strike for higher wages. As a result the employers formed themselves into a Chamber of Commerce to protect the general interests of the trade and also to combat the power of the Unions. When the workforce struck again, in 1836, for improved conditions of employment, the employers, united, were able to resist. The strike lasted five months and the Union was ruined. The pottery workers, however, were kept together by the leadership of William Evans, who was also the editor of a successful Trade Union journal called The Potters Examiner and Workman's Advocate[83].

It was in this climate, during the first year of James' management, that he ran into trouble with the Unions. He installed a speaking tube from his office, which was over the entrance arch, down to the workshops for ease of communication. These speaking tubes had been invented in 1796[84] but in the middle of the 19th century they were adapted for use in the house[85] to connect the various rooms to the servants' quarters. A whistle down the tube was the usual way of calling attention.

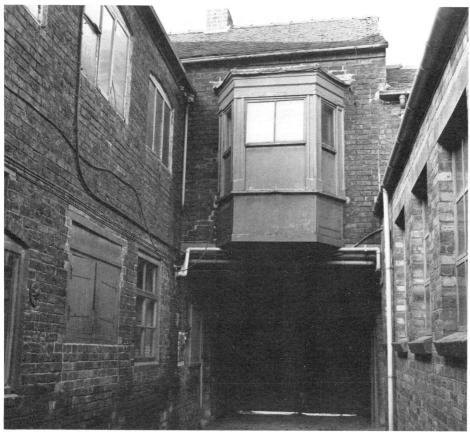

Plate 6. James Dudson's office over the original entrance gates. (Photographed in 1983 after closure of this factory and transfer of operations to Tunstall.

(83) *The Staffordshire Pottery Industry. R. G. Hagger, A. R. Mountford and J. Thomas p.56.*

(84) *Encyclopedia Britannica.*

(85) *Purnell's Encyclopedia of inventions. p.38.*

His figure workers were very suspicious of yet another new-fangled invention and, not understanding it, thought it was to enable James to listen to what they were saying. Actually one had to speak right into the tube for anything but a vague murmur or noise to be heard.

His figure makers wrote to the Potters Examiner[86], part of the letter containing the following :

> "There is an individual who resides in Hope Street, who glories in the name Manufacturer, and who has gotten fixed up in his workshop an apparatus called a WHISPERING PIPE, by which means he can sit in his room and listen to every word that is spoken by his workpeople".

James appears to have lost his temper at this and offered £1,000 for the name of the man who signed the letter, although he does not seem to have been called upon to pay up. William Evans, as editor, made the most of the situation in order to encourage the workforce to join the Union, and gave James the name of "Whispering Tubes Employer[87]".

During these early years of James' management the industry was still divided into the large firms, with plenty of capital, who had a world wide reputation and high quality output, and many smaller ones, who produced basic products and imitated the products of the larger factories. This was not with any fraudulent intention but merely to meet the requirements of purchasers whose tastes were strongly influenced by the larger firms.

The larger factories employed many hands; e.g. Davenports 1400, Thomas Mayer 500, Adams 650, Ridgways 500[88], but the 1851 Census of Population indicates that over 60% of the masters employed less than 20 men. Certainly James Dudson came into the last category for the 1851 Census shows him employing 33 hands (3 men, 12 boys, 2 women and 16 girls).

Nevertheless, small though the factory was, it was producing ware of a high enough quality for James' products to be accepted at the Great Exhibition of 1851, exhibiting china figures.

He also exhibited at the Exhibition of Works of Industry of all Nations in 1862.

(86) *Potters Examiner & Workmans Advocate 22nd August, 1846.*
(87) *Potters Examiner & Workmans Advocate 12th September, 1846.*
(88) *Childrens Employment Commission Report 1842.*

PRODUCTION

James Dudson 1845 — 1882

GENERAL

During the 19th century much of the ceramic production in Staffordshire was superb but there was a large market for cheaper ware which was supplied principally by the very many small potteries in the area.

The Dudson factory produced ware in the middle of this range. The factory was not large in the terms of numbers employed, but the Scriven report, (See p.16-17) described the premises as good, praise not too frequently given to other factories! James Dudson was not producing for the upper end of the market but was providing a decorative, practical and utilitarian range of articles of high quality and great variety. All body and colour recipes, firing notes and comments indicate a desire to produce a consistently high quality article and pride of product, price variation being based mainly on the form of decoration.

During the first twenty years of James' management production was still predominantly of figures and toys. However, stoneware and jasper ware were steadily becoming more important lines until, in the 1860 s, the range of decorations available, in both, was amazing considering the size of the premises and the fact that the firm was still doing considerable business as colour manufacturers.

James, like Thomas, had an extensive range of colours to offer. In 1872 his younger son, William Henry, rewrote all James' recipes in a tidier, more orderly manner and also listed some of Thomas' recipes which had proved their worth. As this book includes various other pieces of information it has proved invaluable. Advertisements of the period mention colours for china, pottery and glass.

That James also did significant business supplying pottery bodies is shown by the above book as there is a section devoted to customer's recipes. This is very discreet:—

Mr. M's	*Best stone jug body*
	Printing body
Mr. A's	*Willow body*
	White stone jug body
Mr. J's	*Earthenware body*
Mr. B's	*White body*
	Earthenware body
Mr. D's	*Printing body*
	Common body
Mr. R's	*Printing body*

An extra page is added dated April 1879

Elijah Birch's	*Black body*
	Sage body
	Blue body

Some light can be thrown on who these customers were, as a notebook compiled at James' death in 1882 listed all the people who owed him money. As they all had folio numbers they were presumably regular customers, but the book containing these numbers is missing. Mr. M. appears to refer to Mayer & Son. Mr. B is probably Elijah Birch. There is no indication of Mr. A and Mr. J but Mr. D. is most likely to be Dimmock & Co., although Davenport & Co. also have a folio number, and Mr. R. is Ridgways. Other potters with folio numbers are:—
Shorters, W. Litherland, Mintons, Burgess & Leigh, Thomas Twyford, C.J. Bailey and Powell & Bishop, although there is no indication as to what they purchased.

Another notebook listing money owed by James at his death tells us that he was purchasing his metal jug and teapot lids from Henry Hall*. Henry Hall was a metal mounter who bought the front part of the New Hall factory from John Aynsley in 1872. He was already the sitting tenant[89]. Business was sometimes in both directions for James, at his death, owed money to Dimmock & Co., Thomas Twyford and Powell & Bishop. This inter-relationship between firms helps to explain the pedigree of some stoneware jugs which have caused confusion. Occassionally jasper ware jugs have been found which strongly exhibit features of being made by Dudson, i.e. shape, foot, rope handle, size and above all body (usually the characteristic brown Dudson body) but the

* *Other names have sometimes been recorded on metal lids used by James Dudson. Examples include T. Booth, James Dixon and Sons. Sheffield and Broadhead and Co.*
(89) *Victoria County History — Vol. 8. p.166.*

jasper sprigs are not those of Dudson, and the jug is named for another factory. It seems likely that the jugs were ordered from Dudson, perhaps purchased as biscuit, but as Dudson's firing was planned for this body, and firing in bottle ovens was very difficult to control, it is more likely that Dudson completed the jugs using jasper sprig moulds lent to them for the purpose. Three Ridgway jugs have been seen of this type, one even having sprigs registered by Ridgway. Presumably, to complete an order a very few jugs or teapots were required not justifying the factory in question manufacturing for themselves. Certainly Dudson were supplying jugs marked with presumably retailers names. Two names appearing from time to time mainly during the 1870 s on Dudson jugs are Paxton and Norwood, (See plate 7).

Plate 7. Brown solid body. "Patent lyt" Britannia metal lid marked James Dixon & Son. Rope handle. "Wheatsheaf, Hops and Divisions." Incised 996. Impressed PAXTON 10.78. 8½″. 1878, (Paxton was a retailer).

Sadly, the records of the first 25 years of production under James' management are non-existent for no factory documents have survived. Earlier this century many records were burnt and samples of previous manufacturing lines were sold to a market trader to produce more space for current production. It is particularly disappointing as during this period many changes were made in production, and therefore many questions arise which are difficult to answer. Fortunately, however, the lack of information does not apply to all lines but is largely confined to figures, china and parian.

Nevertheless some evidence is available in the form of surviving original models for stoneware relief moulded jugs, and nearly 2,000 jasper sprig moulds. These were found on the factory, all thick with soot, but when cleaned formed an excellent basis for research, so now a fairly comprehensive account of lines produced can be given. The collecting of examples has taken considerable patience and perseverence which explains why some pieces illustrated are not in perfect condition.

FIGURES AND TOYS

Production in 1845-65 was probably much the same as that recorded in 1842-44. Obviously some figures would have waned in popularity and been discontinued, whilst new ones would be produced as people and characters caught the public imagination. It can only be presumed that Dudsons were producing much the same as other figure making factories in this period.

A few facts emerge however. It is evident that between 1845 and 1850 James changed from making his best quality figures in porcelain to bone china instead. In 1851 he exhibited at the Great Exhibition and is listed in the catalogue as showing ornamental china figures, (See appendix D p.174).

He is described in the 1851 Census and Trade directories as a china figure manufacturer and later recipe books do not contain a single porcelain recipe, whereas great stress is laid on china production and recipes.

Of course production was not restricted to china figures only. A fine example of an earthenware figure has recently (August 1984) turned up, (Colour plate 2a). This is a tobacco jar in the form of a Turk's head with the top of his turban forming the lid. It is made in earthenware enamelled on glaze, and would be produced 1845-50. In 1845 lidded Toby jugs were being produced but there is not yet any reference to either Turk's head or tobacco jars, so they obviously follow rather later. It is unmarked, but can be very definitely authenticated by comparison with a marked white stoneware vase made c 1860/70 the modelling of which is identical, (Plate 17 p.84).

74

At the end of the 1834 recipe book there are a few recipes of interests

1. *Figure body for firing bisquit and glost together.*

   Bisquit to be fired in the easiest part of the glost oven

   70 lbs blue ball clay

   180 lbs china clay

   135 lbs flint

   100 lbs stone

   28 lbs whiting

2. *Body for figures to stand*

   A china bisquit fire

   42 lbs ball clay blue

   72 lbs china clay

   88 lbs flint

   39 lbs stone

5 times this quantity in one charge very good. This is what I am now using Feby 20/48

J. Dudson

There is another recipe which is rather strange, and is included in the hope that someone will understand it. It is probably a Thomas Dudson recipe — but may be a little later.

Figure Body NZL

13 B ball slip

7 Bouks china slip

6 Bouks flint 32 oz / pint

4 Bouks Cornwall stone

40 lbs whiting

Stain, flux and blue 2 lb. /\pint

There follows the recipe for special glaze "figure glaze NZL" and another for "Figure blue LZ"

"Bouk" is Potteries slang for the unit of measure of the liquid slip.

THE END OF FIGURE PRODUCTION (c. 1865)

Gradually during the 1850 s the factory changed over to a different type of production. The quantity of figures produced must have declined steadily as more relief-moulded stoneware and jasper ware took over manufacturing space and parian and ironstone china were also introduced.

Manufacture of figures was discontinued about 1865. Perhaps the competition in this market was getting very keen as so many factories were producing this type of ware by this time. More probably James found that the market was increasing greatly for stoneware, a line which was a personal favourite of his. His son, James Thomas, was travelling extensively throughout London and the provinces, widening the market and considerably increasing the demand for stoneware in which the firm later specialised.

PRODUCTION OF CHINA

As already indicated there is practically no documentary evidence relating directly to china ware production, other than body recipes. One jug, (See plate 8) is attributed to James Dudson in the 1860 s because of its similarity to his relief moulded stoneware jugs of this period, in particular the pattern called Pansy. Other identified items include the cheese dish shown below. The evidence of directories, advertisements and, above all, the factory 1872 record book points to china being fairly important (as shown below). In this same 1872 book a list of prices being paid to operatives gives a fairly comprehensive list of the articles being made at this time. This list is given on page 101 and, from it, one can deduce what was made in china and / or earthenware. The 1872 recipe book shows great interest in and involvement with china bodies, and some notes to recipes are reproduced. The first page deals with some manufacturing advice:

Mix china bodies in dry state and to give them a fine and solid transparent texture, which constitutes their beauty, sift them through the following lawns. First a No. 10 or No. 12 lawn, second through a No. 14 and lastly through a fine No. 16 lawn,

Plate 8. China jug "Pansy" unmarked 8½".

Plate 9. White china cheese dish. Slip cast. Relief-moulded. "Hops, vines and wheatsheaf." Unmarked. 11" mid 19th century.

and it is well at all times to try your materials by taking a small portion from the bulk, softening it and form it into a small bat, fire and glaze and if specked be sure to reject it as unfit to use.

There are then listed 23 different china bodies, many have had small trial runs and been accepted (one or two rejected), and many have comments on their quality. Obviously these were not all for Dudson use but to supply customers.

No. 1. Superior china body

(Nantgarw china body). *

26 lb bone pounded and sifted

14 lb Lynn sand

2 lb potash

Mix the above well with water. Mould into lumps the size of a brick. Fritt them in a hard part of a biscuit oven. Then pound and grind it for use. Take 40 lbs of the above fritt to 10lbs china clay.

China Body No. 3.

189 lbs bone

120 lbs stone

120 lbs china clay

9 lbs flint

"This body is good without flint, flint being used to stay contraction".

China Body No. 4

"The best casting china body in the Kingdom"

98 lbs bone

49 lbs stone

49 lbs china clay

168 lbs shavings of No. 3 body.

The following body recipes have no comment until No. 13

* *Nantgarw China works, Nantgarw, Glamorgan, Wales, circa 1813-1822.*

China body No. 13

"Fritted china body as good as French".

700 lbs bone

500 lbs Lynn sand

350 lbs Cornish stone

Mix the above well together and mould it into bricks. Fire in the hardest part of the china biscuit oven then pound and grind it for use as follows.

479 lbs of the above fritt

492 lbs china clay

377 lbs bone

177 lbs Cornish stone

50 lbs flint

26 lbs felspar

Various recipes follow marked good or very good and four described as beautiful.

"The two following bodies are for more common and cheap purposes such as printing gold edge line and sprig and common enamelling and for supplying the small gilders. They are good strong and serviceable bodies."

a) For thrown ware	b) For pressed ware
420 lbs bone	420 lbs bone
180 lbs stone	180 lbs stone
200 lbs china clay	160 lbs china clay
80 lbs blue ball clay	60 lbs blue ball clay
10 oz enamel blue for stain	10 oz enamel blue for stain

Later in the book is a recipe for purple china and another for lilac porcelain, both credited to Bailiff Thomas. There is no evidence whether they were ever used by either Thomas or James.

IRONSTONE CHINA

Ironstone china was a popular and fashionable line in the mid 19th century. This was a very strong durable body which stood up well to hard wear and James advertised this line. Three different body recipes are listed which show his attempt to give a consistent fired product using a kiln which could not give the same heat to all ware being fired in it. The recipe differences were to adjust the temperature/time of heat applied during firing in different parts of the bottle oven so the end product was similar. Obviously a serious attempt was made to produce ware to a consistent degree of vitrification. Again the addition of something referred to as frit and calx — presumably added to promote vitrification — does seem to fit with a further attempt to promote consistency of vitrification. No examples have been identified.

STONEWARE BODIES.

Several recipes are included and there is no indication as to which were used, but the comment before the recipes is significant. "Old stone bodies — for service are worth all the bone bodies that can be made and will boil water like a saucepan". James produced kettles in stoneware and water can be boiled in them if they are placed on a trivet before an open fire — although one does not have to be impatient !

Possibly the following is one of the recipes used :

Stone body

    48 parts Cornish stone

    25 parts of blue and brown clay

    24 parts of Cornish clay

    1 part of glass

    1 part of calk

This will vitrify at the temperature of earthenware but must be ringed to be kept straight.

Whatever the recipes, stoneware bodies were used by James not only for his relief-moulded jugs, teapots, etc., but for his jasper ware and mosaic ware, and there is no doubt that they had a high degree of vitrification. It was common practice for the factory to brush glaze the exterior of their jasper ware at this period — and this would not have been possible on porous ware.

It might be of interest at this point to include instructions for placing the ware during firing which is in the 1872 factory book.

"Places in oven where the different sort of ware will fire. Both biscuit and glost together."

ARCH BUNGS.
Bottom with smeared glost jug. Tankard as well. This same ware will fire the height of bags in rings.

BOTTOM MIDDLE OF OVEN
With full glazed ware such as C'sticks, toast racks, soaps, etc.

Full glazed ware will fire in the middle bung also glost flat C'sticks will fire from top to bottom in the middle bung

Full glazed jugs will fire six saggars on the top of the two front middle bungs

The fore bungs will fire full glazed four saggars high

Clayware
White stone jugs will fire anywhere above the bags of the first ring and archers

Sage and drab clay ware fires best from saggars high above the bags

Blue clay ware will fire three saggars above the sage

Teapots 3 or 4 saggars above blue and sage clay jugs

Butter tubs, flowerpots or spitoons above teapots. The extreme top for wavers, kettles, hens, 4s and 6s jugs or large flowerpots

Middle or second ring bottom from saggars high with full glaze flat candlesticks, toast racks, pillar C'sticks, and everything full glaze

Place four or five saggars of clay flat or tall C'sticks

NOTE : Toast racks must be set out with and carried only four saggars high, either clay or glost

Barley and blackberry flower pots only two saggars higher above clay C'sticks
Clay tankard jugs will fire in same as barley and blackberry flower pots

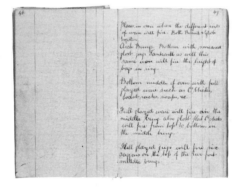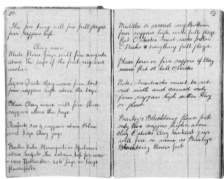

Firing instruction in 1872 book.

STONEWARE — RELIEF MOULDED 1850 — 1880

From early Victorian days jugs were often relief decorated, i.e. the decoration was part of the mould from which they were cast. This type of decoration became popular because it was attractive, yet cheap and easily cleaned. As the jugs were used on the table to hold milk, water or beer etc., the demand was for a decorative article. During the 1840 s Dudson produced jugs of this type, sales being recorded in the 1842 / 44 order book. After his father's death in 1845, James gradually increased his production until it became an important line for the factory and indeed led to their eventual specialisation. The signs are already appearing that James is concentrating on practical and useful articles, many directed towards catering whether in the home or commercially. The list of people owing money to him at his death contains many registered companies, presumably a high proportion being retailers, but one or two names suggest canteen use, e.g. Burton Bros., S. Montague (both these are well known clothing suppliers) and Jacobs & Co. (the biscuit manufacturers).

Plate 10. From left to right:
a) White stoneware broth bowl stand. Relief-moulded floral border. Impressed DUDSON. Diameter 7″. 1870-80 s.
b) White relief-moulded stoneware jug. Britannia metal lid. "Fern". 7½″. This pattern was registered in 1862 but this example has a moulded mark DUDSON 1882.
c) White relief-moulded stoneware cream jug. "Jewel". Impressed DUDSON. 3¾″. 1860-80.

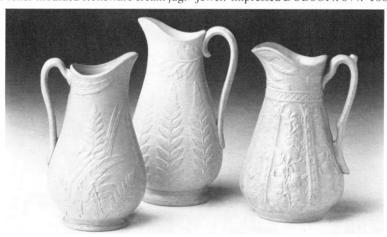

Plate 11 From left to right:
a) White relief-moulded stoneware jug. "Fern Fronds". Impresed 0 otherwise unmarked. 8¼″. 1865-80. This design was first registered by Wood and Sale in July 1864 and was transferred to James Dudson in February 1865.
b) White relief-moulded stoneware jug. "New Fern". Impressed DUDSON 0. 8¼″ 1860-80.
c) Blue relief-moulded stoneware jug. Panelled. Name of pattern unknown. Impressed DUDSON. 5″. Late 1840-50 s

Plate 12. A group of relief moulded stoneware jugs. From left to right:
a) "Scroll" 1860 s. Impressed DUDSON in a triangle. 7½" green. (The modelling of this jug was changed in the 1870 s to widen and flatten the spout).
b) "Boston". 1891-1900. 6" Impressed with curving England.
c) Blue panelled jug with leaves rising vertically from the base. Pattern name unknown. 20¼." Impressed DUDSON on foot. 1850/60 s.
d) "Argyle". Ground enamelled in blue. First registered in 1865, this example 1870 s.

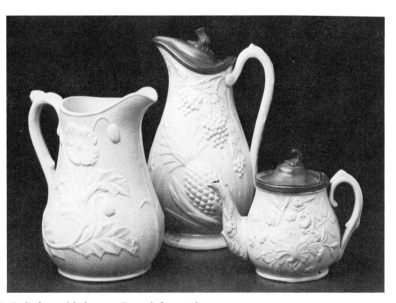

Plate 13. Relief-moulded ware. From left to right:
a) White parian body. "Poppy". Impressed DUDSON. 7¾". 1860 s
b) White stoneware. Britannia metal lid"."New Pineapple". Impressed DUDSON. 9¼", 1860-80.
c) Drab stoneware. Britannia metal lid. "Rose". Impressed DUDSON. 5½", 1850 s.

82

Plate 14. Relief-moulded stoneware jugs. From left to right:
a) Sage green. "New Lily." Impressed DUDSON 8¼"
1860 s.
b) Drab. "Maize." Impressed DUDSON 1860 s
c) Blue. Pattern name unknown. Impressed DUDSON 6."
1850-60.

Plate 15. Relief moulded stoneware jugs 1860 s. From left to right:
a) "Night and Morning," showing Morning,9." Unmarked. 0 impressed on base. See plate 23 for reverse side.
b) "Vine Leaf." Blue. Impressed DUDSON 8¾."

Plate 16. Relief-moulded stoneware. From left to right:
a) White. Britannia metal lid. "Jewel." Impressed DUDSON. 7½." 1860-70 s.
c) White. "New basket." Made in 1975 from the original moulds as a commemorative jug for the firm's 175th anniversary. Limited edition of 500. This information and the jug number is stamped on the base. 8."

The small blue jug (1855-60), (Colour plate 4 jug D) is typical of the late 1850 s with its upward flaring lip but the foot is less well defined than most earlier manufacturers produced. It is worth commenting here that Dudsons found the upward flaring lip elegant and continued to model many stoneware jugs in this way throughout the rest of the century. Another jug of this same period (c. 1850) which is a different shape is shown in plate 18.

Both jugs are made in the same blue body, smear glazed, fully glazed interior, stippled background, but the foot of this one is much better defined than the previous example. Both jugs are impressed DUDSON on the foot rims. Unfortunately they did not mark every piece at this period.

Plate 17. Relief-moulded stoneware. From left to right:
a) White vase. "Turk's head." Impressed DUDSON. 5½." 1870-1880. (See colour plate 2).
b) White. Britannia metal lid. "Cactus." 8." 1860-70 s.
c) White. Britannia metal lid. "Argyle." Impressed DUDSON. 5½." c. 1870. Argyle was registered in 1865. The registration mark was applied at first but later alternative marks were DUDSON or a circular moulded mark, (See p.23).

Plate 18. Blue stoneware jug. Pattern name unknown. Impressed DUDSON. 7¼." Originally produced 1850 s but this particular example is struck glazed and was probably made in 1880 s.

One of the earliest patterns was Tulip. Thomas sold Tulip jugs — some of them lustred. Tulip jugs were a major line for the factory throughout several decades until the turn of the century. They received many different treatments, being made in white or coloured stoneware body, in the 1860s in parian, in the 1870s fully glazed, or enamelled and silvered or gilded etc.. This Tulip jug (identical modelling) was also produced by Samuel Alcock but their pieces are marked and the final treatments differ from Dudson. There are other examples of Tulip jugs around but Dudson may have produced one of the earliest.

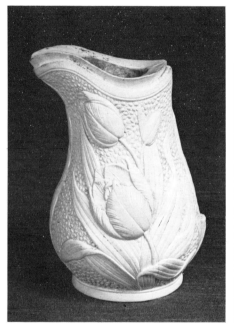

Plate 19. Master model for Tulip jug.

Plate 21. A complete Tulip jug. Blue stoneware.

Plate 20. Master mould and case for Tulip jug.

85

New patterns were introduced from this period onwards but not many of the designs were registered, the following being the only ones.

1855, 6th August 101019. A stoneware jug without a foot, "Pineapple". Note that the pineapple is straight on the jug, a later version (unregistered) has the pineapple sloping, (Plate 13, p.82 and plate 24. p.88).

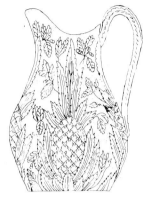

Plate 22. Original drawing of "Pineapple" submitted for registration in August 1855.

1861, 23rd April 140200. Footed stoneware jug, "Barley", (Plate 26, p.89).

1862, 27th February 149673. Footed stoneware jug, "New Fern", (Plate 11, p.81).

1862, 27th February 149674. Footed stoneware jug, "Fern", (Plate 10, p.81).

1865, 13th February 175959. Footed stoneware jug, originally registered by Wood & Sale, William Street Pottery, Hanley in July 1864, was transferred to James Dudson, "Fern Fronds", (Plate 11, p.81).

1865, 23rd December 193844. Footed stoneware jug, "Argyle", (Plate 17, p.84 shows an "Argyle" teapot).

Two more relief-moulded jugs were registered by James' son in 1887 and 1899.

1877 21st January 66351. Queen Victoria Jubilee jug, (Plate 51 p.113).

1899 350300. Baden-Powell/Kitchener commemorative jug, (Plate 53, p.113).

More lines were added to the range of embossed ware until the end of the century, and many were offered enamelled and/or gilded. They were produced in white, sage, drab and blue.
Production is dealt with in greater detail in Appendix J p.201, where a complete list of patterns is given.

Plate 23. Blue stoneware jug. "Night and Morning" showing Night See plate 15 for reverse Morning. Impressed 0.9″ 1860 s.

ARTICLES PRODUCED IN RELIEF MOULDED STONEWARE

Low and tall pear jugs. Sizes 4s, 6s, 9s, 12s, 24s, 30s, 36s

Low and pine teapots with stone covers or metal lids

Sizes 12s, 18s, 24s, 30s, 26s, 72s

Flower pots. Foxglove

Garden pots. Barley, wreath and blackberry

Sugars. Stone covered, also creams

Butters. Barley

Toast racks

Tall candle sticks all sizes

Coffee pots

In any of the following colours: White, blue sage, drab

ENAMELLED RELIEF MOULDED STONEWARE. 1872

JEWEL   Jugs ground enamelled

Jugs enamelled coloured leaved — or spots

Teapots — ground

ETRUSCAN   Jugs — ground enamelled edging

Jugs — enamelled coloured leaves

FERN   Jugs — enamelled coloured leaves

Teapots, jugs, sugar and creams gilded

ARGYLE   Coffee pots — enamelled

Jugs, teapots, creams, ground enamelled

WHEATSHEAF   gilded, (Colour plate 7).

Etc.,

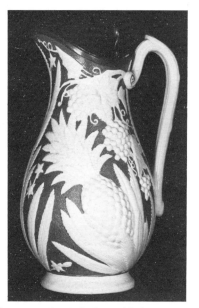 

Plate 24. White relief-moulded stoneware ground enamelled in blue. Britannia metal lid. "New pineapple." Impressed DUDSON. 9½". 1870 s (Compare plates 22 and 25).

Plate 25. White stoneware. "Vine Border." 8". This illustrates a different technique for enamelling this type of ware. Enamelling was popular in the late 1860 s and 1870 s. (See colour plate 6).

Articles Produced in Plain Stoneware Body

| Bread trays | Cheese stands | Egg pots |
| Toast racks | Candlesticks | etc. |

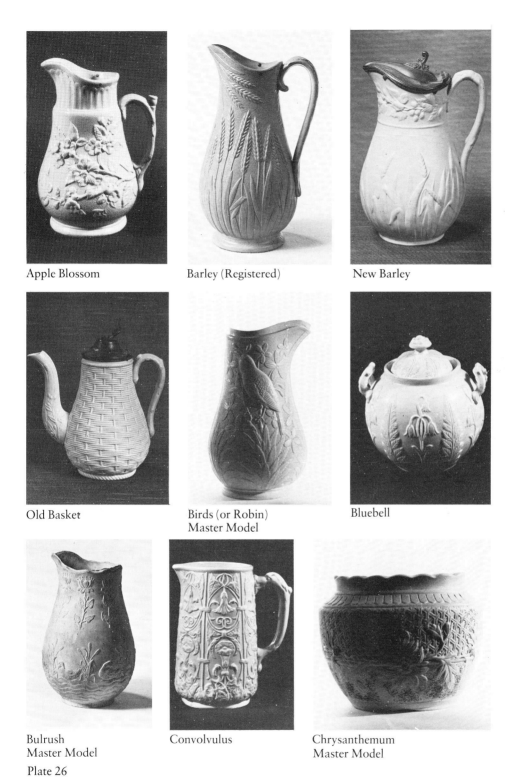

Apple Blossom

Barley (Registered)

New Barley

Old Basket

Birds (or Robin)
Master Model

Bluebell

Bulrush
Master Model

Convolvulus

Chrysanthemum
Master Model

Plate 26

Plate 26 & 26a. Relief moulded stoneware to illustrate various designs. Dates are given in Appendix J p.20.

Damascus

Hazelnut and Squirrel
Master Model

Hazelnut
Master Model

Holly
Master Model

Ivy

Music

New Butterfly

Snowdrop

Sunflower
Master Model

Plate 26 a.

90

JASPER WARE

Reference is made to jasper ware in all existing factory records and it was probably never entirely out of production, with the exception of the Second World War, until discontinued in 1965.

James Dudson developed the stoneware lines, and with his particular interest in this ware produced a very dense, vitreous and high quality body which was used for both embossed and jasper pieces.

All ware is fully glazed in the interior, but the exterior is only lightly glazed by brushing on the glaze and, if examined, brush marks are discernible. Earlier pieces are slip dipped but by the 1860 s and 1870 s mainly coloured bodies were used. The colours of this period were :

Blue and sage. Both of these, when used for jasper ware, are usually of a very delicate pastel shade.

Brown. Various shades of brown were produced at this period. The characteristic brown body used by Dudson was in production at least by 1860, (Colour plate 5 p.63), but note also the reddish brown (called claret brown) of the jug a) also in colour plate 5 and the very light brown of the jug in colour plate 8 (p.66). The jugs in plate 27 and plate 28 a) are very dark brown.

Plate 27. Very dark brown solid body. Rope handle "Chinese Figures". Impressed 12 8 . 7¾". 1880. $\overline{80}$

Plate 28. From left to right:
a) Very dark brown solid body. Britannia metal lid "self-acting" (Toft's patent). "Blind Man's Buff." Unmrked. 7¾". 1870 s. See plate 49 for later adaptation of this pattern for hotels and railways.
b) White relief-moulded stoneware. "Autumn and Winter" showing Autumn. Mark No. 17. 8¼". Fully glazed for catering industry 1900-20.
c) Brown solid body jasperware jug. Britannia metal lid. "Wheatsheaf and Hops." Impressed DUDSON X. 6½". Late 1850 s.

Slate blue — soft grey blue, typical of this period but discontinued after James' death. (Colour plate 5 page 63).

Shapes of jasper teapots and jugs were basically the same as the embossed pieces of the period. The acanthus and bell range of jugs is typical of the 1850s, not only their shape but also the twisted branches forming the handles, (Colour plate 5 p.63). This pattern was also produced on some stoneware pieces which were relief decorated.

Plate 29. A group of pre 1850 jasperware jugs. Footed tankard shape. From left to right:
a) Bright blue slip dipped. Rope handle. "Hunting". Incised 173. 6".
b) Bright blue slip dipped. Rope handle. "Figures". Incised 223. 6¾". (Metal lid missing).
c) Bright blue slip dipped. Rope handle. "Figures and Divisions". Unmarked. 7".
d) Dark green slip dipped. Rope handle. "Cherubs". Incised 13. 6".

The group of jugs shown in plate 29 illustrate features considered to indicate production pre-1850. The shape is quite different from jugs produced later — as is the body, which is very greyish-white. They are slip dipped and smear glazed. Probably James was still producing these articles in the style produced by his father Thomas, a few years earlier. There is no doubt, however, that the jugs were made by Dudson as all the moulds for the jasper sprigs are amongst those found on the factory, and the rope handles are the same as those appearing on the tankard jugs later. Indeed rope handles are a feature of Dudson jugs. Teapots produced from 1860 onwards frequently have relief-moulded spouts.

INCISED NUMBERS

The factory at this period had a system of incising decoration numbers on the base of the jasper ware, frequently but unfortunately not invariably. How early the system was started is not known. It certainly was in operation from 1845 onwards but, as no proved example of Thomas Dudson's jasper ware have been found, it cannot be stated with certainty that it was not introduced a little earlier. There is no doubt that the vast majority of pieces marked in this way are characteristic of James Dudson's production The system ceased with James' death in 1882.

The incised numbers are written in free hand on the base of the clay ware. Frequently they appear to be written by the *same* hand. In particular the three is very characteristic.

173   1679   223   3386   3387

The number gave instructions to the decorator and covered the following :

(a)   The type of handle (where applicable)

(b)   The borders

(c)   The sprigging

(d)   If grooved, the exact number in a certain position

Shape and colour did not come into it unless the piece was to be slip dipped or slip painted. Thus the same number may be found on different types of articles (e.g. a tobacco jar and a jug) providing all the above factors are identical. Occasionally pieces of Dudson jasper ware of this period are found without the incised number. They were probably special orders and not being in general production were not allocated a decoration number.

The system cannot, of itself, be used to date pieces, because the same number, if applicable, continued throughout the period. It is not safe to presume that the number indicates the date at which the decoration was first used. When the system was introduced 1 and 1000 could have been numbered on the same day. However, it is of some interest to note that the four early jugs referred to on page 92 are numbered 13, 173 and 223 whilst the fourth has no number. The acanthus jugs have numbers in the upper 500 s, (p.63).

Because these incised numbers are written in such a characteristic manner they give a strong indication of a Dudson piece, and comparison with known sprigging and positively identified pieces can be used as confirmation. Attention must be drawn, however, to the fact that incised numbers occur on pieces with impressed marks of other factories. Usually these pieces of ware do not look like Dudson and so no confusion occurs. There are, however, exceptions. Dudsons supplied special orders for jasper ware to other factories, and retailers, impressing the customers name and the Dudson incised number on the base. There is a likelihood therefore that pieces that look like Dudson, but are marked with another factory's name, were made by Dudson for a special order, and that the incised number is a Dudson number.

Two impressed names that occur with Dudson incised numbers are Paxton and Norwood. They were probably retailers.

Incised numbers in conjunction with B.P. Co.

B.P. Co. is the mark used by Brownhills Pottery Company Ltd. There appears to have been a special liaison between this factory and Dudson between 1872 and 1882. The Brownhills Pottery was purchased by James Eardley in 1871, and he gave the management of it to his son, Alfred Eardley, and others[90]. Studied advertisements published by the Brownhills Pottery between 1871 and 1882 do not mention jasperware, but during this period it is believed that Dudsons made some jasper ware for them. Several jugs, typically Dudson in every respect and including the Dudson incised number on the base, but with B.P. Co. impressed on the base too, have been found, (See plate 30).

Plate 30. Blue solid body. Cane handle "Hunting." Incised 3191½. Impressed B.P. Co. 6¾." 1870 s.

(90) *Frank Porter — Postal Directory for the Potteries 1887. P.339.*

The blue jug with the vine border and hunting scene, both of which are identical with the Dudson sprigs, is particularly interesting. It is impressed B.P. Co. and has a Dudson incised number of 3191½, the 3 being especially typical. So far most of the examples found have been jugs, but a cheese dish has also been seen, so production was not restricted to jugs.

James Dudson died in 1882, and this seems to coincide with the cessation of Dudson supplying Brownhills. The fact that James Thomas Dudson, on taking over from his father, greatly reduced production of ornamental jasper ware, and concentrated on jasper ware for the catering industry, may well be significant. There is one other interesting piece of information given by Llewellyn Jewitt (p.288) that James Eardley lived in Alsager. This is where James Dudson lived also, and between 1872 and 1882 Alsager was a small village, so they doubtless knew each other well. Some years later (c. 1888 according to their advertisements) Brownhills Pottery Co. manufactured jasper ware themselves. It must be stressed that this later production had no connection with Dudsons. The pieces are marked B.P. Co. but have no incised number. They do not resemble Dudson ware in any way.

Patent Lid
About 1860 a "patent lock lid" came into use for the stone cover for jugs and teapots; as the pot was tilted the lid slipped forward but would not fall out. The patentee so far is anonymous but he licensed James to use his patent. Inside the stone cover is an oval stamp which reads "James Dudson — licensed by the Patentee." The patent was still in use by later members of the family, (See marks p.216).

James steadily expanded his overseas markets and because of this a very characteristic impressed mark sometimes appeared on the base of both jasper and stoneware pieces during the 1870 s. At the same time Dudson was sometimes impressed on the foot but marking the ware was still not common practice. It is usually considered that any ware with England marked on it is post 1890 but as just indicated, Dudson sometimes breaks this rule as pieces exist with both James Dudson inside the stone ware cover and the curving England on the base as well. He *died* in 1882.

JASPER PATTERNS

"Muses"	"Coursing"	"Fern"
"Muses and divisions"	"Hunting"	"New Fern"
"Muses and trees"	"Blind Man's buff"	"Vine"
"Sacrifices and divisions"	"Fern wreath"	"Birds"
"Sacrifices and trees"	"Festoon (vine festoon)"	"Cherubs"
"New sacrifices"	"Albine"	"Muses and ferns"

Plate 31. "Bird and Butterfly."

Plate 32. "Bird and Butterfly."

Plate 33. "Fern Wreath."

Plate 34. "Wheatsheaf and Hops." 1850 s

Plate 35. "Wheatsheaf and Hops." 1860 s.

Plate 36. "Tropical Bird."

Plate 37. Brown solid body. Moulded handle. "Sacrifices." Incised 1677. 7½." 1860-70 s.

Plate 38. Brown solid body. "Patent Lift" metal lid. Twisted branch handle. "Fern and Bluebell." (Ferns are blue, blue bells are white). Incised 617. 7½." c. 1860.

Some of these sprigs are of the same style as those of other manufacturers, but there is usually some difference in the modelling. To compare them thoroughly would be extremely interesting but very time consuming and cannot be gone into at this time.

Plate 39. A group of typical 1860-70 pieces. From left to right:
a) Sage art vase. "Muses and Trees". Impressed DUDSON. 5".
b) Sage covered mustard pot. "Sacrifices". Impressed curved ENGLAND ✤ S. 3½".
c) White relief-moulded teapot. Britannia metal lid "Jewel". Pine shape. Unmarked. 6".
d) Sage teapot. "Cherubs". Impressed inside lid JAMES DUDSON. Licensed by the Patentee, Hanley, Staffordshire. 5". 1860-70 s.

MOSAIC WARE

This is one of Dudson's special decoration designs which was first produced at least by the 1830 s.

To produce this decoration "rollers" or roulette wheels were run around the turned jug or bowl creating a depression on the surface of the article. A contrasting coloured slip was applied through a straw filling up the depression with the slip as the jug was turned. The slip was allowed to dry and then the jug was re-turned, smoothing the surface by removing the top layer and so revealing the pattern of alternating body and coloured slip.

In 1840 a bead and line pattern (Plate 40 p.98) was used between bands of colour. Some of the earlier pieces (1850 — early 60 s) were impressed PATENT MOSAIC with a decoration number also impressed on the base, (See colour plate 6 p.64 tobacco jar).

97

Plate 40. White mosaic pillar candlestick, stoneware. Showing the characteristic "bead and line" in pale blue with black lines. Impressed DUDSON. 8½″. 1860-80.

Plate 41. Pale blue mosaic jug, stoneware. "Bead and line" in black and white. Greek key pattern in bright blue. Britannia metal lid marked T. Booth. Unmarked. 8″. 1860 s.

From 1850 onwards this decoration was applied to stoneware bodies in white, ivory, sage, drab, blue or brown. Earlier pieces were smear glazed or brush glazed. Teapots, jugs, coffee pots, cocoa jugs, bowls, candlesticks, tobacco jars, biscuit barrels and condiment sets were all given this treatment.

Some other factories produced a similar effect by using transfers.

Plate 42. "Hen on Nest". Egg box. Yellow nest. Red on white hen. Impressed DUDSON. 6½″. c. 1860. They were still in production 1880-90.

Plate 43. Slate blue solid body full sized Stilton dish. (Produced in 4 sizes). "Cows and sheep".
Unmarked. 11¼". 1870 s. It's knob has been broken and unfortunately replaced with a
drawer knob. It should have rope. (No. 5 on p.213). These cheese dishes were produced with
a wide variety of Dudson jasper patterns. This one, although imperfect, was chosen because
an earlier example of this pattern has been recorded in blue slip dip on white with rope knob,
otherwise identical to the above. It was incised 247. (1850 s).

Plate 44. Hyacinth blue slip dip on white stoneware, biscuit barrel on stand. "Festoon".
Incised 878 (or possibly 848 if held other way up). Impressed W L 9¾". 1860 s.

Plate 45. Wall plaque in stoneware glazed with blue/green nacreous glaze. "Winter." One of a series of the four seasons which were adapted from Danish sculptures. (Thorwaldsen). Unmarked. 10½″ diameter. Mid. 19th century.

Plate 45a. Similar plaques "Summer" "Autumn."
(All four designs were used on Dudson jugs. Spring has not yet been found).

Plate 46. From left to right:
a) Brown solid body. Straight sided biscuit barrel. Britannia metal lid. "Wheatsheaf and Hops." Unmarked. 6″. c. 1860.
b) Sage green flower pot. "Muses and Divisions." Impressed DUDSON. 6½″. 1860-80.
c) Blue slip dipped on white biscuit barrel. Imperial shape. Silver plate lid. Impressed DUDSON. 6″. 1880 s

TYPES OF ARTICLES PRODUCED 1860 — 1880.

N.B. Some of these articles were made earlier when "toys" were the main production lines.

The list will probably not be comprehensive as no order book is available for this period. Also the firm was always prepared to make for "special" orders.

Jugs
   Relief moulded stoneware — some gilded and/or enamelled
   Jasperware or plain
   Some with metal lids

Teapots
   Pine or low, as above (other shapes)

Coffee pots, tall
Coffee and Tea urns
Kettles.
Eggpots and cups.
Hen boxes (hen on the nest)
Bread trays, large and small
Sugar bowls. Sugar boxes. Cream jugs
Mustards, handled. Peppers and salts
Cheese dishes
Butter dishes
Biscuit barrels
Honey pots
Broth bowls and stands
Bedroom sets (ewers, basins)
Soap dishes
Pressed slop bowls. Pressed slop buckets
Candlesticks. Tall, pillar and flat. Some gilded
Savealls (a device for burning candles completely)
Imitations (?)
Dessert ware, plates and comports, gilded
Table centres, gilded
Spirit bottles, jasperware, some silver mounted, some in pairs in silver stand
Garden pots
Flower pots
Match pots
Spill holders
Beetle traps, tall and low
Spitoons, Ivy or Vine
Nest eggs (for gamekeepers etc.,) brown or green (simulated pheasant egg)
Porous water bottles
Tobacco jars, Mosaic, Turks Head
Vases, Turks Head
Wine or water coolers

12

EXTENSION TO HOPE STREET FACTORY

James Dudson 1845 — 1882

The site next to the factory in Hope Street was owned by John Bedson. He bought it from Outrim and Hindle at about the same time that Thomas Dudson purchased his plot in 1835. He was a master carpenter and established a joinery business there. He got into financial difficulties in 1853, however, and sold some of his land to Timothy Dimmock[91] but this was not to prove enough for he went bankrupt in 1855, and Thomas Keeling and Richard Clarke became creditors to sell his estate "with all convenient speed". Only two lots were sold at the original sale in April 1855 and they were offered again on September 9th, 1856 when once more they failed to sell. Keeling and Clarke, doubting their ability to obtain any money for these premises, called a creditors meeting at the Saracen's Head on 20th November, 1856, and at this meeting Timothy Dimmock received most of these properties in discharge of the debt owed to him by Bedson. Timothy Dimmock died in 1870 and, in March 1871[92] James Dudson bought from his son, James Dimmock, the dwelling houses "No. 91 Hope Street, with land, cottages, large house, outbuildings, joiners workshop and yard — all enclosed in brick walls" and incorporated it into the factory, by this means straightening the front boundary, (See plan 8).

He then began a series of modernisation measures and extensions to the factory. In 1872 he built a new bottle oven — to dry the ware — the two original bottle ovens still being used for firing. These two original ovens were pulled down some years ago but the bottle oven built in 1872 still stands. In 1874 James Dudson considerably improved the factory using R. Scrivener and Son as architects (his son's father-in-law) and W & R Inskip of Longton as builders. Amongst the work carried out was the taking down of the privies and putting in drains and w.c.'s; cellars were put in and the floor of the cellars, the entry and the yard were all paved; flights of steps to all workshops were renewed; all roofs were retiled and the houses were modernised.

(91)*Manorial Court June 23rd 1853*
(92) *Manorial Court, March 30th, 1871.*

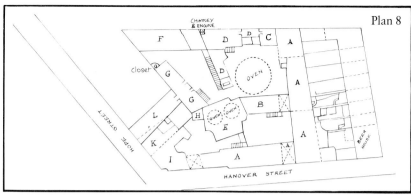

Key　　　　Dudson factory at James Dudson's Death 1882 (from Deeds)

A　Warehouse to workshops.

☒　Office over entrance arch.

B　Warehouse and workshops.

C　Stables and coach-house. Over these — Pressers chamber. Moulds

D　Engine house. 3 horse-power engine. Presses. Blunger and machinery. rooms over. Working moulds and mould shop.

E　Stock room.

F　Two storey building with cellar underneath. Blocks and moulds in block chamber.

G　Two storey building with four stove pots securely fixed, and lead house.

H　Building shed with stock room over.

I　Dwelling house and offices adjoining. 105 Hanover Street.

K　Dwelling house — 91 Hope Street.

L　One dwelling house and shop adjoining — tenant 'Howard'.

Also shows the seven Great York Street houses and the 'Great York Tavern'

Ovens

The two small hovel ovens were the originals with the one to the left being the colour kiln.

The large oven was erected in 1872.

CONCLUSION.

James Dudson retired in 1880 handing over to his son, James Thomas, to whom he left the factory and adjoining houses upon his death on June 6th, 1882. He died at his home in Alsager after a few days illness, aged 70[1] and was buried in the family vault in Hanley Cemetry[2].

His will records that his younger son William Henry received the two houses in Clarence Street, some property at Fenton, a farm at Blakeley Lane, Cheddleton, and £6,000. His wife Jane died in 1886.

(1) *His will — proved 19th July, (No. 540 Somerset House)*
　　Pottery Gazette July 1882, P. 642.
　　Staffordshire Advertiser June 10th, 1882.
　　Evening Sentinel 7th June.

(2) *Factory records record purchase in 1861 for £24.*

13

JAMES THOMAS DUDSON

1841 — 1917

FAMILY HISTORY

Plate 47. James Thomas Dudson.

Plate 47a, William Henry Dudson

James Thomas went to Cobridge school from December 1845 to March 1847 and then had a private tutor, Samuel J. Mellor, from June 1847 to September 1850.

James T. married Elizabeth Scrivener in 1864 and their first child was born the following year. He was christened James Robert. They had a second son, Harry, born in 1874, and three daughters, Evelyn, who died when just 22, Jane, who married Henry Buckley King, a member of a family of flour millers of Hanley and later of Liverpool, and Constance, who never married. Constance was very artistic, and this talent is frequently to be found in members of the family in all generations.

When James T. became owner of the factory, according to his father's will, he was very ably supported by his younger brother. Unfortunately, however, this was only to last for a very short time, for seven months after his father's death,

9. From left to right:

a) Brown solid body. Metal lid missing. Rope handle. 3 turned grooves at base. "Sacrifices and Trees". "Ribbon and daisy" border. Unmarked. 7". 1860-80.

b) Slate-blue solid body. Rope handle. Turned grooves. "Festoon". Incised 1279. Impressed 12. 7¾". 1860-80.

c) Brown solid body. Rope handle. Turned grooves. "Allbine". Incised 967X. Impressed L 12 7¾". 1860-80.

d) Blue slip dipped on white. Twisted branch handle. "Acanthus and Bluebells". Incised 667 Impressed WL 24. 7¾". 1850 s.

e) Dark grey/green solid body tobacco jar. "Sacrifices". Incised 1388. Impressed 10 M. 6". October 1879.

10. From left to right:
a) Brown solid body spirit flask with silver mount and silver covered cork. Hall marked Sheffield 1872. "Game and Vine". Base is hollowed in the centre and incised 3387. 7½". 1860-80.
b) Similar spirit flask, stopper is missing. "Game and Vine". One of a pair, Brandy and Whiskey. 7½". 1860-80. Both are incised 3386. 7½". 1870 s.
c) Dark green slip dipped on sage tall pillar candlestick. Impressed DUDSON ENGLAND S. 8¾". 1890 s.
d) Dark blue slip dipped on blue. "Bird and Bamboo". Impressed DUDSON BROTHERS HANLEY S O D3. (i.e. No 3 vase shape). 4½". 1900-14.

11. Dark blue slip dipped coffee pot. Twisted branch handle and moulded spout. Widow finial which closely resembles the Elijah Mayer widow finial. Turned on an engine turning lathe. Small glazed. 8¾" 1810-25. Unmarked but identified by spout, handle and sprigging. This widow finial was also used again in the 1880 s. (See p.264).

12. Turquoise slip dipped urn. "Rams head and swags." Incised 634. 9¾". 1850 s. Dark blue
slip dipped coffee can and saucer. "Festoon." Incised 1652. Impressed H L 22/4/81. 2½".
1881. Matching cream jug. Incised 1652. Impressed B L 30 $\frac{5}{81}$. 2¾". 1881.

William Henry cut his hand whilst working at the factory. Septicaemia developed and he died on 9th January, 1883, being buried in the family vault beside his father. He left two very young children, James Douglas, (who in due course founded the firm of Dudson, Wilcox & Till), and a daughter, Edith. Their mother Maria, and James T. became their legal guardians to administer the property and money until they became 21.

James T's son, James Robert, now 17 years old was also working with his father but Harry was still too young, being only 8. It was obviously felt that this did not give James T. enough help, for his mother joined the works from 1882 to 1886. They lived in one of the houses on the factory, 105 Hanover Street, whilst William Henry, and his family after his death, occupied John Bedson's old house next door, 91 Hope Street.

Like his father before him, James T. also dealt in property, in addition to potting, but to an even greater extent.

14

PRODUCTION

James Thomas Dudson 1880 — 1898

During the early 1880 s James Thomas, having travelled extensively for the firm for many years, appreciated that the market for supplying the hotel and restaurant trade was expanding and had great potential. He was a shrewd businessman, more commercially minded than his father, and he quickly realised the advantages to the firm in specialising in this direction. The exceptionally strong, vitreous body perfected by his father and the utilitarian, though decorative, nature of the ware made the products ideally suited for this purpose.

Many of the articles already in production were those demanded by this market, and it is possible, even probable, that Dudson were already selling in this field. For example, the introduction of mosaic ware, (c. 1840) a very important and popular catering line for at least 80 years to come, gives some indication of this. Unfortunately, no order book is available for this period and so no information relating to customers supplied is available. From 1885 onwards order books, and other documents, do exist so from then a fairly comprehensive and accurate account of the firm's productions is possible.

The business had flourished and been very profitable under James. His policy had been to offer a very large variety of decorative lines in several colours and patterns, and many attractive pieces were made in jasper and stoneware[93].

Obviously, if larger hotels or shipping lines etc. were to be supplied they would require greater quantities of one line and therefore some rationalisation of the firm's production was necessary to meet the changing market policy.

The market for embossed stoneware was still buoyant, also mosaic, but the jasper patterns were too numerous to be now appropriate, and this was where the start was made.

(93) *Factory models and documents.*

JASPERWARE. (Blue, Sage and Brown solid body).

The first move to rationalise jasper ware was to introduce "a new cheap class of jasperware" as described in the Pottery Gazette (March 1882 p.245). This new range was in "a fairly made body" with decorations copied from Flaxman's muses, sacrifices, coursing and other patterns. Jugs, teapots, creams, sugars, cheese stands, biscuit boxes and marmalade pots were all to be given this treatment. Obviously the new line was intended for the catering market and was offered fully glazed as well as smear or struck glazed. Dudson advertisements from this date include "jasper ware". Strangely this line, although prolific, had never before been specifically advertised, merely included in "decorative ware".

Following the introduction of the new line less suitable patterns were gradually discontinued throughout the next decade.

By 1891 the following patterns were offered :—

Muses and Divisions

Muses and Trees

Figures and Divisions

Figures

Sacrifices and Divisions

Sacrifices and Trees

New Sacrifices

Torches and Trees

Fern Wreath

Ferns

Trees

Hunting

Coursing

Birds

Festoon

Allbine

Blind Man's Buff

Plate 48. Dark green slip dipped on sage body. "Figures and Divisions". Struck glazed. Impressed ODS DUDSON BROTHERS ENGLAND. 6". 1900-20. This vase was first introduced in 1897.

111

The number of patterns was further reduced until in 1898 only the following were offered :—

Muses and Divisions	*New Sacrifices*
Muses and Trees	*Ferns*
Sacrifices and Divisions	

Sales of these were large. The following were sold occasionally :—

Hunting	*Torches and Trees*
Coursing	*Blind Man's buff*

"Festoon" became very popular again in 1900.

Plate 49. Dark green slip dipped on sage. Fully glazed. "Propellor" Britannia metal lid. "Blind Man's Buff." Impressed DUDSON ENGLAND. 7″. 1891-1900.

Plate 50. Dark green slip dipped on sage. "Festoon and Muses." "Special order" tobacco jar November 1897. 8″.

JASPER DIPPED (1897 onwards).
Jasper dipped ware had been largely discontinued by James c. 1860, and sprigs were applied to solid stoneware body. James Thomas continued this policy

until November 1897 when he supplied a special order for dark green slip on sage body. He next introduced a dark blue dip on white in April, 1898, and jasper dipped continued to be offered from then, with dark blue on blue body being a third addition to the range.

Although various modifications had been made for the previously expressed reason, many of the pieces were still highly decorative. For example, the Stilton cheese dishes in their varying sizes and including the new half-moon shaped cheese dishes, which were introduced in the late 1880 s, are still much admired and appreciated.

Commemorative Ware

The firm brought out commemorative pieces of jasperware as appropriate, especially in connection with Queen Victoria and other members of the Royal Family. Many jasper sprig moulds were discovered on the factory and photographs of them are to be seen on pages 225-6.

Plate 51. Queen Victoria's Golden Jubilee. Relief-moulded stoneware jug. Registered January 1887. No. 66351 unmarked. 6".

Plate 52. The jasperware jug for the Golden Jubilee 1887. Unmarked. 6½". Reverse side is sprigged with a similar head of Queen Victoria as plate 51.

Plate 53. A commemorative Boer War jug produced in 1899 with Lord Kitchener on one side and Col. Baden-Powell on the reverse. Dark green on sage glazed.

Sales included Jubilee jugs in all sizes, Jubilee teapots and cocoa jugs in sage, blue and brown. This was the year of Queen Victoria's Golden Jubilee and James Thomas registered a special commemorative jug for production during this year. Another commemorative jug was registered in 1889, a tankard shape with rope handle which had Kitchener on one side and Baden-Powell on the other.

STONEWARE (Blue, Sage, Drab and White bodies).

Relief moulded stoneware remained an important production line, but there was a gradual change in the popularity of some patterns. The first modifications made by James Thomas were to discontinue the slate blue body and then, in 1887, 3 designs, begonia, cane and holly.

By 1890 further changes in design had been initiated and still more were discontinued :—

1889	*Bamboo.*
1893	*Lilian, poppy*
1895/96	*Bulrush, cable, cactus, maize.*
	New fluted, Napier, oak and joy, rye, passion flower, new pineapple, scroll and line border.
1897/98	*Bronze oak, beehive, coral, gladioli, rose & wyth*.*

On the other hand, new designs which appealed more to the changing Victorian taste had been introduced :—

1880	*Ivy* (discontinued 1890)
1884	*New ivy* (discontinued 1893)
1888	*Chrysanthemum* (discontinued 1896)
1890	*Oak and ivy* (discontinued 1900)
	Music (discontinued 1900)
1891	*Boston* (discontinued 1900)
	New leaf (discontinued 1899)
1893	*Floral* (discontinued 1901). Became very popular

Two patterns were supplied, primarily, for special orders so production of these lines was very small:

Fern oak produced in 1886 and 1893 only

Leaf produced in 1890 and 1897 only

"Fern oak" was ordered by a long standing continental customer, L. Chicherio (country not revealed). "Leaf" also went to the continent, possibly Germany or Switzerland, to Herman Schurhoff & Co.

The demand for stoneware on the home market, however, steadily decreased until in 1900/1901 it virtually ceased. So shortly after James T. handed over to his sons (1898) they ran down production dramatically. However, the line was not completely discontinued for orders continued from the continent even up to 1917, in spite of the war.

* *There is no indication as to the design for Napier and Wyth.*

13. Left to right:

a) Dark blue slip dipped vase "Sacrifices and Trees." Unmarked. 4½." 1880 s.

b) Brown solid body tobacco jar. Metal lid missing. "Acanthus and Bluebell." Geometric border. Incised 724. 7½." c. 1860.

c) Brown solid body urn. "Muses and Festoon." Impressed DUDSON BROTHERS HANLEY ENGLAND W. 9½." 1900-14.

d) Blue slip dipped eggcup "New Festoon." Impressed as c).

e) Blue slip dipped scent bottle. "Figures and Divisions."
 Impressed as c). 4¾." 1900-14.

f) Brown solid body jug. Rope handle. Oak border. "Coursing" (hounds on reverse side). Unmarked. 6." 1860-90.

14. Mosaic ware. Left to right:

a) Blue solid body, double lipped cream jug with "bead and line".
Impressed DUDSON BROTHERS ENGLAND AD; 2". 1900-14.

b) Blue solid body jug. Impressed DUDSON ENGLAND AD. 8". 1891-1900.

c) Drab mosaic jug. Impressed DUDSON. 4". 1860-80.

d) Blue solid body jug. "Patent Lift" lid. Rope handle. Impressed DUDSON ENGLAND. 8".
1891-1900.

e) Sage green solid body tankard shape jug. Impressed DUDSON BROTHERS ENGLAND S.
4¼". 1900-39.

f) Brown solid body sucrier. Pewter lid missing. Incised in free hand on the base W. H.
DUDSON MAY 1878. 5½".

116

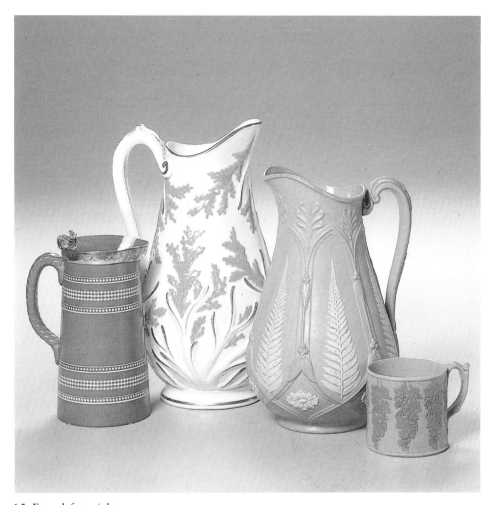

15. From left to right:
a) Brown solid body Mosaic jug with silver plated mount and lid. Rope handle. Glazed. 7".
c. 1870.
b) Enamelled and gilded fully glazed relief moulded stoneware jug "Coral". Unmarked. 10¼".
1870 s.
c) Slate blue (but greyer than usual) relief moulded jug with jasper sprigs attached "Fern and
Lozenge". Incised 385M. Smear Glazed. 9". 1850 s.
d) Buff solid body coffee can. Fabric texture impressed onto wet biscuit body. "Vine". Incised
251. 2½". c. 1850.

16. From left to right:

a) Pink solid body tankard shaped jug. "Floral" and "Decorated." Thick raised enamel decoration. Impressed DUDSON BROTHERS ENGLAND. 5″. c. 1910.

b) Majolica (green/brown) glazed jug. Rope handle. Interior mauve glazed. Impressed ❖ 6½″. c. 1890.

c) Brown slip dipped on blue. Imperial shaped teapot. "Muses and Divisions." Impressed DUDSON BROTHERS HANLEY ENGAND B. 6¼″. 1900-14.

d) Brown slip dipped on blue fruit bowl.
"Dancing." Impressed as c). Diameter 9″. 1900-14.

MOSAIC

The range of mosaic ware introduced so successfully in the 1830/40 s was still extremely popular, and became increasingly so due to its suitability for the catering markets. Orders were larger for this line than any other.

The mosaic patterns were produced on white, sage, blue and brown bodies and could be either fully or smear glazed. This line increased in popularity in the years to come and several designs were produced. For a more detailed description see page 192.

Joseph Lyons and Co. Ltd., of Kensington, London were important customers, from 1885 when records begin, for mosaic ware for their restaurants and in 1908 were to register a specific mosaic pattern for their use exclusively.

MAJOLICA

A characteristic earthenware of this Victorian period is majolica which was introduced into this country by Mintons and which they had exhibited at the 1851 Great Exhibition. Originally, the body was coated with an opaque white glaze but, later in the century, a semi-translucent coloured glaze was used. This popular line was suitable for adapting to a cheaper version and Dudson offered a range of green majolica glazed articles such as the jug shown in colour plate 16, and "Begonia" and "Rose" spittoons. Sales were slightly better for spittoons than tableware but were still small, so Dudsons produced their own new bronze-green plain glaze which was considerably more popular and continued to be an important line offered by the factory until the Second World War.

PARIAN.

Parian was still advertised but evidence does not suggest significant sales of this body. Parian busts of Christ seemed to be the best selling line.

Plate 54. Blue glazed stoneware jug with brown neck, foot and handle. Introduced 1886.

119

COLOURED NECKS ON PLAIN BODY — A new line.
An attractive new line offering brown necks on blue, sage, or pink bodied jugs, teapots, sugars and creams was introduced in 1886 and proved very popular especially for the catering industry. Later, in 1898, a dark blue neck on white body was added to the range.

PATENT LOCK STONE COVER*.
This patented lock cover had been used by James but James Thomas increased its use, and stressed its advantages in his advertisements.

From 1882 he changed the impressed oval mark inside the stone cover from James Dudson to James T. Dudson — licensed by the Patentee, etc.

METAL LIDS.
Silver and electro-plated mounts and lids were offered as an alternative to Britannia metal. Henry Hall, the metal mounter of New Hall Street, was still doing the mounting, at least to 1890.

CUSTOMERS
Ware was supplied to hotels, restaurants, shipping and railway companies not only throughout the United Kingdom but also overseas. The domestic market remained steady also, to wholesalers and retailers such as the Army & Navy Stores and Maple & Co..

A new business was developed supplying ware to firms for use in their canteens such as J & A McFarlane and The Pure Coffee Co. Two important and regular customers, for their restaurants, were Joseph Lyons & Co., and Mecca Ltd. Considerable business was also done with other pottery factories :—

Mintons. From 1889 to 1900 regular orders (at two or three monthly intervals) were placed for "Convolvulus" jugs in white stoneware with patent lift lid.

Furnival and Sons. In 1890 cocoa jugs and jugs in a jasper ware and later that year teapots, in "Convolvulus", and "Argyle" stoneware.

Maddock and Sons. From 1886 to 1891 regular orders were received. For example:—

> Teapots, sugars and creams in white "Argyle"
> Stoneware "ask for instructions."

Numbers were quite large, e.g. 102 teapots in March 1890 and 696 teapots "Convolvulus" in white, sage, blue and brown in November 1890.

---

* Stone cover was the current term in the industry for lids made in the same stoneware body as the rest of the pot.

Also in November 1890 216 teapots were ordered in brown neck on sage and blue, and mosaic, and a further order in April 1891 for white "Argyle" 156 teapots, 30 sugars and 72 creams, again "ask for instructions".

J & G Meakin 1890. 18 assorted jugs for enclosure, and later candlesticks, bedroom sets and flower pots. 1892. 36 sage "Gladioli" jugs with metal covers in 3 sizes "URGENTLY WANTED".

Shorters 36 white "Wheatsheaf" jugs.

Dimmock & Co. 1892. "for H.C. Hawley" 54 jasper jugs 3 sizes, 3 colours.

Ridgways Brown jasper jugs for enclosure (see page 73).

T. Shorter 1897 — "Send to S. Johnson, Hill Pottery, Burslem, for enclosure, 12 plain white teapots and 76 jugs in white "Wheatsheaf".

There is no indication as to how the above were to be back stamped, but the following examples show that Dudson were willing to supply ware with back stamps other than their own.

James Smith. 1899. 48 jugs brown neck on pink "NOT TO HAVE DUDSON ON".

Defries and Sons. 1901. Several orders to be badged in black "North London Rly. Dalston Junction" "get copper plate from Ridgways".

Bennett & Co. Ordered "Convolvulus", "Wheatsheaf", "New lily" and "tulip", jugs to be marked TN d.

M. J. Newton 1894. Sage and blue jugs with brown necks
1. Mark BM East London
2. Mark PLN Algoa Bay
3. Mark $\underline{1440}$ Townskille.
$\qquad$ st

John Taylor
Mark   743   II
                 Co

Customer Unidentified. Mark JFM

An order for "jugs to be marked "FULLALOVE" to be sent to B & S for them to include" (? Bishop and Stonier).

Back stamping to special instructions certainly complicates the identification of the origin of any piece of ware. It may well, however, explain why a few jugs have been unhesitantly identified as Dudson, having all the characteristics, until a different factory's name, incised or stamped on the base, has caused consternation!

Other marks which may be seen from time to time are for example C5, C6, D1, D2, F, F4. These are requested by certain catering firms, and are their own particular code, but they are impressed along with the Dudson mark.

Many small catering establishments specify "seconds" on their order, and consequently Dudson advertisements offer "seconds" for sale sometimes.

Plate 55. Pepper and mustard pots. 1890 s. Slip dipped blue on white. Green on sage. Impressed DUDSON ENGLAND.

COLOUR MAKING
In 1880 the firm was still supplying colours for china, earthenware and glass, but this side of the business was declining rapidly. By 1898 colours and bodies were only produced for their own use.

Finally a quote from "A Descriptive Account of the Potteries 1893 (p.23)......
"Dudson's ware is as well known and as highly esteemed as any product of its class."

Regret has sometimes been expressed by collectors that some of the attractive early lines of Dudson jasperware were discontinued. Had James Thomas, however, not changed the trading policy the firm would probably not be in existence today. Certainly it would not have flourished and expanded into its present position in 1985 amongst the leading suppliers of hotelware in the world.

122

15

CONCLUSION

James T. Dudson

James T. and family lived in the house on the factory until he retired in 1898. Later that year he bought "Ivy House" in Alsager and moved there after transferring the business to his two sons.

He died on 8th April 1917, in his 76th year and was interred in Hanley Cemetry following a service at Wesley Place church in Alsager on 11th April, 1917.

His obituary notice in the Evening Sentinel (April 10th, 1917) contains the following passage :

"The deceased gentleman was a very shrewd business man, and built up an extensive business, providing for special requirements in stoneware used by the catering trade, the shipping companies and restaurants in London and big cities, in addition to having a considerable export trade. In his younger days, in connection with his business, he travelled a great deal to London, and throughout the United Kingdom for many years and was very well known and respected in the trade ......
The deceased never took an active part in public life, but was appointed Justice of the Peace for the County of Chester ten years ago, and regularly took his seat on the bench at Sandbach. Mr. Dudson was connected with the Wesleyan body, and was a generous supporter ...... of the church at Alsager. The deceased was one of the best known men in Hanley, and was much esteemed and respected".

FAMILY HISTORY — A TRAGIC PERIOD

Dudson Brothers 1898 — 1918

Plate 56. James Robert Dudson.

Plate 57. Harry Dudson.

James Thomas Dudson retired in 1898 and handed over the business to his two sons, making them co-partners. The name of the firm was changed from James T. Dudson to Dudson Brothers (registered 7th December, 1899). The eldest of the two sons, James Robert married Lizzie Burgess by whom he had three sons: James Robert (Roy) 1892, Reginald Burgess (Rex) 1894 and Hubert Scrivener 1899, and one daughter Florence Irene 1900. The younger son, Harry, married Elaine Rigby of Alsager and had two daughters. Both families lived in Alsager at "Northern Hey" and "Osborne House" respectively.

To begin with the partnership was very successful, dealing largely with the catering industry both at home and abroad. Many of their pieces were highly decorative as well as utilitarian, and during this period Harry travelled extensively throughout the provinces. His charming personality was a great asset to the business in this field.

However their success was not to last and 1910 ushered in a very tragic period for the family during which it was remarkable that the business survived. In October of that year Harry developed tuberculosis which proved incurable, so in 1912 the partnership was officially dissolved (London Gazette 11.7. 1912) and indeed Harry died in 1913 at the age of 39. James Robert, by now 48, had his two sons working with him, Roy having joined the factory in 1909, and Rex in 1911. When the First World War broke out in 1914 both were called up, Rex into the infantry and Roy into a cavalry regiment. Whilst Roy was serving in Ireland he was thrown from his horse, kicked on the head and suffered brain damage from which he never recovered.

James Thomas came partially out of retirement, but he was now in his seventies so the strain told on him, and on James Robert too. In 1915 Hubert (aged 16) was brought out of school to be trained by them. In 1917 James Thomas died at nearly 76. James Robert developed an illness from which he never recovered, and Hubert, being 18 years old, was called up into the army. This left no male members of the family to run the business and, but for a remarkable works manager and obviously a very loyal workforce, the firm would undoubtedly have closed.

Henry Bagnall had come to work for James Thomas in 1896, and lived at 105 Hanover Street. When all the problems arose, due to war and illness, Henry Bagnall was appointed works manager. His obituary notice later described him as "an ardent worker" and there is no doubt that the family greatly appreciated his service to the firm at this difficult period. The female members of the Dudson family and female relatives on the maternal side should not be forgotten either as some of them worked in the offices.

Hubert served in the newly formed Royal Flying Corps but, when the war ended, he was released quickly, as was his brother Rex, to return to the factory. James Robert, in a codicil to his will, instructed that the business be formed into a limited liability company and Dudson Brothers was incorporated on 22nd May, 1918.

17

PRODUCTION

1898 — 1918

This period really has to be considered in two parts for the outbreak of war in 1914 had its effect upon production and reference will be made to this later.

By the end of the century the transition to supplying solely the catering industry was complete and the company specialised in supplying stoneware and jasper ware.

The market was strongly for decorative lines but tastes were changing and therefore some of the production lines changed also. The first, and most notable, of these was the relatively sudden cessation in demand for relief moulded stoneware in 1900/01. To compensate for loss of this previously very important selling line Dudsons introduced considerable variety into the coloured stoneware range.

At the same time they introduced a new range of pressed ware, primarily jugs, as another alternative. Jasper ware, mosaic and the coloured stoneware bodies, however, remained by far the most important production lines, and together accounted for a very large percentage of the total sales of this era.

RELIEF MOULDED STONEWARE

The market for embossed stoneware ceased, rather abruptly, in 1900/01, as already stated, and most lines were discontinued. A small number of continental firms, mainly in Switzerland and France, and one firm in America, continued ordering up to 1917.

Orders continued to France throughout some of the war years, although not to the war zone.

The following lines remained in production :—

DESIGN	DATE DISCONTINUED
Fern	*1903*
Kensington	*1903*
Lily	*1903*
Convolvulus	*1905*
Foxglove	*1905*
Star	*1910*
Argyle	*1911*
Autumn and Winter	*1911*
Damascus	*1911*
Registered Barley	*1913*
New Lily	*1914*
Jewel	*1917* (home market 1910)
Night and Morning	*1917*

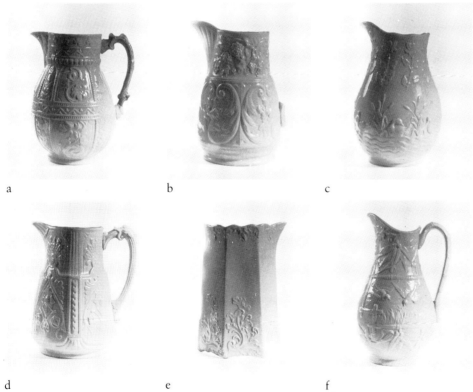

a   b   c

d   e   f

Plate 58. Pressed ware master models. Many are based on the relief moulded stoneware patterns but the spout has often been flattened. All fully glazed.
a) Damascus, b) Scroll, c) Duck, d) Boston, e) Fluted f) Birds.

127

PRESSED WARE

This new line, introduced c. 1882, was lighter and more modern than the stoneware of the previous century, which it partially replaced. Articles were produced in blue, sage or white body. Jugs were the most frequently sold line. They were pressed into two half moulds of the type shown in plate 58 p.127 They were produced in patterns with rather angular handles. The following order received 15/11/1901 gives an indication of sales. "MacMahon, Broadfield & Co — 6 crates of Duck and Star each crate to consist of 96 sets (48 Duck, 48 Star) ⅓ blue and ⅔ sage". Orders are recorded in a working production book.

In addition to jugs the range included flower pots, plates which were green glazed and rushfoot dishes.

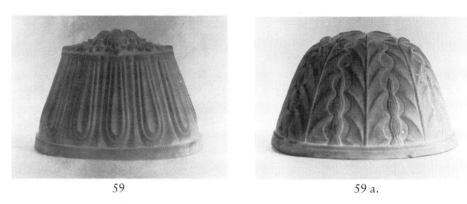

59   59 a.

Plates 59. 59 a. Two terracotta master model blancmange moulds "Fluted". "Pea".

JASPERWARE

By 1901 the number of jasper patterns had again been reduced, to five only :—

Muses and Divisions	*Trees*
New Sacrifices	*Ferns*
Muses and Trees	

"Ferns" and "Trees" were primarily used on cheese dishes and large flower pots. Two new patterns were introduced in the next two years. The new additions were :—

Festoon	*1902*
Dancing	*1903 (February)*.

Festoon had been in production previously, but when it was reintroduced in 1902 it was not in its original form of vines with leopards head and curving ribbons, but with festoons of roses, which linked draped roundels. Dancing was based on the Flaxman figures, (Plate 69 p.145 shows both).

128

This jasper ware was a very strong selling line, and undoubtedly the introduction of a cheaper version to supply the catering industry was a clever move.

JASPER DIP
This was greatly in demand also. Dark green slip on sage green body had been introduced just before the turn of the century, and in 1900 dark blue on light blue body was added to the range. (In 1923 black slip on white body was produced).

It is interesting to see that some restaurants and hotels had their jasper ware orders badged also. The Grand Hotel, Eastbourne and the Birmingham Coffee Company were amongst the first to do this. Jasper dip, like jasper solid body, could be supplied "unglazed" or "glazed". Unglazed was never completely without glaze but was always smear glazed, with a fully glazed interior.

Plate 60. Group of 1890 s jasperware. All marked DUDSON ENGLAND.
a) Dark green on sage. Match pot. 3½″.
b) Sage green. Pepper pot. Metal top. 2″.
c) Dark green on sage glazed. Vase. 6″.
d) Dark blue on white. Sugar bowl. 4″. Introduced 1898.

Plate 61. Jasperware 1880-1913. From left to right:
a) Dark green on sage glazed. Low vase. "New Festoon." 3".
b) Dark green on sage. Vase "Acanthus." 6".
c) Dark green on sage. Vase. "Acanthus and Bluebell." 6".
d) Brown stoneware inkwell. Introduced 1882. 2".
e) Dark blue on white. Marmalade jar. Silver plated lid. 3".

MOSAIC

This was another extremely important selling line in white, blue, sage or brown bodies, either glazed or unglazed as above.

This process has already been described (p.97). Several new designs were introduced, two of which were registered. The first, an imperial shaped teapot with dark green chain mosaic was registered on 4th January, 1908. Rd. No. 518575. On 15th February, 1908 an indenture was entered into between Dudson Brothers and Joseph Lyons and Co. Ltd., "of Cadby Hall, Kensington — Merchants, Purveyors and Refreshment Contractors" by which Dudsons transferred all rights to this design for 10/- to the exclusive use of J. Lyons in the United Kingdom, but retained the right to sell the design abroad.

The other design, a green bead and line, was registered 18th February 1909, No. 537475.

130

Mosaic was sometimes produced with a coloured neck, e.g. blue neck on sage mosaic or brown neck on sage mosaic, and also sometimes gilded.

537475   518575

BADGED MOSAIC

Mosaic was frequently badged, and several of the railway companies favoured this line. Of these, The Great Eastern Railway Company was probably the largest customer. Dudson mosaic hollow ware was made to accompany flat ware of corresponding colours, produced by Doulton and Minton.

Before 1907 orders came direct to Dudson. Between 1907 and 1911 orders for their badged ware (teapots, jugs, etc.,) were placed mainly by Doulton but sometimes by Minton. After 1911 orders came direct to Dudson again. They used glazed blue mosaic badged F.E.R. Co. in black. Other railway companies ordering were : The Lancashire and Yorkshire Railway Co., who ordered teapots, jugs, etc., in glazed bronze-green and stamped L & Y on the base, and also sage green body with dark green neck badged L & Y on the side of the pots; the North London Railway, Dalston Junction and Victoria Station, London.

Cafetaires* were often produced in mosaic. These were produced in two sizes, large and small, and were an early form of coffee percolator. Two forms were made. The earliest, introduced c. 1885, consisted of a cylindrical tube which was filled with boiling water, and then immersed in a jug containing hot water. The top which was placed on the cylinder was in two parts, the lower perforated, the upper a curved dish in which was placed the coffee. This was then covered with a lid. Steam came through the perforations and drew the flavour out of the coffee. A smaller version was introduced after 1900 in which the percolating principle was the same, but a teapot with a handle at right angles to the spout was used. The teapot was filled with boiling water and kept over a low source of heat.

* From the French "Cafetières" — an anglicised version.

COLOURED BODY STONEWARE

This was another very important production line, accounting for just as high a percentage of sales as either jasper ware or mosaic. This type of ware was adapted more than any other to meet the changing market, in that plain coloured stoneware body was no longer as popular, and something more colourful and decorative was often demanded. Therefore, articles produced in the coloured body stoneware were given a contrast neck, or wide band, in some other colour as follows:—

Pink body: green neck   *Sage body: dark green neck*

brown neck   *brown neck*

blue neck   *blue neck*

Blue body: brown neck

dark blue neck

Articles were sometimes made more elaborate by gilding, or even having a broad band in heavy gilt. Another very decorative form was described as "decorated". The wide band, in this product, was of deep raised enamel on which were painted sprays of flowers. These pots might also be "floral" which entailed small individual flowers, usually white with green leaves, being stuck on at random round the base of the pot. "Floral" could be combined with "decorated" and possibly "heavy gilt" too.

Gilding was very much in demand, and could be supplied on any piece. Articles which were treated in this way were tea and coffee pots, cocoa jugs, tankard jugs, bowls and biscuit jars and teapot stands. The biscuit barrel, (Colour plate 17) and the small tankard jug, (Colour plate 16) are examples.

Of course not all coloured stoneware was decorated. A few orders were received for plain articles with customer's badge, but they were certainly in the minority.

Match pots and match stands were produced during this period and were a very popular export line. (Plate 60 p.129).

Dudson exported mainly to the United States of America, Canada, Ireland, the Continent and India. Decorations or colours would be supplied to harmonise with any customer's special scheme.

1914 — 1918

The outbreak of war was almost coincidental with Harry's death and James Robert's illness, and, for these reasons, there was a considerable reduction in the range of articles made, and the more elaborate decorations were stopped. Orders for jasper dropped dramatically in 1915, and gilding, "decorated" and "floral" were completely discontinued. Jasper dipped ware, dark blue on white, and dark green on sage, were still produced with muses and divisions being the most usual pattern, but an old pattern which had been re-introduced, birds, was also sometimes ordered, (Plate 63 p.134).

The coloured stoneware was, of course, the principal production line in brown, blue, sage and white bodies. Coloured necks, although less popular, were still in demand but banding and badging had gained in popularity. Mosaic remained the attractive and sought after line that it had been for nearly half a century, and bronze-green glaze was still selling well.

Plate 62. Bright blue on white glazed jug. "Muses and Divisions." Impressed DUDSON BROTHERS HANLEY ENGLAND. 5½." 1900-39.

Plate 63. Three vases. Dark green slip dipped on sage. Struck glaze. 7", 7" and 6". 1890-1914. Sage handled vase is unglazed. 6". 1950-65.

PRODUCTION LINES 1882 — 1917

Jugs.
  In jasperware, embossed stoneware, plain coloured body stoneware and mosaic.
  From 1886 — brown neck on coloured body.
  Shapes:— Tankard, Cambridge and Wide and Pear.

Teapots.
  In jasperware, embossed stoneware, plain coloured
  body stoneware and mosaic.
  Shapes:— Pine, Bute, Imperial, Greek, Pear.
  Stafford and Rockingham

Bowls and cream jugs
Cocoa pots (earlier Etruscan shape)
Coffee pots. pierced and covered
Kettles   Beakers
Broth bowls and stands
Cheese dishes, 4 sizes. New half-moon shape introduced 1898
Butter dishes and covers
Biscuit barrels and biscuit boxes
Marmalade jars and honey pots
Condiment sets
Blancmange or jelly moulds. 3 patterns. Leaf, fluted and pea
Art vases
Flower pots. Lily, Foxglove, Barley, Wreath and Blackberry, also Jasperware
Tobacco jars. Match pots
Nest eggs
Bedroom sets. Soap dishes
Cuspidores
Spittoons in Old Ivy, New Ivy and Vine
Stoneware bottles — Blue, buff and sage
                    Trees and flowers, enamelled blue
                    Birds and Wreath
                    Apple Blossom
Parian busts of Christ

134

18

DUDSON, WILCOX & TILL LTD.

1902 — 1926

JAMES DOUGLAS DUDSON 1879 — 1967

The Dudson involved in the founding of this firm was James Douglas Dudson, born 1879, the son of William Henry Dudson. His father had died from septicaemia at a young age when Douglas was only 4, leaving property and money in trust for his son until he became 21, and it was this money which enabled Douglas, shortly afterwards, to set up the business. He went into partnership with Albert Wilcox and (? Geoffrey) Till to manufacture earthenware at the Britannic works, High Street, Hanley, just four years after his first cousins, James Robert and Harry took over the production at Hope Street.

Plate 64. Douglas Dudson.

Douglas married May Baines, whose family owned Baines colour works, and they went to live in School Lane, Longsdon. They had two children, Eric and Joan.

The firm was successful for many years, specialising in attractive earthenware dinner and tea services. The marks they used are shown on page 224.

Dudson, Wilcox & Till supplied Woolworths, and these orders accounted for such a high proportion of the factory's output that when Woolworths cancelled their orders suddenly in 1926 the firm was forced into bankruptcy.

Douglas' daughter Joan trained in art and sculpture, and until her marriage was engaged in freelance modelling. Some of her models were sold to Coalport, four to Mintons (for export to America) and a few to Wades and Midwinter.

Plate 65. Figure designed and modelled by Joan Dudson 1922. Signed J. Dudson and dated 1922.

17. Left to right:
a) Ginger brown solid body teapot "New Sacrifices" Pine shape.
Impressed DUDSON BROTHERS HANLEY ENGLAND. 5″. 1900-20.
b) Dark blue slipped dipped. 'A' shaped vase. "Bulrush".
Impressed DUDSON BROTHERS HANLEY ENGLAND. 10″. 1900-20.
c) Sage green biscuit barrel, silver plated mount and lid. "Floral" and "Decorated". c. 1910. 7″.
d) White on white jasperware handled and covered sugar. Glazed. Impressed DUDSON
BROTHERS HANLEY ENGLAND D. 3″. 1900-20.

18. 1950-1965 jasperware

a) Salmon pink slip dipped teapot. Imperial shape. "New Sacrifices." Mark No. 20 (p.223). 6".
b) Salmon pink slip dipped cream jug. "Dancing." Mark No. 20. 12¾".
c) Dark blue slip dipped Portland vase. "Dancing." Stamped Jasperware made in England since 1800. 7½".
d) Sage solid body commemorative tankard. "Worcestshire County Cricket Club Champions 1964." Impressed B.Y. Mark No. 20.5¼". Edition limited to 200.

19. 1950-1965 jasperware. From left to right:

a) Sage green E.R. Commemorative mug. 4″. 1953.

b) Blue solid body jug. "Festoon." Vine border. (Compare with plate 9) Mark No. 20 8″.

c) Nutmeg solid body tobacco jar "Hunting." Mark No. 20 6¾″.

d) Salmon pink slip dipped fully glazed bowl with floral sprigs with removable inner container. Mark No. 21 6″.

20. 1950 s Vitrified hotelware. From left to right:
"Melody Sage", "Country Fair", "Melody Marone" (Country Fair designed by Helen Dudson).

19

HUBERT SCRIVENER DUDSON

1899 — 1964

REX DUDSON 1894 — 1929

Plate 66. Rex Dudson.

Plate 67. Hubert Dudson.

As Hubert's two older brothers died without marrying, the running of the business eventually passed solely into the control of Hubert and his family.

Hubert married Helen May Wilkes at St. George's Church, Newcastle-under-Lyme on 22nd June, 1921. May was the only daughter of Charles Wilkes, the outstanding modeller at Burgess & Leigh's factory in Burslem. During the 1930 s Charles Wilkes and his apprentice, Ernest Bailey, designed most of Burgess & Leigh's brightly coloured, embossed jugs, decorated with animals, birds and people, which are known as Flower Jugs.

Hubert and May had three children, Derek Hubert, born 1st August 1922, Charles Bruce, born 19th December, 1926 and Helen Sylvia, born 22nd September, 1935.

May's brother, Frank Wilkes came to Dudsons as Works Manager (later Works Director) from 1929 until his retirement in 1973.

PRODUCTION BETWEEN THE WARS 1918 — 1939.

After they returned from the war, Hubert and Rex jointly ran Dudson Brothers Ltd., with Hubert, not yet 20 years old, in charge of production. He must, at this stage, have been grateful for the experience of his works manager, Henry Bagnall. Rex, only a few years older, concentrated on the sales side and together these two young men guided the company through the difficult post war years.

Production was exclusively of vitrified stoneware, especially the coloured body stoneware in which the factory had specialised for so long — sage, blue, buff, white and pink (pink body was restarted in 1934 using a different stain). All the output was directed towards hotels, restaurants, shipping lines, etc., for which the body was so eminently suitable.

The same basic body was used throughout being decorated, according to demand, in any of the following ways a) plain, b) band and/or line, c) badged, d) jasper, e) mosaic. As production capacity was limited and principally hollow ware was manufactured an agreement was reached with the Globe Pottery Co. Ltd. for Ridgways (Bedford works) Ltd. to supply any additional vitrified hotelware which Dudsons required. This agreement was signed on the first of February, 1923, with Hubert later becoming a Director and minor shareholder in Ridgways.

In 1925 Rex went into partnership with his friend, Guy Forshaw, in a mail order business. They were very early in the field for this form of marketing and had considerable success, offering ware from other pottery factories in addition to Dudson. However, the partnership was destined to be short lived as Rex developed tuberculosis, which became progressively worse, so necessitating its dissolution (18th May, 1928). Rex died a year later at the age of 34. His obituary notice in the Evening Sentinel (22nd May 1929) shows him to have been a keen sportsman and well liked bachelor who took an active part in the life of Alsager where he lived.

Obviously, Hubert felt the loss of his brother keenly, the more so as Henry Bagnall had died in 1927 (March 15th). He, therefore, asked his brother-in-law Frank Wilkes to join him as works manager and this Frank did as soon as he could be released from his current position.

In the early 1930 s Joseph Lyons Ltd., enquired whether the factory could increase supplies if substantially larger orders were placed with them. To

142

comply with this Hubert bought into another factory but when the promised orders failed to materialise he was forced to sell out at a considerable loss, obviously adding to the company's problems at this period.

Hubert decided, therefore, to expand the wholesaling side of the business to meet the wider requirements of his catering customers. He factored many Ridgway lines, some glass and cutlery and also bone china. This latter was made for Dudsons by Salisbury Crown China Co., Longton; Wildblood, Heath & Sons Ltd., Longton; and Hammersely & Co. (Longton) Ltd., and explains why bone china of this period can be found back stamped Dudson Brothers as each factory was supplied with a special rubber stamp.

Jasper was being produced, the amount varying according to demand. Due to the cheap range of jasper, using the Flaxman moulds, which James T. Dudson brought out in 1882 there was already a great similarity between Wedgwood sprigs and Dudsons, sometimes the only differences being the order in which they were arranged, borders and dividers. Of course Dudsons marked their ware clearly so confusion cannot really occur.

PRODUCTION 1918-30
Production was restricted to definite lines as shown by catalogues produced in 1920 and renewed in 1930.

PLAIN STONEWARE, glazed
White, sage, blue. Pink was not made in this period.
Bands were sometimes added as follows:

> Dark blue on white body
> Dark green on white body
> Brown on white body
> Light blue on white body
> Dark green on sage body

Note that wide bands were produced, with one exception, on white body. Prior to 1920 coloured bands (necks) were produced on coloured body, especially brown necks on sage or blue.

BRONZE-GREEN WARE, glazed
White ware was dipped in bronze-green opaque glaze, (See p.190).

LEADLESS PATTERNS, glazed
Available on teapots — includes "brown neck and mosaic sage."

MOSAIC, glazed
The "bead and line" decoration could be added to any shape. White, sage, blue and brown coloured body. Usually the lids were made of stoneware but jugs could be fitted with metal covers if desired.

DUDSON'S WORLD-FAMED STONEWARE.

LEADLESS PATTERNS,
AND BROWN NECK & MOSAIC SAGE

No. 3

No. 5

No. 4

No. 2

No. 6

No. 7

Brown Neck & Mosaic Sage

WOOD, MITCHELL & Cᵒ Lᵀᴰ LITHOS HANLEY

Page from 1920 s catalogue.

Plate 68. Three 1920 s teapots, jasperware. From left to right:

a) Black slip dip on white introduced 1923. Imperial shape. 3¾″ "Dancing".

b) Dark blue on blue "Dancing". 6¼″. Imperial shape.

c) White on white. Pine shape. 4½″.

Plate 69. Jasperware 1900-1939. From left to right:

a) Buff teapot. Pine shape. "Muses and Trees".

b) Blue slip dipped pine shape teapot "New Festoon". 4″.

c) Flower pot dark green on sage. 4½″. "Dancing".

d) Dark blue on blue stoneware teapot with spout right angled to the handle. 4½″. Stamped "L.N.E.R. Hotels". This is the shape that was used as the base for the cafetaries too.

145

Articles produced

Teapots —	Nine sizes, 5 pints down to 8 fl. oz. capacity. All stone covered. The teapots were specially designed to minimise the risk of broken spouts and handles.
Coffee Pots	Also cocoa jugs. Seven sizes, 3 pints down to 8 fl. ozs capacity.
Jugs —	Ten sizes, 4½ pints down to 4 fl. ozs capacity.
Creams —	"Toy" (tankard shape) 10 to the pint "Newgate" (tankard shape) 14 to the pint "Pic" (two lips) 30 to the pint "Small size" (tankard shape) 40 to the pint
Bowls —	Slop or sugar bowls in four sizes, 24s, 30s, 36s and 42s. Also "individual" and "straight" shape.
Teapot stands —	Small and large.
Egg hoops —	also footed egg cups.
Butter dishes —	also jam dishes.

PRODUCTION 1930-39

Very similar to the previous decade but some new lines were offered.

PLAIN STONEWARE

White, sage, blue as before but buff was now added.
Pink re-introduced in 1934 but in a different shade. The complete range of articles were made in all colours. Banded colours were available as before.

BRONZE-GREEN WARE

This glaze on white ware was available as before but two new lines were added:
1. Dark green glaze on white ware.
2. Powder blue on white ware.

LEADLESS PATTERNS

These patterns and "brown neck on mosaic sage" are no longer included in the catalogue.

MOSAIC

As the previous decade with the addition of two new patterns:
1. Black check and line
2. "Black Gordon." (See appendix G, p.193).

Articles produced

As before with some additions:

Teapots —	Bute shape added to the range, (See p.216). The stone lids for all sizes of "Imperial", "Pine" and "Bute" shapes were identical so they could be interchanged.
Cruet Sets —	Three pieces which were not on a stand.
Beakers —	

Vases —	"A" shape and No. 3 shape were now produced in plain body.
Bowls —	A footed bowl now available in 4 sizes.
Egg cups —	A footless egg cup now produced in addition to the former hoops and cups.
Ashtrays —	
Plates, cups and saucers —	These were made in Ridgway Hotel-china and back stamped DUDSON.

JASPERWARE 1918—39

Coloured bodies
Pale blue and sage green. Pink added 1934.

Patterns
"Muses and divisions", "Muses and trees", "Dancing", "Festoons" and "New Sacrifices".
"Music and trees" was discontinued c. 1930
"Festoon" was now draped roundels with rose swags in place of leopard heads and vine swags.

Dipped jasper

Brown dip on white body, unglazed
Light blue dip on white body, unglazed
Black dip on white body, unglazed — introduced 1923
Dark green on sage body, unglazed
Dark blue on blue body, unglazed

In the early 1920 s dark blue dip on blue body was produced fully glazed specially for the London and North Eastern Railway hotels. Later it became popular for other hotels e.g. The Grand Hotel, Eastbourne who also had their badge added. Dark green on sage body became popular, c. 1930, when fully glazed.

Shapes
Some shapes and articles were offered in jasper which were additional to the main range:

Flower pots — 8½, 7½, 6½ and 4½ inches in height
Biscuit jars
Scent bottles
Ring stands
Puff boxes
Vases — Four new shapes added

Although it is described as unglazed all Dudson jasper was lightly glazed at least. The inside was glazed in the usual way and the outside "struck" with glaze, i.e. the inside of the saggar (the rough earthenware vessel which contained the ware during firing) was coated with glaze. As the glaze was volatile a proportion was transmitted to the articles contained in it.

The jasperware of this period was never identical to Wedgwood and was always marked Dudson.

EXPORT MARKETS 1918-39

All these lines were exported through the company's agents to several parts of the world. Agencies were established in New Zealand, New York, Argentina, Brazil, Uraguay, Paraguay, Holland and South Africa. South Africa was an important market and the South African agents, Ross-Elliot & McKellar in Durban secured an interesting order from the Nationalised Southern Rhodesia Railways in the 1920 s. This was for white ware glazed with bronze-brown and badged in gold.

SECOND WORLD WAR 1939 — 1945

In 1942 Hubert Dudson's health broke down. Investigations showed that he had contacted T.B. at the time of his brothers death which, in spite of tests, was not appreciated at the time. This necessitated a period of treatment, so his wife, May, was created a director. She assisted with the financial side of the business, and gave valuable service acting as go-between her husband and the factory. Once again, however, the company had reason to be thankful for the loyalty and hard work of the work's manager, Frank Wilkes, and of all the work force, in keeping production going under very difficult war time conditions.

PRODUCTION DURING THE WAR

During the period there was a Pottery Trade Concentration Scheme and Dudsons made an agreement with R. Edwards & Co., St. James Street (12.8.42) under which Dudsons agreed to pay Edwards £66.13.4 on the 8th day of each month to compensate them for loss of trading. Dudsons took some of Edwards operatives and the remainder were released for war service. Final payment was made on 6th May, 1946.

There was also a Limitation of Supply Act which restricted manufacturing output at each factory. This necessitated selection of orders, from time to time, when the total could not be supplied.

The double spouted teapot shown in plate 70 is interesting. This was used by the army during the war.

148

Plate 70. From left to right:

a) Blue solid body teapot stand. Diameter 7".

b) Dark blue on blue cream jug "Muses and Divisions" 2½". 1890-1920.

c) An early electric kettle. 9". 1920-30

d) Brown double spouted stoneware teapot made for the Army in the Second World War. 6½". 1939-45.

20

POST WAR TO PRESENT DAY

1945 — 1984

Plate 71. Derek Dudson.

Plate 72. Bruce Dudson.

Derek joined his father, Hubert, in 1947, after training at Ridgways' Bedford works under Mr. Philip Bailey, the Managing Director, and at the North Staffordshire Technical College with Dr. Webb. His first job was to get jasper ware into production again and to recapture and build up some of the pre-war markets. He was particularly successful in the United States and, at the request of the American agent, a special new backstamp was introduced for jasper ware destined for this market. However some ware stamped in this way inevitably found its way on to the home market. (See marks, p.222).

At the same time the more important side of the business, the vitrified hotelware, was being developed very rapidly and successfully after the war time restrictions were lifted. Coloured bodies and, a little later, decorated wares were again permitted.

In 1949, however, Ridgways' Bedford works was sold to Lawleys Ltd. When the existing agreement to supply Dudson brothers requirements of vitrified hotelware expired, in 1950, a new agreement, satisfactory to both sides, could not be found and Hubert Dudson resigned from his directorship of Ridgways.

The company decided, therefore, that the time had come to make their own full range of vitrified hotelware and, for this purpose, Albert Pottery in Hobson Street, Burslem, was purchased. An existing registered company, J.E. Heath Ltd., owned by Dudson Brothers Ltd., was used for the "new" factory. The J.E. Heath name came from the late London and South East agent who had previously run the Dudson showroom in Charterhouse Street, London, for many years.

At the new factory some shapes were produced similar to those previously purchased from Ridgways to ensure continuity of supply to Dudson's customers.

It was not immediately recognised, but this triggered off a most exciting period in the history of the firm. Like all companies the business had had its ups and downs since its inception. It was now to emerge from a long period when survival was remarkable and recovery was due to courage, perseverence and, above all, hard work on the part of all concerned.

Early in 1951 Bruce, Hubert's younger son, joined the company, having first qualified as an engineer. Very shortly afterwards he had to take charge of J.E. Heath Ltd., as his brother, Derek, developed poliomyelitis in the summer of that year. Bruce studied pottery at the North Staffordshire Technical College to assist him in his task.

Derek returned to work in 1952 and, shortly after, the opportunity arose to purchase the Grindley Hotelware Co. Ltd., in Tunstall, which Hubert did in May of that year. This factory had been purpose built by W.H. Grindley & Co. Ltd. to make hotelware and had established markets in Canada and Australia. Derek took over these markets when he became managing director of this company.

During the 1950s the home market was greatly expanded under Hubert's guidance. Nevertheless, it could not absorb the total production of the two factories. It was decided, therefore, to expand the overseas markets and to widen the area to which goods were sent. In particular the Canadian and Australian markets, already developed, were expanded by Grindley Hotelware, and J.E. Heath developed a new market for their lines in Canada.

Steadily the output of the group increased and, in 1965, the production of jasper ware was discontinued. It was with great regret that such an attractive line, and one with which the family had been associated for more than a hundred years, was finished but the output was relatively low and interfered with main stream production.

Hubert continued to control the group almost until his death in 1964. Derek and Bruce then took over as joint managing directors.

The group enjoyed success in opening up one overseas market after another, and experienced exciting growth in the existing markets, especially Canada and Australia. The group expanded within the capabilities of the companies to finance such expansion. Markets were secured in countries where the group had never previously been known. For example Greece, a traditionally conservative market, had purchased 90% of its hotelware from Germany and yet within three years Dudson sales exceeded German sales. Success was also achieved in Italy, Switzerland and Sweden; traditional porcelain markets which had to be convinced to change to vitrified hotelware.

At the opposite end of the spectrum great success was achieved in converting the traditional earthenware markets, such as Ireland, to purchase instead the more expensive product. To cope with continually increasing demand both Grindley Hotelware and J.E. Heath factories were extended at later dates.

What was the reason for the group's continuing success? In the first place, undoubtedly, the experience of more than a hundred years of making stoneware, in particular coloured stone ware. This, with an intimate knowledge of pottery bodies, led to a very fine quality vitrified body being produced. Furthermore they made coloured vitrified hotelware bodies. At this time these were not made by their competitors. Other firms produced coloured bodies only in china or earthenware.

The biggest seller of the colours produced was sage, a beautiful soft shade of green, which was first produced in the solid body jasper ware and stoneware of the 1860 s. The colour was modified slightly for the hotelware body and is a colour unique to Dudsons and one with which they are immediately associated. For a long time it was a great success in markets all over the world and is still being sold today.

Other colours included drab, later called buff, which was discontinued in the early 1960 s. Buff was replaced by nutmeg, still in production today. Pink was also discontinued in the early 1960 s and blue was discontinued in 1965. In addition to the white body four coloured bodies are in production today, sage, nutmeg, bamboo and cream.

The second reason for the group's continuing success arose from the first in that the special body, being so suitable for catering ware, resulted in Dudsons specialising in this market from 1900 onwards. If you are selling one type of ware only any problems which arise must be solved quickly, or methods for increasing productivity must be devised speedily. This is perhaps not quite so

21. 1960 s Vitrified hotelware. From left to right:
"Carnival."
Brown glazed decoration "Camelot." Article shapes designed by Martin Hunt.
"Totem."

153

22.1970 s Vitrified hotelware. From left to right:
"Diabolo."
"Gloriana."
"Avalon." shape designed by Michael Kitt
"Bohemia." speckled, matt glaze.
"Astral," speckled shiny glaze.
Stacking cups.

23. Dudson Fine China. 1980 s. From left to right:
"Iona", "Lugano", Tahiti", Monaco.

24.Dudson Fine China. 1980 s.
Customer specials, including gold band and line "Valencia." Black wrapover edge "Capri."

acute for firms making earthenware as well as "Vit". Urgency has sometimes led Dudsons to demand modified, or new, equipment from their suppliers ahead of general demand.

There are several examples where Dudsons have been first, or at least very early, in the field.

1. They were the first vitrified hotelware companies to use sand setter rings for placing bungs of clay ware, for bisque firing, in order to improve the straightness of the biscuit ware (1951).

2. They were the first English hotelware companies to aerograph edge patterns. ("Melody" produced by J.E. Heath was their first).

3. The group were very involved, perhaps more than any other factory, in the development of underglaze lithography, and the change to underglaze water slide transfers.

4. The group were one of the first in the development of gas fired intermittent kilns.

5. They were largely responsible for the development of an underglaze band and lining machine in the late 1960 s.

6. In the 1970 s the group were involved with Podmore & Sons in developing the first conversion of Podmore's vibro energy mill for use in the pottery industry to clean and de-sand biscuit ware.

7. They were the first vitrified hotelware companies to adjust their glazes to resist detergents.

8. They were the first English companies to produce dark brown glaze on vitrified hotelware, (See colour plate 21).

9. The first oval dish edge-sponging machine was developed for Dudsons.

Perhaps the family-inherited trait of determination to overcome difficulties, together with the fact that they have always trained as potters which enabled them to be in overall charge of production, have played their part in company success. However, most important of all, the companies have always been exceptionally well served by loyal staff and employees to whom much of the success must be attributed.

It is sometimes considered that vitrified hotelware is a somewhat inferior product of the pottery industry, and that, because it is thicker than bone china, it is easier to make. In fact that is not true. Of course it does not have the beauty of the finest bone chinas and other decorative articles. It is essentially a practical product which, nevertheless, must have beauty and quality in its own way. It is more expensive than earthenware and must, therefore, give long and durable service to the caterer. Not only for this reason, however, must it have strength but also to resist chipping. In many world markets health regulations prohibit the use of chipped ware in restaurant service. The Dudson group have been continuously engaged in improving the strength of the body, and they were prime movers in the creation of the British Standard for vitrified hotelware in 1966. This was revised in 1980, being reduced from 1% water absorption to ½%. This lower figure has been used by the Dudson group for many years.

Plate 75. An example of 1980 s vitrified hotelware speckled honeyglaze "Cotswold".

Unlike ware destined for the domestic market all decoration (with the exception of gold and platinum) must be underglaze to withstand the abrasion of continual stacking and unstacking, and the chemical attack from the more aggressive dishwash detergents.

There are other problems which present a challenge to the designers too. Generally speaking, the decoration must be only on the rim of the plate and must be such that it can remain in service for a considerable time, cost of re-equipping a restaurant being so costly. There will always be some establishments who choose to use domestic ware but having the right design is equally important to caterers choosing vitrified hotelware. Designs have to be offered to suit a very wide range of decor, so not only traditional patterns are needed but also very up-to-date designs, often in the van of fashion. From 1950 onwards Dudsons have used the full range of design facilities. These include consultant designers, in-house design, free lance artists including local art students, and also a considerable amount of special design work for specific customers. Examples of designs typical of the different decades can be seen in colour plates 21-24.

Plate 73. Ian Dudson.

Plate 74. Max Dudson.

Derek Dudson died in 1975, much respected in the industry for his great courage in the face of disability and for his foresight and technical knowledge. Two of his sons, Ian and Max, work in the group. Ian was created production director of J.E. Heath Ltd., in 1976, and managing director of this factory on 20th April, 1978. Shortly after this Bruce made him joint managing director with himself of Dudson Brothers Ltd.

The name of the Tunstall company was changed from The Grindley Hotelware Co. Ltd., to Duraline Hotelware Co. Ltd., in January 1979. Duraline was already a recognised trade name and registered back stamp, so the change avoided the confusion which had often arisen with another manufacturer having a similar name.

Sadly, production at the Hope Street factory became no longer economically viable in 1980, and production from there was moved to the Duraline and Heath factories. At the same time new offices and showrooms for Dudson Brothers Ltd. were erected on a site adjoining Duraline Hotelware Co. Ltd. at Tunstall. The original factory is now used only for warehousing.

After some years of research the group has taken another important step forward with a major development under Bruce's direction. In 1983 a new china body was put into production, which, to the best of the company's knowledge, is the first body of its kind to be made in the world. This produces thinner, whiter translucent ware which is yet stronger than their vitrified ware. All the decoration can be applied underglaze and it is, therefore, not only a beautiful but a practical product, specially designed to meet the needs of the food service industry. (See colour plates 23 & 24 p.155).

159

The rise from a relatively small factory, with output of restricted lines, to a group in the forefront of its field is remarkable. Not only have the numbers employed increased tenfold, but mechanisation has also increased productivity — all in the space of thirty-five years.

Surely Richard and Thomas Dudson would approve of the group of companies and their performance today.

APPENDIX A

THE ARCHEOLOGICAL DIG.
EXCAVATION AT DUDSONS POTTERY, HANLEY

BY ANN ROBERTS, B.A. (MED. HISTORY AND ARCHEOLOGY)

The excavation was carried out in a yard onto Lower Hanover and Hope Street. The size of the area under excavation was limited by the yard still being used as a loading bay for the factory.

Each deposit on the site was removed in the reverse order in which it was laid down. Towards one end of the dig, the depth was such, that a ladder had to be used for access. In all, about seven feet of deposits were removed, much of it pottery and kiln waste. Each deposit or structure found was numbered, and a description follows.

1.	This extended all over the area excavated and can be described as a "demolition layer" dating from the 1950's when the site was levelled during alterations to the factory. It contained bricks, black and red ash and recent pottery from the late 19th and 20th century.
2, 4, 5.	This group comprised of two blue brick floors, cut into by two runs of drain pipes. Possibly they made up part of the factory formerly on the site.
6.	Before the floors and drains were laid, dark red ash was used to level the ground.
11.	This was a brick wall of three courses broken at one end by a round cast iron grid set into it. The wall stretched right across the area excavated and continued into the baulks at either side.
9.	Abutting onto the iron grid in wall 11 and continuing across the site at right angles to it, was a sagger drain. This was made up of broken saggers closely laid together side by side.
8, 12.	The drain was filled and surrounded by black ash. This deposit covered the area excavated at this depth, and contained parian ware, some master moulds for this ware and pottery from the late 19th century. These layers are the first of a whole series of tipped deposits on the site.

10.	This deposit covered most of area excavated after the removal of 9, 8 and 12. It contained compact material, particularly marl and clay and was again tipped onto the site.
15.	The next layer to be uncovered yielded most pottery; this deposit containing ash and clay amongst other materials, mid and slightly earlier 19th century pottery, including willow patterned, mocha and other decorated wares but no parian. This layer abuts onto 21 in a fairly straight line across the site.
16, 17, 18, 20.	These were composed of tipped material — stiff clay, ash, bricks, kiln waste and kiln furniture. Some 19th century decorated pottery was founded along with clay pipes and stems.
21.	Is important in that it contains pottery roughly one hundred years older than that found elsewhere on the excavation. The pottery — salt glazed ware, cruder Midland purple, and butter pot sherds, was in a mixture of stiff clay, rubble and coal. As there is no layer or humus between this and the preceeding layer, it is believed that this is yet another type of material. Possibly it was dug from another site and brought here, during the search for a workable clay. The tipping of layer 21 is probably contemporary with the other tipped layers described above.
22.	This was the first deposit on the site, and the final layer of tipped material to be reached. It was made up of dark purple ash, clinkers and 19th century pottery.

Finally, at roughly a depth of seven feet, stiff yellow clay was uncovered. This was proved to be the natural, untouched surface of the area excavated.

THE POTTERY

A large number of pottery sherds and two complete vessels were recovered from the excavation. Much of this came from the tipped deposits on the site, and the overall similarity of the pottery found, suggests that all or most of the tipping was done by the same factory. However, this cannot be said about the tipped layer 21 which contains pottery one hundred years older than the rest.

For ease of description, the types of pottery found have been placed in several broad categories.

EARTHENWARE

This is much the largest group and contains hand painted, transfer printed pottery, mocha and stripped ware and plain white glazed pottery. Numerous types of willow patterned ware was found, particularly in layer 15. Notable

162

pieces include a delicately painted, almost complete lid, the major part of a mocha ware jug, and a delicately painted bowl.

PARIAN WARE
Most sherds come from 12 and 8, and include white, grey and white with blue background types. The two complete vessels found are of pale grey parian decorated with cherubs, floral patterns and scrolls.

LUSTRE
A relatively small amount of this ware was found, but this was compensated for by the range of colour amongst this group. These included gold and silver, and pink lustre, wares. The best example found was an almost complete lid decorated with dark pink lustre bands on a white background.

BLACK BASALT
This group includes glazed and unglazed and machine burned basalt.

NOTTINGHAM TYPE WARE AND STONEWARE
A number of these types were found.

FIGURES, etc.
Several fragments were found, including part of a head from a Staffordshire dog, part of a parian figure with hands clasped in prayer, and part of a cottage. This was in the form of a box with holes in the base, and the roof as the lid. It was probably a pastille burner, (See colour plate 2, p.20).

The following categories are of pottery mostly found only in layer 21.

SALT GLAZED WARE
Various types were found, some decorated with linear patterns, some were salt glazed with black iron lead glaze "poured" over them.

MIDLANDS PURPLE WARE AND COARSE WARE
This group is made up of the numerous coarse red bodied wares found in layer 21. Many can be identified as butter pots, and vessels such as panchons and salters from the style of the rims found.

SLIPWARE
A small amount of slipware was found, including 3 sherds of jewelled ware patterned in brown.

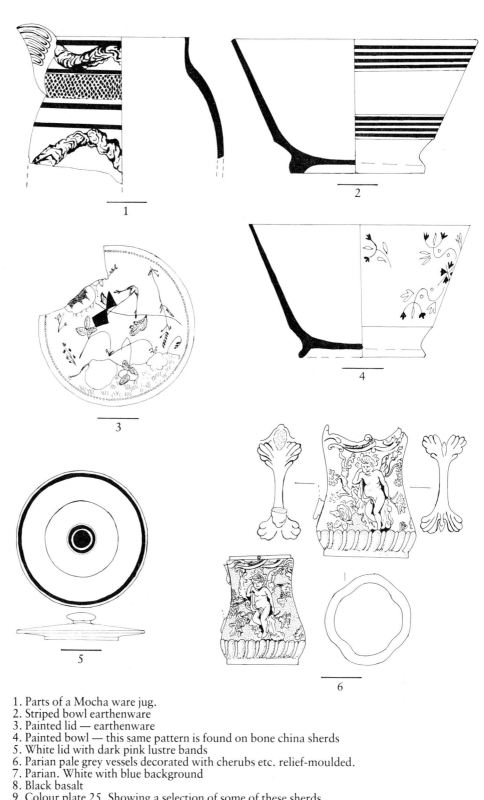

1. Parts of a Mocha ware jug.
2. Striped bowl earthenware
3. Painted lid — earthenware
4. Painted bowl — this same pattern is found on bone china sherds
5. White lid with dark pink lustre bands
6. Parian pale grey vessels decorated with cherubs etc. relief-moulded.
7. Parian. White with blue background
8. Black basalt
9. Colour plate 25. Showing a selection of some of these sherds

164

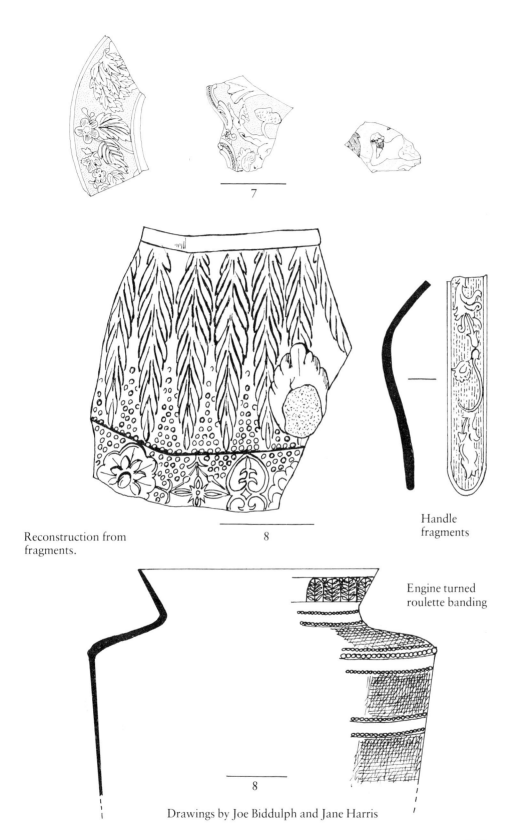

7

Reconstruction from
fragments.

8

Handle
fragments

Engine turned
roulette banding

8

Drawings by Joe Biddulph and Jane Harris

165

Authors comment

As described by Mrs. Roberts, there was only one possible site for the excavation. During the 20th century all the original brick floors had been covered with concrete and to penetrate this would have risked damage to such an old building. It was fortunate that the only site available was so close to the position of the original bottle oven, and because of this several sherds were found as she has described.

The dig was originally requested in the hope that sherds of early Staffordshire figures would be found so making it possible to identify some of the figures listed in the order books.

Unfortunately, relatively few of these were recovered but nevertheless the sherds were very interesting in that they correlated with the other early factory production lines, i.e. lustre, black basalt, hand painted china, underglaze transfer prints, etc.

Some of these sherds can be seen in colour plate 2 and in colour plate 25 and the excellent drawings produced by members of the Archeological Society show greater detail so clearly.

It is not possible at this stage to comment further than has already been done in references in the text. Future research, however, may be rewarding, particularly with regard to transfer printed pottery.

25. A selection of sherds from the Archaeological excavation.

166

APPENDIX B

SOME NOTES ON THE KEELING FAMILY

Robert Keeling. Baptised 24.12.1758 Newcastle parish register, "Robert — son of Samuel Keeling". His burial is recorded in St. Marks (Shelton) parish register as follows — "buried 16th December, 1835, aged 77, of Bucknall Road, Hanley.

ROBERT KEELING'S FAMILY
1. *Thomas.* c.1780 — 1812. Married Jane Dale on the 6th September, 1802 at St. Giles, Newcastle-under-Lyme. They had 2 sons, both baptised at Bucknall, Samuel on 29th March, 1803 and Thomas on 15th September, 1805. Thomas senior died on 23rd October, 1812, and his will (17.10.1812) tells us that, although he was a potter when he married, at the time of his death he was a victualler and owned "The Red Lion" public house in Hanley. He referred to his brother Isaac, and another brother Daniel "Engraver, Shelton" was one of his executors.

2. *Daniel.* Local directories of the period show that Daniel was an engraver in Broad Street, Shelton. His death is recorded in the Staffordshire Advertiser, 24th February, 1844, which gives his age as "in his 60th year".

3. *Isaac.* As for Thomas and Daniel, no baptism has been found for Isaac either. Mankowitz and Haggar (P.282) give his dates as 1789 — 1869 and tell us he was a designer and engraver at Wedgwoods, but that in 1811 became a Wesleyan Minister. The Wesleyan Historical Society have records of two of his stations; Bradwell in 1816 and Southport up to 1864. His will shows he left Southport in 1864 and went to Earby in Yorkshire, whether to a new ministry or into retirement is not clear. His will was proved 9th October, 1875. He was the author of many pamphlets, books and sermons, and a great collector of paintings, as his will also shows. His "brother Enoch — Cashier" was his executor.

4. *Enoch.* He was baptised on 12th January, 1791 at St. Giles Newcastle-under-Lyme. In 1818 he was a book-keeper at the Etruria works and lived in

Edmund Street (Parsons and Bradshaw Directory). He is listed as a commission agent in 1835 (Pigot and Co.) possibly he was helping in the firm of Keeling and Mayer in Charles Street, Hanley. In 1851 he lived at Tinker's Clough Cottage, Shelton, and owned Nos. 2 and 3 Edmund Street (Electoral Roll) and there are several letters in the Wedgwood collection (at Keele University) which indicate he was still cashier at Wedgwoods. He handled several orders from Samuel Keeling and Co. to Wedgwoods.

Robert Keeling had four other children:
5. Jacob baptised 11.11.1792 St. Giles, Newcastle-under-Lyme.
6. Ralph Ratcliffe baptised 13.3.1796 St. Giles, Newcastle-under-Lyme.
7. Jesse baptised 22.6.1801, Hanley Tabernacle.
8. Maria baptised 24.10.1803, Hanley Tabernacle.

ROBERT KEELING'S GRANDSONS (SONS OF THOMAS)

Samuel Keeling, earthenware manufacturer, took over John Glass' manufactory in Bucknall Road (Pigot.1836). He had a factory in Market Street from 1840 — 1852. Llewellyn Jewitt (P.310) says "This Samuel Keeling was great nephew to the patentee James Keeling...." He goes on to say that Samuel "one of the patriarchs of the potteries resided in partial retirement at Rocester" and that his firm Messrs. Keeling & Adams had three mills for grinding potters materials at Hanley. The Eastwood mill, a flint mill, which we are told was earlier a combination of two parts, one a pottery worked by Wm. Baddeley, the other a silk mill worked by William's brother James Baddeley. The other two mills were the Botteslow mill and the Albion mill. Thomas Dudson granted Samuel Keeling and his partner Thomas Adams a mortgage of £1,000 on the Eastwood mill in 1844 (See p.35). Samuel died between 1872 and 1878.

Thomas Keeling. Thomas was a partner in the firm of J. & T. Dimmock & Co., timber merchants and boat builders in Stoke-on-Trent and other places. He was co-executor of Thomas Dudson's will with James Dudson (Thomas' son) and, as much of the estate was left in trust, they were closely involved in many transactions throughout their lives.

In 1872 Josiah Dimmock and Thomas Keeling were the only partners in the timber firm, Thomas Dimmock having died earlier. Then Thomas Keeling died on 22nd May, 1872 and his brother "Samuel Keeling of Rocester, flint miller" and his "nephew, Thomas John Keeling of Hanley, timber merchant", were his executors. He left all his shares in the timber firm to his nephew. Thomas Keeling lived in Howard Place, Shelton.

Some notes on James Keeling. Potter of New Street, Hanley.
He was born in 1762. This was deduced from the notice of his death in the Staffordshire Mercury 12th August, 1837, which says he was 75. He married

twice, a gravestone in St. Johns parish churchyard, Hanley, records the death of "Saray, wife of James Keeling, on December 24th, 1785 — aged 23". James was also 23. He married again, in his early 30's, to Sarah Dimmock. They had 10 children (Hanley Tabernacle records):—

SARAH	born 16.10.1796 – (married John Condor)
MARTHA	born 14.8.1798 — (married Rev. R. W. Newland)
ELIZA	born 16.1.1801 — (married John Burton)
ANN	born 22.10.1803 –(married Samuel Burton)
THIRZA	born 15.9.1805
RUTH	born 27.9.1809
JAMES	born 8.12.1812
ISABELLA	born 6.2.1814
THOMAS	born 21.5.1816
CATHERINE	born 20.8.1819

Sarah became a member of the Tabernacle shortly after her marriage to James, but, although James was a regular attender some years later, and served on church committees, he never became a member. James was a highly respected earthenware manufacturer in New Street, Hanley, who specialised in dinner and tea ware which was transfer printed underglaze. He took out two patents in 1796.

1. 20th June, 1796 "A preparation or substitute for white lead, red lead, calcined lead or other similar preparation of lead, for glazing and enamelling earthenwares, porcelain and china wares, also useful in the making of glass and enamel."

2. 5th July, 1796. "Constructing, erecting and making ovens, kilns and fireplaces used in baking and hardening porcelain, china and earthenware."

He also owned one third of the copyhold earthenware manufactory in Hanley which was occupied by Wm. Hackwood the younger — a house in High Street (occupied by John Condor) and a farm at Cheddleton (his will proved October 27th, 1837). His executors were Thomas Dimmock of Shelton, potter, and Timothy Dimmock of Shelton, timber merchant. His New Street pottery was already being run by his sons-in-law Samuel and John Burton. He was also one of the partners in Keeling, Toft & Co. A notice in the Staffordshire Advertiser (September 20th, 1806) recording a change in partnership within this firm, lists four of the partners as James Keeling, Thomas Toft, Philip Keeling and Thomas Dimmock amongst others. Philip Keeling was probably James' nephew, (See Dimmock tree, p.9).

SOME NOTES ON THE DIMMOCK FAMILY

Thomas Dimmock. (junior) was a potter and according to John Ward 1843 (page 388) had three factories, one in Hanley, one in Shelton and an enamelling and gilding establishment adjoining the Kings Head in Shelton. Godden gives the following information c. 1818-59 in Albion Street. 1830-50 in Tontine Street.

Timothy Dimmock and his brother Josiah founded a firm of timber merchants at Etruria (J. & T. Dimmock & Co.) Thomas Keeling was also a partner in this business.

Mary Dimmock married Thomas Keeling who left his estate to his "brother-in-law James Keeling as devisee in trust". His will (10.7.1810) shows that he also was a potter in Shelton, but does not state where, and that they had two sons, Philip and Daniel.

APPENDIX C

THOMAS DUDSON

POTTERY PRODUCTION 1819 — 1825 (EARLIEST RECORD AVAILABLE) AND 1834

N.B. Many of these lines may have been produced earlier, and similarly many would continue in production for years to come.

TYPES OF POTTERY BODIES MADE :—

Stoneware — smear glazed — white and brown
Black basalt. Also smear glazed
Caneware
Pearlware
Opaque china
Granite china
Chalk body
Jasper
China (containing bone ash)
Flatware body
Common white body
Body for printed ware

Coloured Bodies:—

Blue, green, brown, cane, drab and black.

Different smear glazes are given for the various coloured bodies. Also a recipe for painted glaze.

PRODUCTION LINES

BLACK BASALT
Sometimes gilded

CHINA TEASETS
"Grecian", "Bute" and "Evening" shapes.
Hand painted, outside and/or inside cups
Gilded
Transfer printed

PRODUCTION LINES continued

TRANSFER-PRINTED WARE
Blue and white
Pink and white
Blue — green and white
Brown and white

JASPERWARE
Blue slip dipped

DIPPED WARE
Blue, brown, French grey, olive green, cane and drab dips.

Articles produced

Teapots —	Oval, round, round capt., cottage in sizes 12, 18, 24, 30 s
Coffee pots —	Oval, round in sizes 4, 6, 9 12 s
Jugs —	Round (several patterns)
	Dutch
	Roman
	Dipt
	Brown milk
	Blue figured (Jasper)
	Brown necked
	in sizes 12, 18, 24, 30 s
Mugs —	also tooth mugs
Bowls —	Breakfast, round, brown, dipt
Sugar bowls —	Oval, round
Sugar boxes —	
Creams —	Oval, round
Cups and saucers —	Cut, fluted and various shapes
Coffee cups —	
Coffee cans —	
Dinner plates —	
Breakfast plates —	
Ewers and bowls —	Oval and round
Muffins—	
Egg cups—	
Chamber pots —	
Salts —	also salts on feet
Teapot stands —	
Cake plates —	
Slop bowls —	

This list is not comprehensive as it is compiled from the few early books found in the factory safe, (See p.24). Indeed some of the body and colour recipes included in these books indicate the likelihood of other types of ware, popular at this time, also being produced by the Dudson factory.

No books are available between 1825 and 1834. Another gap occurs between 1834 and 1842. During the 1830 s production of figures, animals and "toys" (chimney ornaments) was greatly increased to become the main line.

CHANGES INDICATED BY THE 1834 BOOK

FIGURES AND ANIMALS
No records exist to show when production began but the following recipes in this book indicate they were in production by this date:
a) Recipes for figure bodies — (several) including "blue figure body", and their glazes.
b) Colour recipes for stumps, hares, horses, ground and flesh.

BODY RECIPES
The number of pottery body recipes has increased considerably from the two earlier books. They give the following pointers to production:
a) Ironstone body
b) Lomoss body
c) Mortar body
d) Several recipes for "Stone Jug Body" and a receipt for "Smear glaze".
e) Jasperware now being made in the stoneware body "Jasper dipped"

Coloured body recipes
Drab, turquoise, lilac, sage, buff, blue.
Brown, chocolate, cane, green.
They were either smear glazed or painted with glaze.

APPENDIX D

PRODUCTION FROM 1842 — 1844

A comprehensive order book is available for 1842/44 and all the lines being produced have been classified as follows. Figures and animals were made in 3 different bodies, 1) porcelain, 2) a very white firing earthenware, 3) common earthenware. There is no means of telling which body is used other than the price at which the article was sold. This, of course, may not be infallible as modelling and hand painting will be more complicated on some articles than others.

FIGURES	1842/44 ORDER BOOK
Nelson — 4 different sorts	*6/- a dozen*
Napoleon	*9/- and 6/- a dozen*
Napoleon and Turks	*5/- a dozen*
Napoleon on horse	*3/- a dozen*
Wesley	*8/- a dozen*
D. O'Connell	*6/- a dozen*
Wellington	*6/- a dozen*
Albert & Queen Victoria	*2/6, 5/- and 14/- a dozen*
Boy on goat	*5/-, 6/- and 8/6 a dozen*
Mother Goose	*6/- a dozen*
Mother goose and yews	*6/- a dozen*
Jim Crow	*12/- a dozen*
Falstaff	*7/- a dozen*
Punch and Judy	*6/- a dozen*
Cupid	*5/- a dozen*
Tam O'Shanter	*6/- a dozen*
Babes in the Wood	*6/- a dozen*

New Babes in the Wood	6/- a dozen
Babes with trees	6/- a dozen
Elements	6/- a set, or 3/- & 6/- a dozen
Seasons	6/- a set, or 3/- & 6/- a dozen
Large seasons	16/6 a set
Charitys	6/- a dozen, & 3/- a dozen
Faith, Hope & Charity	6/- a set
London Criers	7/6 a dozen
Bird catchers	6/- a dozen
Thousand marbles	8/- a dozen
Fowl girls and boys	5/- a dozen
Rabbit boy and girl	6/- a dozen
Turk and bird	2/6 a dozen
Sweep and yews	6/- a dozen
Boy on dog	9/- a dozen
English shepherd	6/- a dozen
Scotch shepherd	6/- a dozen
Sitting shepherds	5/- a dozen
Basket shepherds	6/- a dozen
Stallion and shepherd	5/- a dozen
Shepherd and harper	2/6 a dozen
Thatchers	5/6 a dozen
Mowers	6/- a dozen
Wood cutters	6/- a dozen
Harvest figures	6/- a dozen
Haymakers	6/- a dozen
Fruit gatherers	7/- and 7/6 a dozen
Gardeners with spades	6/- a dozen
Double gardeners	6/- a dozen
Tinkers	7/- a dozen
Basket figures — (others)	7/- a dozen
Scotch sportsmen	6/- a dozen
Scotch bottle figures	10/- each (introduced 1844)

FIGURES	1842/44 ORDER BOOK
Harpers	*5/- a dozen*
Fiddlers	*6/- a dozen*
Minstrels — 2 varieties	*6/- a dozen*
Cap minstrels	*6/- a dozen*
Fettered minstrels	*6/- a dozen*
Tambourine player	*2/6 a dozen*
Accordion player	*6/- a dozen*
Accordion and turk	*6/- a dozen*
Turk and piper	*2/6 a dozen*
Piper	*2/6 a dozen*
Piper and bird on grave	*6/- a dozen*
Brigands	*6/- and 2/6 a dozen*
Turks	*6/- a dozen*
Standing turks	*7/6 a dozen*
Turk and sailor	*6/- a dozen*
Turk and bird	*2/6 a dozen*
Sailor	*6/- a dozen*
Sailor and lass	*6/- a dozen*
Smugglers	*6/- a dozen*
New smugglers	*14/- a dozen*
Snuff taker	*4/- a dozen*
Spanish lovers	*14/- a dozen*
New Spanish lovers	*15/- a dozen*
Bachelors	*15/- a dozen*
Umbrellas	*7/- a dozen*
Courtship	*10/- a dozen*
New courtship	*12/- a dozen*
Mistletoes	*10/- a dozen*
Grandfather	*14/- a dozen*
Father, mother and children	*6/- a dozen*
Sitting figure with child	*6/- a dozen*
Parent figures	*6/- a dozen*

Uncles and aunts	*6/- a dozen*
Sofa figures	*10/- a dozen*
Sofa turks	*12/- a dozen*
Double figures	*2/6 each*
Large figures	*4/- each*
Large Chinese figures	*3/6 each*
Large chinese figures — pair	*10/- or 5/- each*
Large Byron	*5/- each — often sold by the pair for 10/-*
S.S. Women	*6/- a dozen*
S.S. and young	*3/- a dozen*

NOTE: many of the figures were also done in white and gold.

DOGS

More expensive lines

POODLES — *possibly porcelain*

Rough sitting up blue	*26/- a dozen*
Rough sitting up yellow	*24/- a dozen*
Poodles — blue and also yellow	*24/- a dozen*

SPANIELS

Rough sitting up blue	*26/- a dozen*
Rough sitting up yellow	*24/- a dozen*
Sitting up Spaniels blue	*26/- a dozen*
Sitting up Spaniels yellow	*24/- a dozen*
Roughed Spaniels	*30/- a dozen*
Roughed dogs blue	*30/- a dozen*
Large scroll dogs	*36/- a dozen*
Corner dogs	*26/- a dozen*

Medium price lines — good quality earthenware

Greyhounds	*9/-, 10/6 and 12/- a dozen*
Borzoi dogs	*9/-, 10/6 and 12/- a dozen*
Large spaniels	*15/- a dozen*
Dog and monkey	*10/- a dozen & 6/- a dozen*

Medium price lines — good quality earthenware

Dog, *hare and staghounds*	*6/- a dozen & 8/- a dozen*
Dog and sheep	*18/- a dozen*
Dog, pups and wildcat	*5/- a dozen*
Blue spaniels	*5/- a dozen*
Blue rough spaniels	*5/- a dozen*
Dog and sitting figure with child	*6/- a dozen*
Dog and cat on cushion	*5/- a dozen*
Dog and cat in basket	*6/- a dozen*

Cheap range — earthenware

Terrier dogs	*3/- a dozen*
Dog and pups	*3/- a dozen*
Dog and turks	*3/- a dozen*
Dog and bird sitting up	*3/- a dozen*
Dog and bird lying down	*3/- a dozen*
Roughed dogs	*3/- a dozen*
"Dunce" dogs	*4/- and 2/6 a dozen*
Red spaniels	*3/- a dozen*
Dog and duck	*2/- a dozen*
Buff or blue dogs	*2/2 a dozen*
Blue spaniels	*1/9 a dozen*
Blue springer spaniels	*1/6 a dozen*
Red spaniel on yellow pedestal	*1/10 a dozen*
Dog and kennel	*9d a dozen*
Dogs	*1/- a dozen*
Dog and cat in basket	*1/- a dozen*

CATS

Cat and barrow	*12/- a dozen*
Cat and rabbit	*6/- a dozen*
Wild cats	*6/- and 5/- a dozen*
Cat in basket	*6/- a dozen*
Cat and dog on cushion	*5/- a dozen*

Cat and dog in basket	6/- a dozen
Cat and soldiers	5/- a dozen
Cat and sweep	5/- a dozen
Cats	1/10 a dozen
Cats	7½ a dozen
Cats	7/6 a gross
Cat and cottage	9d a gross

OTHER ANIMALS

Monkey and kennel	6/- a dozen
Stag and thistle	4/6 a dozen
Rough sheep	22/- a dozen
Blue sheep	1/10 a dozen
Fox heads	1/6 and 2/- each
Small blue birds	2/- a dozen

INKWELLS

Ink and dish	6/- each
Sofa inks	10/- a dozen
Grandfather inks	12/- a dozen
Round inks	6/- a dozen
Round blue inks	6/- a dozen
Napoleon inks	6/- a dozen
Child and bird	5/- a dozen
Turk inks	5/- a dozen
Cupid inks	5/- a dozen
Babe inks	6/- a dozen
Toby inks	5/- a dozen

ANIMAL INKS

Large spaniel inks	10/- a dozen
Dog inks	9/- and 3/- a dozen
Shepherd inks	3/- a dozen
Chinese inks	5/- a dozen
Basket inks	6/- a dozen

ANIMAL INKS

Dog inks	*36/- a dozen*
Rabbit inks	*6/- a dozen*
Greyhound inks	*6/- a dozen*
Dog and monkey inks	*6/- a dozen*
Dog and pups inks	*6/- a dozen*
Pointer dog inks	*6/- a dozen*
Monkey inks	*5/- a dozen*
Large sheep inks	*6/- a dozen*
Fox and monkey inks	*6/- a dozen*
Cat and jug inks	*5/- a dozen*
Cat and rabbit inks	*4/- a dozen*

COTTAGES

Flower cottages	*10/6 a dozen*
Blue cottages	*15/6 a dozen*
Swiss cottages	*9/- a dozen*
White and gold cottages	*10/- a dozen*
"New"	*14/- a dozen*

EARTHENWARE COTTAGES

Round	*5/- and 3/- a dozen*
"New"	*5/6 a dozen*
Thatched	*5/6 a dozen*
Blue thatched	*5/6 a dozen*

CASTLES

White and gold porcelain	*9/- a dozen*
Castles — unspecified	*4/-, 2/6 and 7½d a dozen*

CHINESE TEMPLES

10/- a dozen. and *18/- a dozen* — a "New Model" produced in 1842. (i.e. Chinese temples, at least, were in production prior to 1842).

EWERS AND BOWLS

Leaf ewers and bowls	*4/- each*
Tulip ewers and bowls	*4/- each*
(Unspecified) ewers and bowls	*4/- each*
* Plaided ewers and bowls	*2/- each*

LUSTRE

Cups and saucers	*3/- a dozen*
Jugs and basins	*4/- a dozen*
Jugs — 3 varieties (not described)	*2/3, 3/-, and 3/6 a dozen*
Jug — New pattern	*4/6 a dozen*
Mugs	*2/3 a dozen*
Cans	*1/4 a dozen*
Basins	*1/6 a dozen*
Vases	*3/6 a dozen*
Lustre vases Gothic	*8/6 a dozen*

PRINTED WARE

Recipes for underglaze printing include the following colours : Flo-blue, green, pink, black, brown, olive green and chrome green

"PRESENT" WARE

Mugs	*5/6 a dozen* (Lynmouth is frequently ordered).

TEA SETS PRINTED

1/6 a dozen

DINNER SETS PRINTED

4/6 a dozen

COMMEMORATIVE WARE WITH A VIEW OF THE THAMES TUNNEL OPENED 1843

Mugs	*6/- a dozen*
Cans	*15/- a dozen*
Tunnel mugs — gold	*3/5 each*
Tunnel spill jars	*1/6 a dozen*

* Scotch plaid

"VIEW" WARE

View cans and mugs	*1/4 a dozen*

CANS "PRINTED N.P."

CANS "PRINTED N.P."	*1/4 a dozen*
also "Name" cans and mugs	*4/6 a dozen*

MUGS

Present	*5/6 a dozen*
.Thames Tunnel	*6/- a dozen*
Name	*4/6 a dozen*
View	*1/4 a dozen*
Lustre	*2/3 a dozen*
Sportsmen	*6/- a dozen*
Assorted	*2/3 a dozen*

CANS

Printed	*1/4 a dozen*
Gilded	*2/- each, i.e. 24/- a dozen*
Name	*4/6 a dozen*
Cans gilded	*24/- a dozen*
View	*1/4 a dozen*
Lustre	*1/4 a dozen*
Thames Tunnel	*15/- a dozen*
Porcelain	*15/- and 16/- a dozen*
Leaf	*1/4 a dozen*

BASKETS

Shell	*21/- each*
Oval redicule *	*5/- a dozen*
Flat	*5/- a dozen*
Blue	*6/- a dozen*
Redicule	*5/- a dozen*

* Sometimes spelt ridicule

TAPER OR SPILL HOLDERS

Vine taper holders	*26/- a dozen*
Vine taper holders	*6/- a dozen*
Blue taper holders	*6/- a dozen*
White and gold tapers	*6/- and 3/- a dozen*
Stag tapers	*4/6 a dozen*
Thames Tunnel spills	*1/6 a dozen*

JUGS. These are produced in quite large quantities and sell steadily, often "assorted."

Stoneware —	*White, blue or buff*
Figured —	*3/-, 4/- and 6/- a dozen* (i.e. Jasper)
Flowered —	*4/- each*
	hand painted enamel 6/- each (See plate 4, p.22).
Tulip —	*4/- and 8/- a dozen* (probably stoneware).
Lustre —	*2/3, 3/-, 3/6 amd 4/6 a dozen*
Blue striped —	*3/6 each*

TOBY JUGS

Porcelain —	*36/- a dozen*
White and gold —	*5/- and 10/- a dozen*
Earthenware —	*10/6 a dozen*

LARGE TOBY JUGS WITH COVERS (Introduced 1843)

Original —	*2/- each*
New shape	*2/5 each* (not described)

FLOWER TUBES

Matt blue	*36/- a dozen*
Flower	*8/- a set*
Blue flower	*3/- a set*

VASES

Flower small	*£1. 6s. 0d the set*
Prince	*3/- the set*
Lustre	*3/6 a dozen*
Lustre — Gothic	*8/6 a dozen*

MISCELLANEOUS

Cornucopias	*2/6 a set*
Daila stands (Dahlia?)	*2/- a set*
Tea sets — printed	*1/6 a dozen*
Dinner sets — printed	*4/6 a dozen*
Cups and saucers	*3/- and 5/- a dozen*
Lustre cups and saucers	*3/- a dozen*
Extinguishers	*2/- a dozen*
Sweet William and black edge	*6/- a dozen*
Lussau (?)	
Artificial fruit	*8/- a dozen*
Custard cups, middle size	*5/6*
Boxes, Japan	*12/- 10/- and 8/- a dozen*
Boxes, Napier	*5/- and 5/6 a dozen*
Tray with raised flowers	*15/- each*
Redicules. 2 sorts	*5/- a dozen*
Oval redicules	*5/- a dozen*

TEAPOTS
Round and pressed
These were being supplied in coloured body, presumably stoneware body, the following colours being available.

Blue, turquoise, sage, lilac, drab. buff, cane, green, brown, chocolate

Although no orders are recorded Dudson was able to supply them in bone china too.

APPENDIX E

FIGURE AND ANIMAL PRODUCTION IN MID 1850 s

This list is written at the end of the 1842/44 order book and covers piece rates payable to makers. Whether these are the only lines in production or are new additions to the 1840 s range it is impossible to determine.

FIGURES

Reaper lovers	*Soldier and sailor*
Harvest lovers	*Large sailors return*
Sitting harper	*Wheat figure, new*
Sitting shepherd	*Sportsman and clock*
Scotch drummer	*Polka clock*
Scotch gardener	*Boat figures*
Tree figure	*Water carriers*
Gypsies	*Churn figures*
Flag, sailor and lass	*School boys*
Well figures	*Bower gardeners*
Gate and figures	*Jug, figures and bower*
Theaday and Willin	*Basket gardeners*
Venus with cupid	*Flag figures*
Double soldier and sailor (blue)	*Double clock figures*
Double soldier and sailor (tall)	*Soldier clock stand*
Dog, figures and bird	*Parrot figures*
Grape gatherers	*Fountain figures*
Double soldiers	*Beehive figures*

FIGURES

Swan figures

Omar Pasha

Uncle Tom

Uncle Tom, Eve and boat

ANIMALS

Sheep and stump

Dog and stump

Goat and stump

Cow

Cow with child

Cow cut out at mouth

Lions, 3 sizes

Zebras, large

Donkeys, large

Basket Spaniels

Poodles

Double rabbits

Stag and garland

Stag and children

Goat and young

Goat and figure

Goat and child

Rabbit bowers

OTHERS

Bowers

Boats

Two baskets and scarf

Blue topped cottages

Clock and bower

Lidded Toby jugs

Toby tobacco jar

Turks head tobacco jar
(See colour plate 2)

Mosaic tobacco jar
(See colour plate 6)

CRUCIFIXES

In 21 different sizes (not detailed).
Body not specified.

TOILET WARE

Paint and gilded

Some gilded borders,
narrow or broad

28 different numbers
(without description).

Two named patterns
"Gold grapes and lines"

"Vermicelli gold"

N.B. Some figures now were made in Parian body in addition to earthenware (and ? china).

It is believed that the Parian busts of Christ, which were a popular selling line in the 1880 s, were modelled in the 1850 s/ 60 s.

Production of pottery figures gradually decreased during the 1850 s as other lines took over. According to contemporary advertisements figure production ceased c. 1865.

APPENDIX F

VARIOUS PRODUCTION LINES

1. **BLACK BASALT**
   In production 1819-22 (earliest records available).

   Round "capt" teapots — several sizes. Oval teapots, Cream jugs, Sugar bowls. These were sometimes gilded.

   The jug in plate 2 was identified by means of the Archeological dig. Other pieces were also found, (See appendix A, p.165).

2. **LUSTRE WARE**
   1823 and 1834 books record lustre recipes
   (not known if it was produced earlier).
   Silver, gold, copper, tin, blue and pink

   Earliest examples have so far been found on Tulip jugs. Pieces of silver resist lustre were uncovered in Archeological dig, (See appendix A, p.163).

   Present knowledge is insufficient to identify other lines. At first special details were picked out in lustre (Tulip jug). The later (mid 19th century) Tulip jug is copper lustred with the flowers and leaves enamelled, (p. 21).

   The following articles were sometimes lustred:
   Cups, saucers, jugs (several shapes), basins, mugs, cans, vases, and gothic vases.

3. **TRANSFER — PRINTED WARE (under glaze)**
   In production from 1819 (earliest record available). Still in production in 1842. In 1819-25 the following underglaze colours were used on white body:—
   Blue, Pink, Blue-green, Brown.

   Pink and white "Landscape" tea services were made for Bentley & Wear in 1819.

A considerable quantity of printed sherds have been recovered in the Archeological dig showing various patterns and borders. These will form the basis for future research at a later date, (See colour plate 25, p.166).

The 1842-44 order book records sales in flo-blue, blue, green, pink, black, brown, olive green and chrome green. Tea sets, dinner sets, mugs, cans, spill jars and a special Commemorative range with a view of the Thames Tunnel, opened 1843. This type of ware was probably discontinued by 1850.

3. IRONSTONE CHINA

No examples have yet been identified, so no details can be given.

5. PARIAN

Parian was an important production line during the late 1850 s — 1860 s (contemporary advertisements). As no order or record books are available for this period very few pieces have so far been identified.

Jug (a) in plate 13 (p.82) is identical to those made in the Stoneware body and for this reason has been identified as Dudson. Probably other relief moulded patterns were similarly produced.

Small relief moulded jugs in pale grey parian in a "Cherub" pattern have been uncovered in the Archeological dig. The cherubs are similar to the jasperware cherubs of this period, (See appendix A and colour plate 25).

Evidence from the dig also suggests that figures were produced in parian. Small flowers clustered on a plinth and other layer flowers suggest this (see colour plate 2).

Prices paid to makers in 1850 record 21 different sizes of Crucifixes. The body is not specified but may well have been parian as later (1882-89) parian busts of Christ were produced. These busts were almost certainly modelled in 1850/60 s.

6. CHINA

1819-22 china tea services and coffee cups, cans and saucers were produced.

a) Purple and gold pattern — Grecian shape

b) Pink landscapes - burnished gold — Bute shape

c) White with gold edge and line

d) "Other patterns" — not described (See colour plate 25 p.166)

e) Tea and coffee ware for John Daniel, New Hall Pottery, not described, (See p.38).

c. 1840. White china cheese dish (plate 9 page 76) enamel decorated bowls and other lines.

1830 s-65. China figures and animals (in addition to earthenware range).

1860 s. China jugs, e.g. Pansy jug (plate 8 page 76).
China articles were produced from the same moulds as the relief moulded stoneware.

c. 1870. china production gradually phased out.

7. MAJOLICA AND BRONZE GREEN WARE

Majolica glazed ware was introduced 1885/86 using the stoneware body. Mainly on a) Plain tankard jugs (colour plate 16b p.118).

b) Spittoons in "Begonia" and "Rose" relief moulded patterns.

Majolica did not prove popular and it was discontinued in 1910 when Bronze-Green glazed ware was introduced (1910-1939). This was a very popular and important production line until 1939.

8. PRESSED WARE 1882 — c. 1918

Introduced 1882 as lighter and cheaper than the relief moulded stoneware. Produced in blue, sage and white earthenware. Jugs were most popular line but flower pots, butter pots and green glazed plates and rushfoot dishes were also produced.

Patterns — were all adaptions of the moulded stoneware patterns.

New fluted	Scroll
Damascus	Coral
Jewel	Star
Argyle	Duck (old Bulrush).
Fern oak	Convolvulus
(Plate 58 p.127).	

9. TOBACCO JARS

Production started in 1840 s

Toby — 1840 s to 1860 s

Turk's Head — late 1840 s to 1900 (Colour plate 2 p.20).

Mosaic — 1840 s to 1880

Rustic — c. 1900 to 1920

DUDSON'S WORLD-FAMED STONEWARE.

BRONZE GREEN

GLAZED

Teapot

Jug

Jug (metal covered)

Cream "Pic"

Cafétaire (complete)

Bowl (Straight Shape)

Butter or Jam Dish

Teapot or Jug Stand

Egg Hoop

Cocoa Jug

Vase No. 4 Shape

Coffee Pot

WOOD MITCHELL & C° L™ LITHOS. HANLEY

A page from a 1930 s catalogue.

10. PLAQUES
Moulds for the production of plaques exist on the factory

1) Oblong	Dick Turpin
	Sacrifices
	Tam-o'shanter
2) Round	Night
	Morning
	Spring, Summer, Autumn, and Winter

Blue/green glazed plaques are shown in plates 45 and 45a.

11. HENBOXES (Hen Tureens) HEN-ON-THE-NEST
See plate 42 page 98. These were made throughout the second half of the 19th Century.

Usually unmarked but sometimes have DUDSON impressed on foot rim.

MOSAIC WARE

1840 TO EARLY 1960s

LEADLESS PATTERNS 1900 — 1930

In these patterns a depression was created on the turned surface of the pot which was then filled with contrasting slip. (Greater detail is given on page 97). (See colour plate 14, p.46).

"*MOSAIC*" always contains the characteristic "bead and line".

Sherds uncovered during the Archeological dig indicate this pattern was started in the 1840s in conjunction with underglaze bands of colour.

The earlier pieces, c. 1850s, have *PATENT MOSAIC* impressed on the base along with an impressed decoration number.

The tobacco jar in colour plate 6, page 64, is impressed 120.

1860 —   Stoneware body was used in white, ivory, blue drab,
1880
             sage green and brown

             Pieces may be brushed glazed, struck glazed or fully glazed.

             They were inlaid with a variety of coloured slips.

             Articles given this treatment :—

             Teapots, coffee pots, cocoa jugs, tankard jugs, bowls, candle-sticks, tobacco jars, biscuit barrels and condiment sets.

1880 —
1900   Ivory and drab coloured bodies discontinued. Inlay normally in black slip now.

1900   Brown neck and mosaic sage introduced, (See page 144). Also other coloured necks, e.g. blue neck on sage mosaic, or brown neck of blue mosaic etc. These were discontinued c.1920 and brown neck on sage mosaic was discontinued in 1930.

BADGED MOSAIC
Mosaic was frequently badged for hotels, but more especially for Railway companies. The Great Eastern Railway Company was probably the largest customer. (G.E.R. on blue mosaic).

1908/9 Two new mosaic designs were registered

1)   4th January, 1908. Rd. No. 518575.
     Imperial shaped teapot with dark green china.
     On the 15th February, 1908 this design was indented to the exclusive use of *J. Lyons & Co.,* in the home market. Dudsons retained the overseas rights.

2)   18th February 1909. Rd. No. 537475.
     Registered for 15 years, expired 18th February, 1924. This particular design was in production in the 1860s and 1870s but it was registered as *"A Statement of Novelty — the design in dark green on a white body is the novelty."* (page 131)

These mosaic lines were discontinued by 1930.

1930   Mosaic now "bead and line" only in black fully glazed.
        Mosaic was discontinued in the early 1960s.

LEADLESS PATTERNS
1900   Leadless patterns numbered 1 — 7 were introduced, (See p.194).

The designs were produced in the same way as mosaic but did not include the "bead and line."

They were produced with green slip decoration on white stoneware body.

By 1930 They were discontinued.

c. 1930 Two new designs introduced with black slip decoration on white body.

1)   Black Gordon

2)   Black check and line

They were discontinued in 1939.

Some Mosaic and Leadless patterns

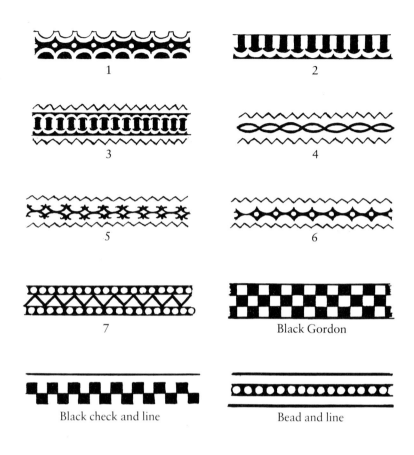

1

2

3

4

5

6

7

Black Gordon

Black check and line

Bead and line

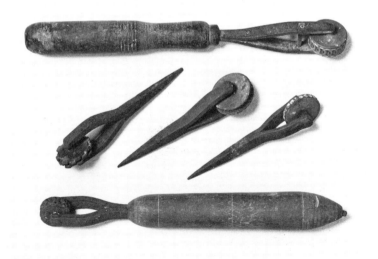

A few of the rollers used for producing mosaic patterns.

APPENDIX H

PLAIN COLOURED BODY STONEWARE

1870 s   Some articles such as bread trays, candlesticks, cheese stands, toast racks, egg pots, etc., were produced in plain coloured stoneware bodies, blue, green, brown, drab and white.

These might be left perfectly plain or were sometimes gilded.

The earliest known example of Dudson badged ware was produced in this period — A "Mitre" badged jug — i.e. A Bishop's mitre stamped on a plain blue stoneware jug.

1886   Contrasting brown necks on blue, sage or pink jugs, teapots sugar and creams were introduced, (Plate 54, p.119).

1898   Dark blue neck on white body added to the above range.

1900   Demand for badged ware increasing.

1900/01 Sudden cessation in demand for relief moulded stoneware, and plain coloured stoneware no longer as popular. As a result considerable variety introduced in coloured stoneware range.

e.g. contrast necks or wide bands on tankard shape.

     A.   Pink body — green, brown or blue necks

         Sage body — dark green, brown or blue necks

         Blue body — dark blue or brown neck

         These could be gilded, or have a broad band in heavy gilt.

195

B. "Floral"—white flowers and green leaves scattered around the pot at random.

"Decorated" — wide band of deep enamel on which were painted sprays of flowers.

"Floral" and "Decorated" were sometimes combined and were possibly "heavy gilt" too. (Colour plates 16 & 17 p.p.118 and 137).

1915   "Floral" and "Decorated" were continued.

1914/18 Coloured stoneware was badged and/or banded.
Coloured necks still produced — less popular.

Bronze-green glaze popular, (See p.190).

1918/39 Production now exclusively of vitrified stoneware, especially coloured bodies:— sage, blue, buff (replaced drab in late 1920 s), white and pink.

Pink body was discontinued during the war, i.e. 1918, restarted in 1934 using a different stain.
Treated as follows:—

a)   Plain glazed — perhaps badged

b)   Banded glazed — dark blue on white

                    dark green on white

                    brown on white

                    dark green on sage

N.B. With the one exception these are coloured bands on white body. Prior to 1920 coloured contrasting bands were on coloured bodies.

Bronze green glaze on white body continued until the end of the 1930 s.

Two new lines were introduced during the 1930 s
1)   Dark green glaze on exterior of white ware

2)   Dark blue glaze on exterior of white ware

POST WAR TO PRESENT DAY
Coloured vitrified hotelware bodies:—

Drab   — later called buff was discontinued in early 1960 s

Blue   — discontinued in 1965

Pink   — discontinued in early 1960 s.

Sage, nutmeg, bamboo and cream are still in production.

APPENDIX I

BADGED WARE

1860 s   Earliest known example is the *Mitre* badge i.e. a bishops mitre stamped in black onto the jug. This was produced for Acme Patents and was supplied until c. 1910.

1894   Sage and blue jugs with brown necks were badged for hotels in South Africa.

        a) BM   East London

        b) PLN   Algoa Bay

        c) $\frac{1440}{SE}$ Townsville in Australia

1897   Blue mosaic ware badged *FULLALOVE*

1900   Demand for badged ware increasing

1900/06   RAILWAY BADGES

1901 a)   *North London Rly. Dalston Junction* in black

      b)   *G.E.R. Co.* on blue mosaic (Great Eastern Railway).

1905 a)   *G.N.R. Dining Car* on both sides of sage green teapots.

      b)   *G.N. Rly Co.*

      c)   *Steam Packet Co.*

1910 Blue mosaic jugs, badged in black

OLD ORKNEY WHISKY

With *"Blurton Bros"* stamped on base jug.

Only one badge book remains on the factory for the earlier years. This is dated 1926. The following are a few reproductions from it.

A SELECTION OF BADGES SUPPLIED IN 1922

1. Cosens & Co. Ltd.
Weymouth

2. Pacific steam Navigation
Liverpool

3. Isle of Man Steam Packet
Co. Ltd.

4. The Leith, Hull &
Hamburg Steam Packet Co.

5. The Pacific Steam
Navigation Co.

6. Royal Mail
Steam Packet Co.

7. London North Eastern
Rly.

8. Great Northern Rly. Co.
Ireland

9. Rhodesia Railways

10. Bristol Zoo

11. Good Year
Tyre & Rubber Co.
Wolverhampton

12. W.D.&H.O. Wills.
Bristol

13. High Commissioner for
S. Africa in London

14. Spencers. India

15. Grand Hotel. Calcutta

16. Inglis Ltd. Sydney,
Australia

17. F. Hawes. Takapuna,
New Zealand

18. Clarke. Ireland

19. Royal Berkshire
Hospital

20. Grand Hotel
Eastbourne

21. St. Pancras Borough
Council

22. Merton College,
Oxford

23. Queens College,
Cambridge

24. Marlborough College,
Wiltshire

APPENDIX J

RELIEF MOULDED STONEWARE

1830 s
Evidence exists, in the form of recipes, that smear glazed stoneware was being produced. No examples.

1840 s
A stoneware "Tulip" jug was already in production by 1842.

LATE 1840 s — 1850 s — Characteristics of the Period
a)   Coloured stoneware bodies — blue green, drab in addition to white

b)   Frequently unmarked but some have DUDSON impressed on the foot rim

c)   Typical shape — weight well towards the base

d)   Foot not very well defined — unlike many other manufacturers at this period

e)   Background usually stippled

f)   Handles represent stems, branches or bark

g)   The rim is sometimes flat but an upward flaring lip is more usual

h)   Floral decoration, well defined, in high relief often in panels

i)   Loose running plant patterns also

j)   At present no gothic figures are known

In **1855** "Pineapple" was registered. This design has the pineapple upright. Later pineapple jugs have the pineapple slanting.

Fashion for heavily decorated jugs was beginning to fade.

"Basket" was introduced. Tankard shape was becoming more popular.

1860 s — 1900

White, drab, blue, slate blue and green bodies. Majority of patterns were introduced in 1860 s. In 1870 s there was a fashion for enamelling and/or gilding parts of the design.

Lines were mainly discontinued in 1900 but a few were exported up to 1917.

N.B. Combinations of two designs on the same jug have been seen. Perhaps these form some of the designs as yet unidentified.

COMPLETE RANGE OF ARTICLES MADE IN RELIEF-MOULDED STONEWARE

Teapots	12s. 18s. 24s. 30s. 36s.	Metal or stoneware lids
Jugs	6s. 12s. 24s. 30s. 36s.	Metal mounted lids or plain
Creams	30s and 36s.	Metal mounted lids or plain
Sugars	18s. 24s. 30s. 36s.	Stone lids or plain
Butters	24s. 30s.	Could have stands and lids
Coffee pots	18s. 24s. 30s. 36s.	Metal or stoneware lids
Kettles	18s. 24s.	Metal or stoneware lids
Broth bowls	24s. 30s.	With stands and covers
Slop bowls	30s.	With or without stands

Patterns which were regularly produced in this complete range were :

Argyle, Convolvulus, Damascus, Chrysanthemum, Fern, Jewel, Poppy, Boston and Rose.

The remaining designs appear to have been produced in jugs only, either plain or with metal lids.

RELIEF MOULDED STONEWARE

DATES

Design	Introduced	Discontinued	Illustration
Argyle (registered)	1865	1911	Plate 17 p.84
Apple blossom	Mid 19th C.	c. 1880	Plate 26 p.89
Autumn & Winter	1860 s	1911	Plates 28 & 45 pp. 91 & 100
Barley (registered)	1861	1914	Plate 26 p.89

New Barley	Late 1870 s	1914	Plate 26 p.89
Basket	1850 s	1900	Plate 26 p.89
New Basket	1887	1895	Plate 16 p.89
Beehive	1860 s	1898	No example
Begonia	1860 s	1887	No example
Birds (also called Robin)	1860 s	1900 Home 1903 Export	Plate 26 p.89
Bluebell	1860 s	1901	Plate 26 p.89
Boston	1891	1900	Plate 12 p.82
Bulrush	1860 s	1895	Plate 26 p.89
Cable	?	1896	No example
Cactus	1860 s	1896	Plate 17 p.84
Cane	?	1886	Plate 82 p.207
Chrysanthemum	1860 s	1896	Plate 26 p.89
Convolvulus	Mid 19th C.	1905	Plate 26 p.89
Coral	Mid 19th C.	1898	Colour Plate 4 p.22
Damascus	1860 s	1911	Plate 26 p.89
Fern (registered)	1862	1902	Plate 10 p.81
New Fern (registered)	1860 s	c. 1900	Plate 11 p.81
Fern Fronds (registered)	1865	c. 1880	Plate 11 p.81
Floral	1893	1901	Plate 81 p.207
Fuschia	1850 s	c. 1880	Colour plate 4 p.22
Gladioli	1860 s	1898	Colour plate 4 p.22 Plate 80 p.206
Hythe	?	1890	Unidentified
Hazelnut	1850 s	1882	Plate 26 p.89
Hazelnut and Squirrel	1870 s	1882	Plate 26 p.89
Holly	1860 s	1890	Plate 26 p.89
Ivy	1860 s	1890	Plate 26 p.89
New Ivy	?	1893	No example
Jewel	1860 s	1910 Home 1917 Export	Plate 16 p.83
Jubilee	1887	1887	Plate 22 p.86
Kensington	?	1894	Unidentified

Design	Introduced	Discontinued	Illustration
Lilian	?	1892	Unidentified
Lily	1850 s	1893 Home 1903 Export	Colour plate 4 p.22
New Lily	1860 s	1902 Home 1914 Export	Plate 14 p.83
Maize	1860 s	1896	Plate 14 p.83
Music	1890	1900	Plate 26 p.89
Night & Morning	c. 1860	1901 Home 1917 Export	Plates 23 p.87 and 15 p.83
New Fluted	1870 s	1896	Unidentified
Napier		1896	Unidentified
New Butterfly	1860 s	1900	Plate 26 p.89
Old New Flower	?	1899 Home 1902 Export	Plate 16 p.83
Oak & Ivy	189-	1900	Unidentified
Oak and Joy	1893 only	A "SPECIAL"	Unidentified
Passion Flower	1860 s/70 s	1896	Unidentified
Pineapple	1855	1860 s	Plate 21 p.85
New Pineapple	1860 s	1896	Plate 13 p.82
Pansy	1860 s	1900	Plate 8 p.76
Poppy	1860 s	1882	Plate 13 p.82
Robin (see Bird)	1860 s	1900 Home 1903 Export	Plate 26 p.89
Rose	1850 s	1897 (few sales after 1880)	Plate 13 p.82
Rye	?	1894	No example
Scroll	1860 s	1895	Plate 12 p.82
Spring & Summer	1860 s	1900	No example
Star	?	1900 Home 1910 Export	No example
Snowdrop	?	1900 Home 1905 Export	Plate 26 p.89
Sunflower	1860	1896	Plate 26 p.89
Tulip	1840 s	1900	Plate 20 p.85
Vine Leaf	?	1900	Plate 15 p.83

Vine Border	?	1894	Plate 25 p.88
Wheatsheaf	1860 s	1901	Colour plate 7 p.65
Wyth (Withe)	?	1898	Unidentified

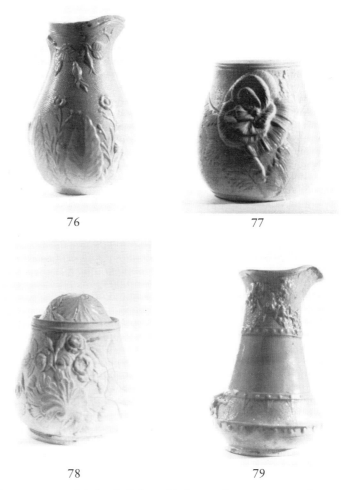

76   77

78   79

Four master models for Relief-moulded ware. Pattern names unknown.

Plate 80. Master model of "Gladioli" — note that modelling has varied slightly from the original. (See colour plate 4, p.22).

Plate 81. Master Model "Floral"

Plate 82. Master Model "Cane"

Plate 83. Master Model. Pattern
name unknown

Plate 84. "New Fern"
registered 1862

APPENDIX K

JASPERWARE

PRE-1850 s

1819   Earliest factory record available gives evidence of the production of jasperware (See colour plate 11 p.107).

1840-45 Only a small quantity of jasperware produced.
        Blue figured jugs, i.e. blue slip dipped on white body.

1850 s — 1882

1850 s   Production steadily increased

Earlier pieces were all jasper dip, i.e. white stoneware body slip dipped in colour : See plate 29 page 92.

Dark blue	— Colour plate 11 p.107
Bright blue	— Colour plate 9 p.105
Light blue	—
Soft green	— Colour plate 8 p.66
Pink	— Colour plate 6 p.64

Solid jasper was re-introduced at the end of the 1850 s, i.e. coloured stoneware bodies :

Blue ⎰ Soft delicate	— Colour plate 7 p.65
Sage green ⎱ shades	— Colour plate 7 p.65
Brown — several shades	— Colour plate 8 p.66
Claret brown — a red brown	— Colour plate 5 p.63
Slate blue (discontinued 1882)	— Colour plate 5 p.63

Jasper Dip continued in production as well but was largely phased out at the end of the 1860 s.

SHAPES

During 1850 — 60 s shapes were often similar to the stoneware shapes.

Low bellied with flat rims

Round bellied with upward flaring lip

TANKARD

Tankard shape was produced in quantity. The earliest tankard jugs had a small turned foot and slightly sloping sides and were probably produced at the end of the 1840 s and early 1850 s, (Plate 29 p.92).

HANDLES

On the early designs handles were made to simulate foliage or twisted branches, or stylised animals.

Other handles were relief moulded, as were spouts
Tankard jugs were usually given "rope" or "cane" handles

INCISED NUMBERS

A system of freehand incised design numbers on the base of the ware was introduced c. 1850 (exact date unknown). System ceased in 1882.

These incised numbers are a useful guide to the identification of Dudson pieces with certain reservations, (See p.93). The first number found to date is 13, (See Plate 29 p.92). Incised design numbers of 3500 and upwards have been found. A list is being compiled but is a long way from being complete.

Some designs, became standard lines and were sold over long periods. These are dealt with in more detail below.

Photographs of the sprig moulds found on the factory are on page 219. It is hoped that these will assist in the identification of less frequently produced patterns. Unfortunately the sprigs are not a comprehensive collection either.

Caution

a) Pieces of ware cannot be dated by means of the incised design number because once in use it continued throughout the 30 years. Low numbers must be early but numbers from 1 — 1000 could have been allocated on the same day on existing ware.

b) Some identified pieces of Dudson jasperware do not have a design number. They may pre-date the system or be special *"one-off"* orders which were not allocated a design number.

c) Dudson ware with the incised design numbers on the base was sometimes marked with the customer's name instead of Dudson. This was very prevalent in the 1870 s and names appearing regularly are PAXTON, NORWOOD, B.P. CO. (Brownhills Pottery Co. — see Page 94) and RIDGWAY. Other pottery companies and retailers names occur.

MODELLING
A great variety of sprigs was introduced from 1850 onwards but the names of the modellers are not known. It is known that Charles Dudson did some modelling c. 1840 — 1850. Some of the sprig moulds are signed J. Dudson — others are incised G.G. and many are incised B.

DESIGNS
Several jasperware sprigs were modelled from designs of the relief moulded stoneware. In the 1850 s — 60 s jasper sprigs were sometimes applied to the relief moulded stoneware as well as to plain shapes.

JASPERWARE DESIGNS

1850 s or earlier
So far the following have been identified as being in production by this date.

Muses	—	Colour plate 8 p.66
Cherubs	—	Colour plate 8 p.66
Hunting	—	Plates 29, 30 and colour plate 19, pp.92, 94, 139
Sacrifices	—	Colour plate 9 and plate 37, pp.105, 96
Bluebell & Acanthus	—	Colour plate 5 and plate 38, pp.63 & 96
Bluebell & Fern	—	Colour plate 6 p.64
Tropical bird	—	Colour plate 8 p.66
Figures & Divisions	—	Plate 48 and plate 29 pp.111, 92
Figures & Trees	—	Plate 29 p.92
Thistle Wreath	—	Colour plate 6 p.64
Thistle & Shamrock Wreath	—	
Night & Morning	—	Frontispiece
3 un-named patterns on urns	—	p.213
Filigree Fern	—	Colour plate 5 p.63
Pattern name unknown	—	Colour plate 11 p.107

1860 — 1880

A great variety of sprigs was introduced which were assembled in various ways. The following were the basic designs.

Allbine	—	Colour plate 9 p.105
Bird	—	Plate 30 p.94
Bird and Butterfly	—	Plate 31 p.96
Bird and Bamboo	—	Colour plate 10 p.106
Japanese Bird	—	Plate 36 p.96
Tropical Bird	—	Colour plate 8 p.66
Blackberries	—	
Blind Man's Buff	—	Plate 28 p.91
Bluebell and Acanthus	—	Colour plate 5 p.63
Bluebell and Fern	—	Colour plate 6 p.64
Cherubs	—	Colour plate 8 p.66
Cherubs & Divisions	—	Colour plate 17 p.137
Chinese figures	—	Plate 27 p.91
Coursing	—	Colour plate 13 p.115
Fern & Wreath	—	Colour plate 8 and plate 33 p.66, 96
Ferns	—	
Fern & Bulrush	—	A fern and a Bulrush crossed
Filigree Fern	—	Colour plate 5 p.63
Festoon	—	Colour plate 9 and plate 44 pp.105, 99
Hope	—	Plate 46 p.100
Hunting	—	Plate 29 p.92
Muses	—	Colour plate 8 p.66
Muses & Divisions	—	Plate 46 p.100
Muses & Trees	—	Colour plate 7 p.65
Muses & Ferns	—	
Night & Morning	—	Frontispiece
Sacrifices & Divisions	—	Colour plate 10 p.106
Sacrifices & Trees	—	Colour plate 9 p.105
New Sacrifices	—	Colour plate 18 p.138

Vine	—	Plate 58 p.127
Wheatsheaf, Vines & Divisions	—	Colour plate 5, p.63 and plate 34 p.96
Wheatsheaf, Vine, Hops & Divisions	—	Plate 46 p.100
Wheatsheaf, Vine, Blackberries & Divisions	—	
Vines & Gamebirds & Divisions	—	Colour plate 10 p.106

Between 1880 and 1891 the number of designs was gradually reduced until in 1891 the following were offered.

1891

Allbine, Birds, Blind Man's Buff, Coursing, Ferns, Fern Wreath, Festoon, Figures, Figures & Divisions, Hunting, Muses & Divisions, Muses & Trees, Trees, Sacrifices & Divisions, Sacrifices & Trees, New Sacrifices, Torches & Trees. (This is mentioned for the first time).

See above list for illustrations.

NOTE The **MUSES** have changed — they are now identical to the Flaxman models.

1898

Designs were further reduced by this date to:—

Muses & Divisions	—	Plate 66 p.141
Muses & Trees	—	Plate 59 p.128
Sacrifices & Divisions	—	Colour plate 10 p.106
New sacrifices	—	Colour plate 17 p.137
Bird & Bamboo	—	Colour plate 10 p.106
Ferns	—	
Hunting	—	Plates 29, 30 pp.92, 94 and colour plate 19 p.85
Coursing	—	Colour plate 13 p.115
Torches & Trees	—	
Festoon	—	Colour plates 9 and 13 p.p 105, 82
Blind Man's Buff	—	Plate 49 p.112

1899

A commemorative jug was registered. Tankard shape, rope handle with Baden-Powell on one side and Kitchener on the other.

1901

Three main patterns only:—

"Muses & Divisions." "Muses & Trees" and "New Sacrifices."

Trees," and "Ferns" were used on cheese dishes and large flower pots.

Two new patterns were introduced:—

1902 "Festoon" — (which replaced the original vines and leopards heads).

roses and draped roundels — (plate 59 and p.128).

1903 "Dancing" — based on the Flaxman models (plate 66 p.141).

These 5 designs continued until 1939. Jasper was discontinued during the war. From its reintroduction in the late 1840 s until it was finished in the 1960 s these five main patterns were produced but many of the original mid 19th Century moulds were also reproduced. See marks for special back stamp for this period.

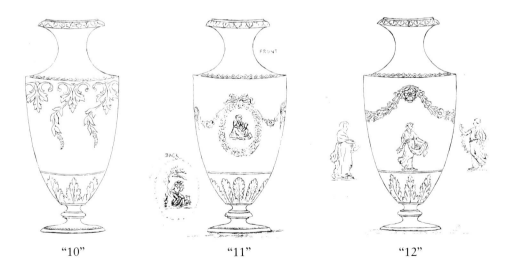

"10"   "11"   "12"

Three un-named patterns. Original factory drawings. Numbers "10", "11" and "12." 1880 s-1920 s. Urns were produced from c. 1830 at least.

Plate 85. Brown solid body. Wine or water cooler. Brush glazed. Blue ferns and white bluebells. Incised 455. Impressed B. 12½". 1870-80 s.

Also produced in red, blue, buff or lilac. Capacities 2, 3 or 4 pints. Other decorations include mosaic and enamelling.

SHAPES

Only one pattern book remains amongst the earlier factory records. This covers a few of the designs and shapes produced between 1880 — 1917.

It is impossible, therefore, to produce line drawings to give anything approaching a comprehensive range of shapes.

Any of the earlier shapes which have been identified positively are included in the photography. There is no point reproducing the same articles again, especially as photographs are more accurate than drawings.

There is, however, a small amount of information available, with regard to some lines, which has been collected from various sources and in particular the book referred to above. These shapes are drawn below.

First, however, it must be pointed out that whilst as many shapes as possible were kept standard and were produced unchanged for several decades, Dudsons did not sell only to the retail trade from c. 1890 onwards. They supplied a "service" to the restaurant and catering industry also and indeed from c. 1900 onwards supplied this market only. They frequently therefore had had to modify their shapes and designs to suit their catering customer's needs. As a result the actual range of shapes is very large and shape cannot be the only criterion in identifying Dudson.

e.g. A throwers size book (c. 1890) gives the following dimensions for the same article to be supplied to two different customers, namely a "toy" tankard shaped cream jug.

a) Carricks   2 $\frac{9}{16}$" high,   1 $\frac{1}{8}$" across top,   1 $\frac{3}{4}$" across base

b) Flemingo   2 $\frac{3}{4}$" high,   1 $\frac{3}{8}$" across top,

         "a medium thick bottom which narrows inside"

This is only one of several examples.

SHAPES

Cambridge

Imperial

Pine

Bute

Rockingham

Tankard Shape Cocoa Jug

Tankard Shape Coffee Pot

Cafétaire

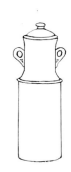

Cafétaire

Blancmange Mould
'Leaf'

Art Vase

Biscuit Jar No. 4

Cheese Dish

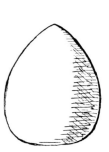

Nest Egg (actual size)

VASES

1

2

3

4

5

6

7

8

D. Shape

HONEY POTS

Stratton
516

512

517

513

217

METAL FINIALS

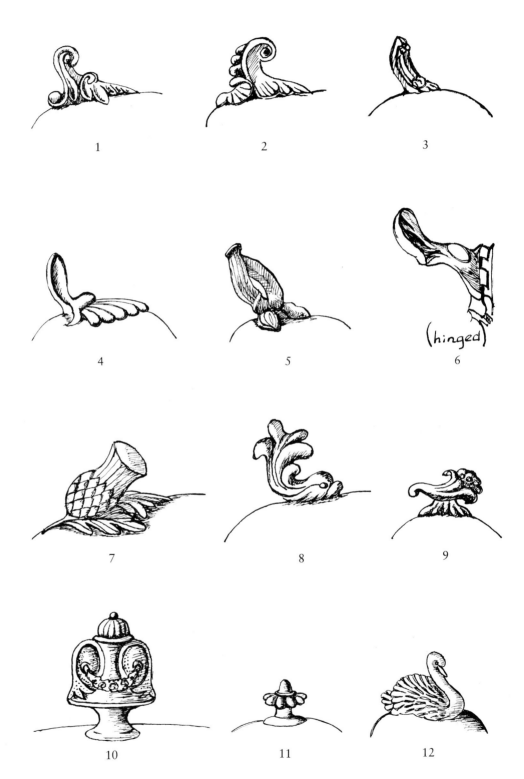

1

2

3

4

5

6
(hinged)

7

8

9

10

11

12

STONEWARE FINIALS & KNOBS

1

2   3

4   5

SPOUTS

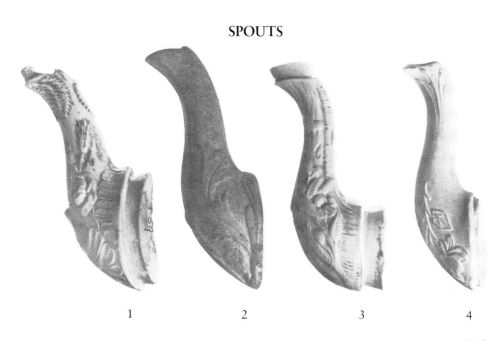

1   2   3   4

SPOUTS Continued

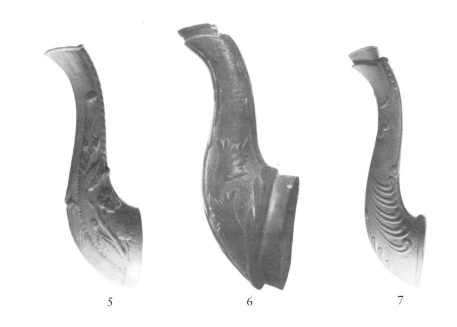

5   6   7

HANDLES

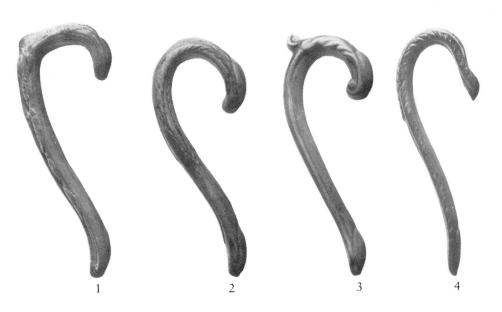

1   2   3   4

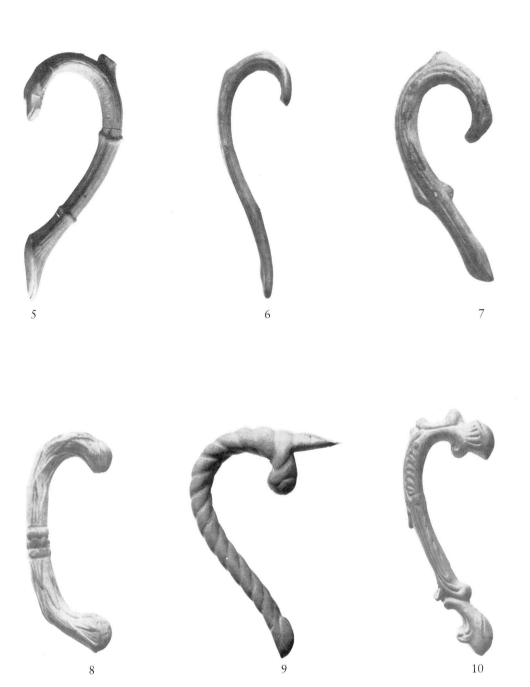

5

6

7

8

9

10

221

MARKS

Most ware was unmarked prior to 1880 but the following marks sometimes occur.

1		1830 — 45	Painted on base.
2			Incised on base
			Impressed on base
			Impressed on base
			These marks appear fairly regularly throughout the 19th Century.
3	R DUDSON	1825 — 1838	RICHARD DUDSON moulded mark.
4	DUDSON	1845 — 1882	Sometimes impressed on foot especially on relief moulded stoneware and mosaic.
5	3386 and other numbers	Mid 1840s — 1882	These incised decoration numbers occur on the base of Jasperware.
6	JAMES DUDSON LICENSED BY THE PATENTEES HANLEY STAFFORDSHIRE	1845 — 1882	Impressed inside stoneware lids. "James DUDSON Licensed by the Patentee. Hanley, Staffordshire".
7	JAMES T. DUDSON LICENSED BY THE PATENTEES HANLEY STAFFORDSHIRE	1882 — 1898	Impressed inside stoneware lids. "JAMES T. DUDSON. Licensed by the Patentee. Hanley, Staffordshire.
8	ENGLAND	1870 — 1899	Impressed on base

9		Moulded registration diamonds occur for:—
	1855	Pineapple
	1861	Barley
	1862	Fern
	1865	Fern Fronds
10	1865 — 1868	Moulded registration diamond for 23rd December 1865 with title "Argyle". DUDSON was frequently impressed with this mark also.
11	1868	After 1868 the following moulded circle was sometimes used to mark "Argyle" ware.
12	1891 — 1899	Impressed on foot.
13	1891 — 1899	Impressed on foot
14	1882 onwards	Impressed on base
15	1900 — 1936	Impressed on foot.
16	1900 — 1936	Impressed on base or foot.
17	1900 — 1936	Impressed inside stoneware lids.
18	1930 — 1936	Printed mark
19	1936 — 1945	Printed mark
20	1945 — 1965	Printed mark specially designed for the American market.
21	1945 —	Impressed or printed mark. Year numbers occur with this mark. Other DUDSON BROTHERS marks occur all are dated.

223

22	1950 —	Printed mark. J. E. HEATH LTD.
23	1952 —	Printed marks used by GRINDLEY HOTELWARE CO. LTD. The name of this company was changed in 1979 to DURALINE HOTELWARE CO. LTD. Other marks are used by these two factories also — all are date marked.
24	1902 — 1926	Printed or impressed marks. DUDSON WILCOX and TILL LTD.

OTHER MARKS WHICH OCCUR

INITIALS *L . B . S . W . H*		Makers and/or ornamenters marks.
NUMBERS *12 24 6*		These refer to the size of the pot.
DATE MARKS *10 . 78* *3* *80* *7* *82*	late 1870 and 1880 s	Ware was sometimes dated:— October 1878 March 1880 July 1882
RETAILER'S NAMES e.g. PAXTON NORWOOD MILLWARD BRENT	1870 s — 1880 s	Dudson pieces may be marked with Retailers names. DUDSON is NOT added.
Other Factory names e.g. RIDGWAY B. P. CO. LTD.	Occurs in all decades until 1950	Dudson pieces may be marked with the names of other factories. DUDSON is NOT added.

MOULDS FOR JASPERWARE SPRIGS

Illustrated below are the sprigs found in the cupboard at the factory. This is not the complete range — others are constantly being found on known Dudson pieces.

Information was recorded of incised and impressed marking on these sprigs.

Scale: Black line represents 2½ cms

COMMEMORATIVES

1. Young Queen Victoria
   and Albert

2. Queen Victoria —
   Middle Age

3. Queen Victoria —
   old age

4. Prince Edware &
   Princess Alexandra

5.

6. Lord Roberts
   of Kandahar

7. Col. Baden Powell

8 Sir Redvers Buller

9 Lord Kitchener of Khartoum

225

COMMEMORATIVES continued

10　Royal Canadian
　　Mountie

11

12　George Washington

13　William Pitt

14

15

16

17

18

19

20

21

22

23

24

25

26

27

28

29

30

31

3

CLASSICAL

33

34

35

36

37

38

39

40

41

42

43

44

45

46

47

48

49

50

51

52

53

54

55

56

57

58

59

231

60

61

62

63

64

65

66

67

68

69 70 71

72 73

74 75

233

CHERUBS AND PUTTI

76

77

78

79

80

81

82

83

84

85

86

87

88

89

90

91

92

235

93

94

95

96

97

PLAQUES

98 Night — After Thorwaldsen

99 Night — After Thorwaldsen

100 Night

101

102

Morning — After Thorwaldsen

103 Autumn

104 Autumn

105 Winter

106

107

108

109 John Gilpin

110

HUNTING

111

112

113

114

115 COURSING

116 GAME BIRD

117 BIRD

239

118

119

120

121

122

123

124

125

126

127

128

129

130

131

132

133

134

135

241

136

137

138

139

FLOWERS

140

141

142

143

144

145

146

147

148

149

150

151

152

153

TREES

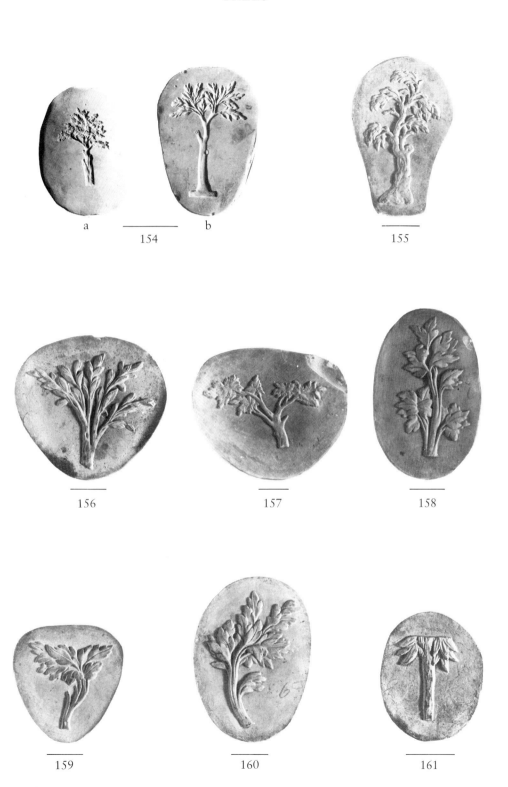

a   b
154

155

156   157   158

159   160   161

162   163   164

165   166   167

168   169   170

171

172

a   b
173

174

175

176

177

178

179

180

181

182

183

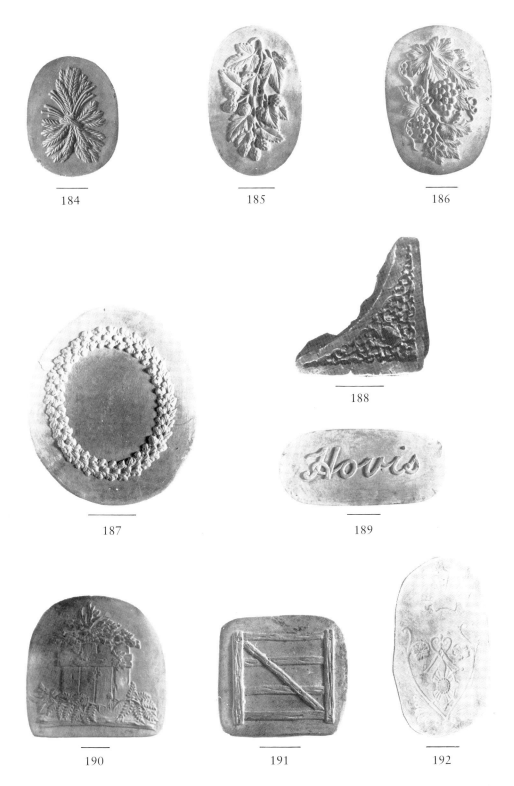

184

185

186

187

188

189

190

191

192

a   b
193

194

195

196

197

198

199

200

201

202

250

DIVIDERS

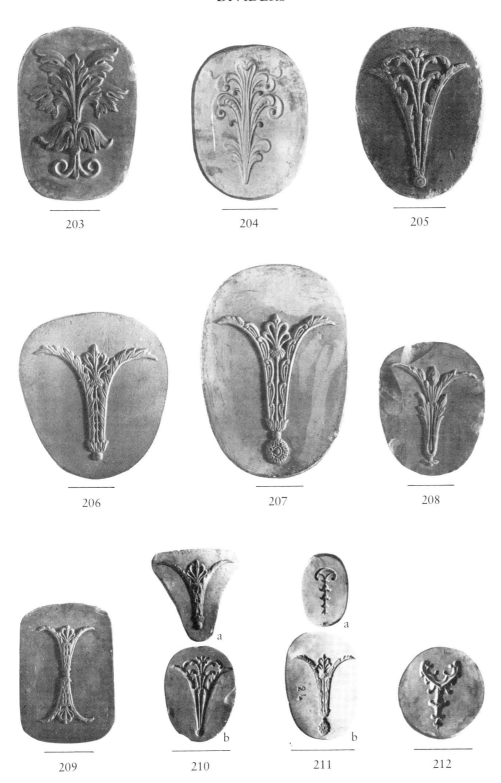

203   204   205

206   207   208

209   210   211   212

251

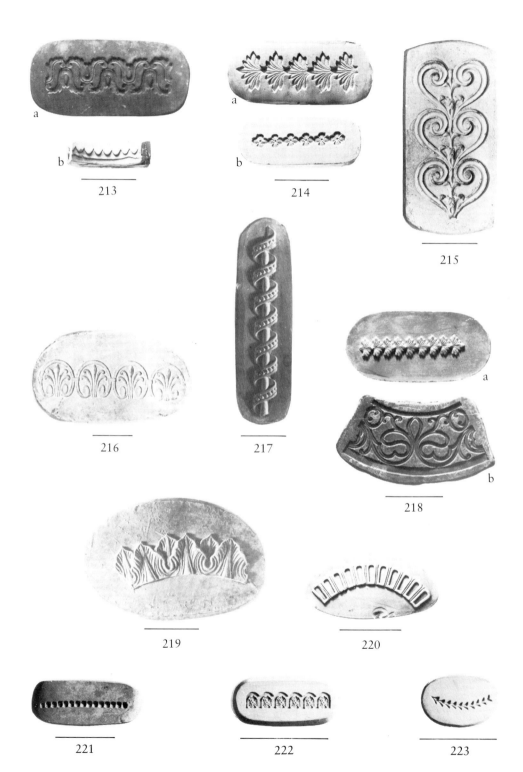

a

b

213

a

b

214

215

216

217

a

b

218

219

220

221

222

223

224

225

226

227

228

229

230

231

232

233

234

235

253

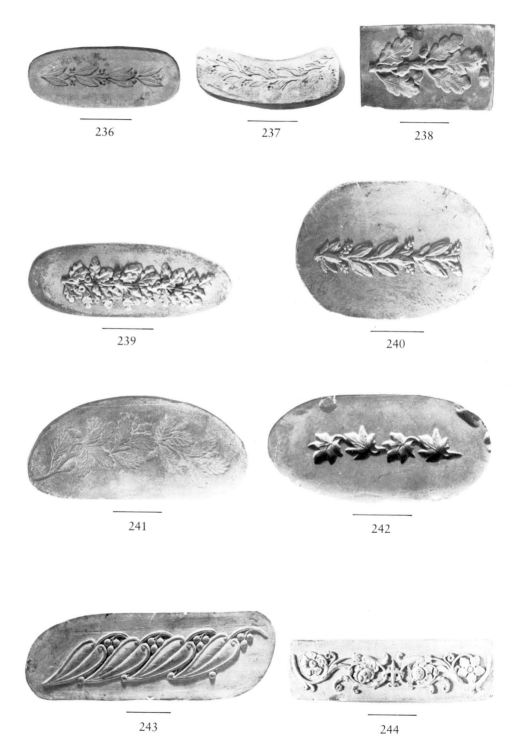

236

237

238

239

240

241

242

243

244

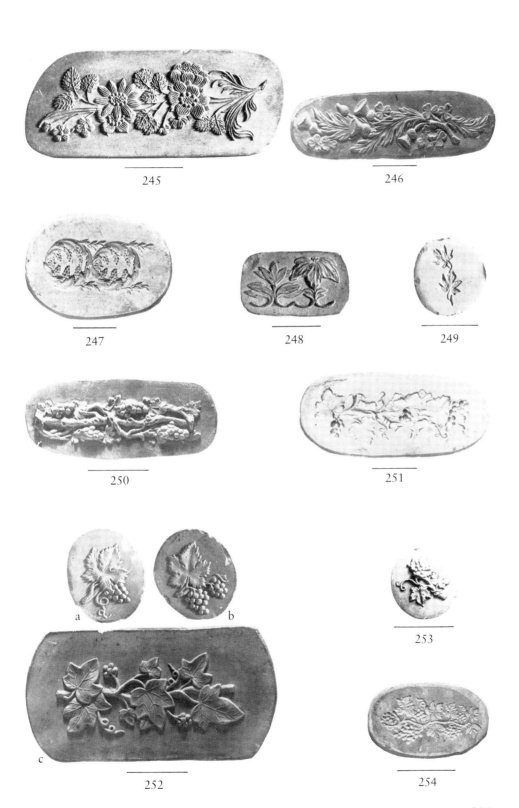

245

246

247

248

249

250

251

a

b

252

c

253

254

255

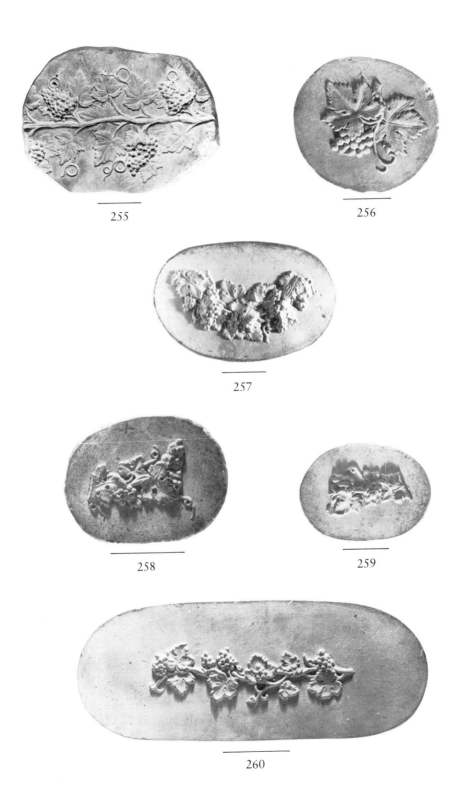

255

256

257

258

259

260

FESTOONS

261

262

263

264

265

266

267

268

269

270

271

272

273

274

MOTIFS

275

276

277

278

279

280

281

282

283

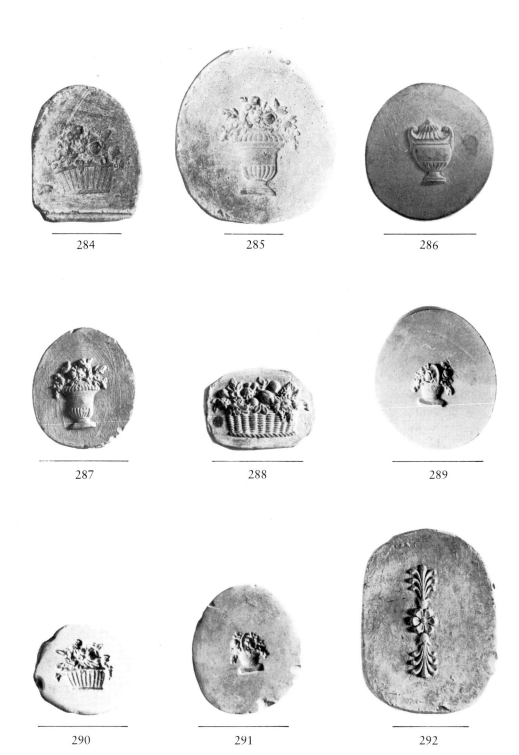

284

285

286

287

288

289

290

291

292

293

294

295

296

297

298

299

300

301

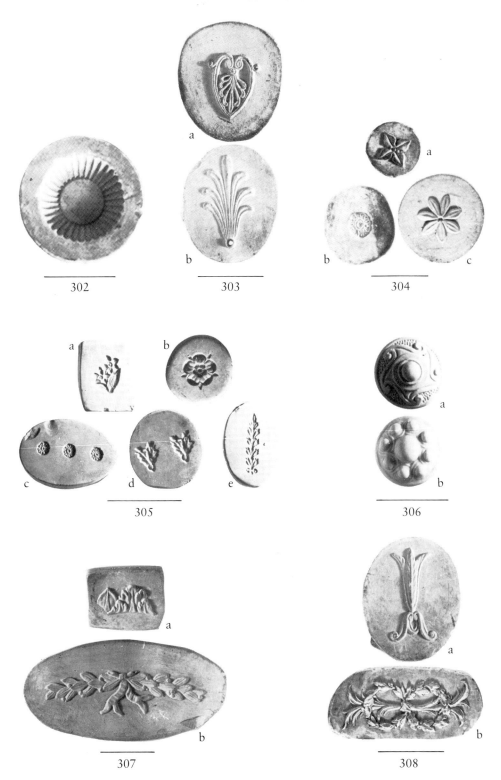

302

303

304

305

306

307

308

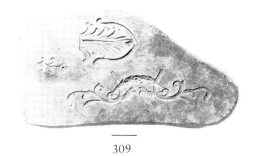

309

310

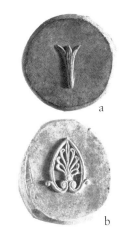

a

b

311

312

313

314

MANUFACTURERS, IMPORTERS, WAREHOUSEMEN AND AGENTS.

A page from SILBER & FLEMING'S ILLUSTRATED CATALOGUE. c. 1880

Note: All these lines were in production in the 1860 s and 1870 s, and some in the 1850 s.

BIBLIOGRAPHY

Local Directories

1818   *Staffordshire Directory. Parsons and Bradshaw*

1822/23   *Newcastle & Potteries Directory.*

1830. 1835   *White's History, Gazetteer & Directory of Staffordshire*

1869. 1870's   *Keates Gazetteer and Directory*

1870   *J.G. Harrod & Cos. Postal & Commercial Directory of Staffordshire — 2nd edition.*

Journals

Pottery Gazette (later the Pottery Gazette & Glass Trade Review).
Pottery Gazette Diaries — (1907, 1910/11).

Other Publications

F. Burchill & R. Ross	*History of the Potters Union* (1977).
Children's Employment Commission	*Appendix to 2nd report of Trades and Manufacturers Vol. 2.* Reports and evidence from sub-commissioners 1842.
G.A. Godden	*Encyclopaedia of British Pottery & Porcelain Marks* (1970).
G.A. Godden	*An Illustrated Encyclopedia of British Pottery & Porcelain* (1968).
G.A. Godden	*British Pottery — An Illustrated Guide.* (1980).
R.K. Henrywood	*Relief-Moulded Jugs 1820 — 1900* (1984) Published by Antique Collectors' Club.
Robinson, Son & Pike	*A Descriptive Account of the Potteries* Illustrated, 1893 Hanley Section.
Simeon Shaw	*History of the Staffordshire Potteries,* 1829
Victoria County History	*Volume 8.*
John Ward	*History of Stoke-on-Trent,* 1843.

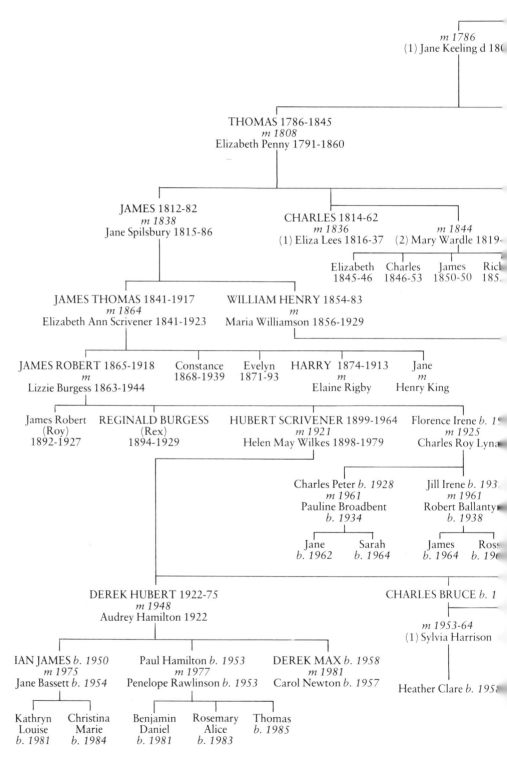

m 1786
(1) Jane Keeling d 18(

THOMAS 1786-1845
m 1808
Elizabeth Penny 1791-1860

JAMES 1812-82
m 1838
Jane Spilsbury 1815-86

CHARLES 1814-62
m 1836   m 1844
(1) Eliza Lees 1816-37   (2) Mary Wardle 1819-

Elizabeth   Charles   James   Rich
1845-46   1846-53   1850-50 185.

JAMES THOMAS 1841-1917
m 1864
Elizabeth Ann Scrivener 1841-1923

WILLIAM HENRY 1854-83
m
Maria Williamson 1856-1929

JAMES ROBERT 1865-1918
m
Lizzie Burgess 1863-1944

Constance
1868-1939

Evelyn
1871-93

HARRY 1874-1913
m
Elaine Rigby

Jane
m
Henry King

James Robert
(Roy)
1892-1927

REGINALD BURGESS
(Rex)
1894-1929

HUBERT SCRIVENER 1899-1964
m 1921
Helen May Wilkes 1898-1979

Florence Irene b. 1
m 1925
Charles Roy Lyna

Charles Peter b. 1928
m 1961
Pauline Broadbent
b. 1934

Jill Irene b. 193
m 1961
Robert Ballanty
b. 1938

Jane
b. 1962

Sarah
b. 1964

James
b. 1964

Ross
b. 19(

DEREK HUBERT 1922-75
m 1948
Audrey Hamilton 1922

CHARLES BRUCE b. 1

m 1953-64
(1) Sylvia Harrison

IAN JAMES b. 1950
m 1975
Jane Bassett b. 1954

Paul Hamilton b. 1953
m 1977
Penelope Rawlinson b. 1953

DEREK MAX b. 1958
m 1981
Carol Newton b. 1957

Heather Clare b. 195

Kathryn
Louise
b. 1981

Christina
Marie
b. 1984

Benjamin
Daniel
b. 1981

Rosemary
Alice
b. 1983

Thomas
b. 1985

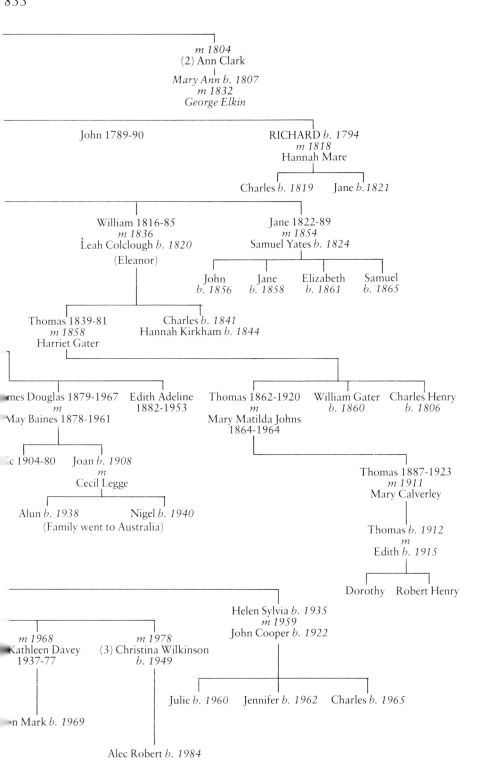

m 1804
(2) Ann Clark

Mary Ann b. 1807
m 1832
George Elkin

John 1789-90

RICHARD *b. 1794*
m 1818
Hannah Mare

Charles *b. 1819*   Jane *b.1821*

William 1816-85
m 1836
Leah Colclough *b. 1820*
(Eleanor)

Jane 1822-89
m 1854
Samuel Yates *b. 1824*

John
b. 1856

Jane
b. 1858

Elizabeth
b. 1861

Samuel
b. 1865

Thomas 1839-81
m 1858
Harriet Gater

Charles *b. 1841*
Hannah Kirkham *b. 1844*

mes Douglas 1879-1967
m
May Baines 1878-1961

Edith Adeline
1882-1953

Thomas 1862-1920
m
Mary Matilda Johns
1864-1964

William Gater
b. 1860

Charles Henry
b. 1806

c 1904-80

Joan *b. 1908*
m
Cecil Legge

Thomas 1887-1923
m 1911
Mary Calverley

Alun *b. 1938*   Nigel *b. 1940*
(Family went to Australia)

Thomas *b. 1912*
m
Edith *b. 1915*

Dorothy   Robert Henry

Helen Sylvia *b. 1935*
m 1959
John Cooper *b. 1922*

m 1968
Kathleen Davey
1937-77

m 1978
(3) Christina Wilkinson
b. 1949

Julie *b. 1960*   Jennifer *b. 1962*   Charles *b. 1965*

n Mark *b. 1969*

Alec Robert *b. 1984*

267

GLOSSARY

BACK STAMP	The factory's mark placed on the underside of the ceramic object.
BISCUIT (OR BISQUE)	Ware that has been once fired.
BLACK BASALT	A fine black stoneware body.
BODY	The ingredients from which pottery is made.
BOTTLE OVEN	The old type of intermittent kiln made up of a free standing bottle shaped structure inside which was the beehive shaped firing chamber. The ware was placed in saggars before being fired in it.
BRONZE-GREEN WARE	White stoneware bodies were glazed with a bronze-green coloured opaque glaze.
BRUSH GLAZING	The application of glaze by brush to the exterior of biscuit ware by hand.
CHIMNEY ORNAMENTS	Pottery and porcelain items made for display on the mantlepiece, often having a flat back.
DRAB	The name given by Dudsons to one of the range of colours in which they produced their stoneware.
EARTHENWARE	Pottery which is not vitrified, i.e. it is opaque and porous if not covered with glaze. It is fired below 1200°C.
EGG HOOPS	A double egg cup in which both the upper and lower parts are shaped to hold the egg. The cups are slightly different in size and can be used either way up.
ENAMELS	Ceramic colours derived from metallic oxides which are applied over the glaze. The ware is then refired at a low temperature.
ENGINE TURNING	Term often used to mean eccentric turning, i.e. turning in a horizontal plane to incise geometric, diced and fluted decorations in leather hard body.
FESTOON	A garland of inter-woven flowers or leaves designed to hang in a curve.

FLATBACK FIGURES	A pottery figure made for placing on mantlepieces. From the mid 19th Century they replaced the earlier figures which were modelled with greater detail in the round. As the back was flat, without modelling, they could be produced cheaply in large numbers.
FLUX	A substance added to the body and glazes to lower the fusion point during firing.
FRIT	Part of a glaze recipe which is melted and reground prior to inclusion in the glaze mixture. Fritting is executed to :—
	1) make soluble minerals insoluble.
	2) make harmless injurious substances (among other things).
IMITATIONS	It has so far proved impossible to identify these articles. They were made "large" and "small" and sold by the gross.
IMPRESSED	Indented into the soft clay (i.e. before firing) by means of a stamp. Many factory marks were impressed.
INCISED	Marks scratched by hand into the soft clay (i.e. before firing) with a sharp pointed instrument. See impressed and back stamp.
IRONSTONE CHINA	A stronger, more durable body than earthenware but cheaper than china. Usually colourfully painted.
JASPERWARE	A hard fine-grained stoneware body (barium) introduced by Josiah Wedgwood and perfected by 1774. Several Staffordshire manufacturers produced this type of product. During the 19th Century the term Jasper (or Jasperware) became widely used for a range of stonewares with contrasting hand applied relief decorations. There are two forms :
	a) solid Jasper in which the white body is stained throughout with metallic oxides to produce a number of different colours. Blue was most used.
	b) Jasper dip. A white body coloured on the surface only but later coloured bodies were surface coloured with a contrasting coloured slip.

LUSTRE	A technique of decoration in which the ware is given a thin metallic coating, either completely covering it or outlining parts of the design.
NEST EGGS	Small pottery replicas of bird's eggs made in pale brown and sage green which were used by game-keepers to encourage birds to lay.
PARIAN	An unglazed biscuit porcelain which resembles unpolished marble. It is usually white but later specimens are tinted.
PITCHER MOULD	An absorbent mould made of lightly fired clay from which the relief decorations (sprigs) were produced for applying to the surface of Jasperware.
PRESS MOULDING	The process of shaping ware by pressing damp clay into moulds. These moulds were made from an original hand modelled prototype. The ware was often made in several parts which were later joined with liquid clay slip.
REDICULE	(Sometimes spelt Ridicule). A basket shaped like a Victorian ladies reticule handbag.
SAGGAR	A rough clay vessel in which the ware was placed during firing in a bottle oven to protect it from smoke and flame.
SAVEALL	A contrivance for holding a candle end in the candlestick whilst it is burning so it can burn to the end.
SHARD OR SHERD	(Both spellings are used). Broken pieces of pottery uncovered during excavations.
SLIP	Potters ingredients mixed with water to a creamy state.
SMEAR GLAZING	A very thin application of glaze applied in the form of a vapour.
SPRIGS	Small decorative motifs formed in moulds for attaching to the surface of ware (sprigging).

STONE COVER	A lid made in the same stoneware body as the rest of the pot.
STONEWARE	A vitrified body that fires between 1200° — 1300°C. It is very hard and strong, opaque and non porous. Stoneware in this context refers to the basic white stoneware and not the buff coloured stoneware used for bottles, etc.
STRUCK GLAZE	A very thin application of glaze in the form of a vapour. This was achieved by placing fully glazed and unglazed pots in the same saggar.
TOYS	A 19th Century derivative of the 18th Century contemporary term image toys i.e. figures or chimney piece ornaments.
TRANSFER PRINTING	Applying a printed design to the surface of ware by means of transfer paper.
TURNING	Trimming or shaving the article to remove unwanted clay. See ENGINE TURNING. A method of finishing the ware which is done on a lathe. While being rotated the pot is brought into contact with tools of various kinds.

These give greater precision, remove imperfections or incise rings. Geometric decoration is done on an engine-turning lathe. |
| UNDERGLAZE | Decoration applied to the body of ceramic ware before glazing. |
| VITREOUS | Having glass-like characteristics. Firing stoneware bodies to a high temperature (1200°C upwards) results in partial vitrification which renders it impervious to liquids. It is therefore unnecessary to add a glaze unless for decorative reasons. |

The pieces of pottery shown in the three following plates were acquired when publication was practically complete. The information they contribute is too important to omit but it was too late to comment in the text.

Plate 86. Blue slip dipped on cream body covered mustard pot. "Figures." Incised. 147. Impressed 0.4." c. 1855.

Plate 87. Dark blue slip dipped jug, twisted branch handle. "Geraniums." Incised 542.
7¼". c. 1860.

Plate 88. Sage green solid body relief-moulded stoneware jug. Panelled with geometric motifs. Pattern name unknown. Impressed DUDSON. 7″. 1855-60.

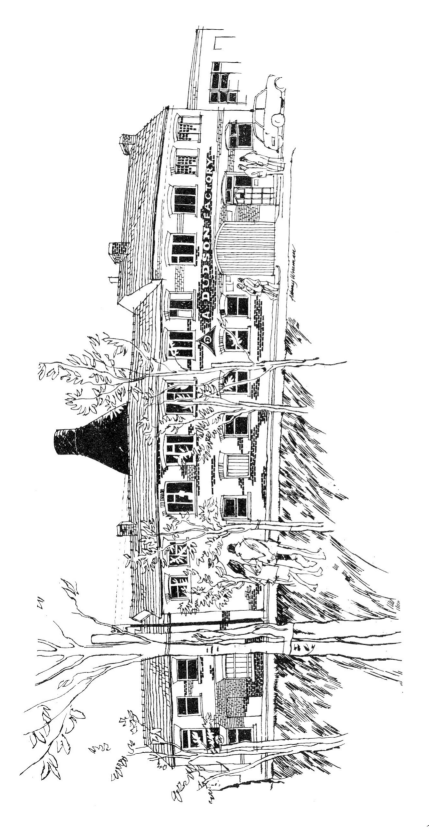

Plate 89. Pen and Ink drawing of the Hope Street factory. c.1975.

275

Plate 90. The J.E. Heath factory 1985

Plate 91. The Duraline factory 1985

INDEX

ADAMS, Boyce, 67
ADAMS, Thomas, 36
ADAMS, William, 31
Aerograph edge patterns, 157
Albert Pottery, Burslem, purchased, 151
Albion Bridge, 36
Argentina, agency established, 148
Army and Navy Store, as customer, 120
Alsager
   "Hope Villa", 67, 103
   James Eardley in, 95
   "Ivy House", 123
   "Northern Hey", 124
   "Osborne House", 124
Ashworths, 14
Australia, export to, 151, 152
Aynsley John, 72

Back Lane, 35, Pl.1, 62
Baddeleys, 10, 14
Baddeley, Edward, 5
BADDELEY, Hannah (later Mare) 12, 13, 14
BADDELEY, James, 36
BADDELEY, John, 5
BADDELEY, Ralph, 5
BADDELEY, Sarah, 9
Badged Ware
   jasper, 129
   mosaic, 130
   railways, 131
BAGNALL, Henry
   Works manager, 125, 142
   death of, 142
BAGNALL, James, 32
BAGNALL, Sampson, 32
Bailey, C.J., as customer 57, 72
BAILEY, Ernest, designer for
   Burgess and Leigh 141
BAILEY Philip managing director for
   Ridgways
   Derek trained under 150
Baines Colour Works, 135
BAINES, May (later Dudson), 135
Baltimore, export to, 45
Band and Line underglaze, 157
BEDSON, John, Master carpenter, 34, 102

Bennet & Co., as customer, 121
Bentley & Wear,
   transfer-printed ware for, 39, 40, 47, 54
Bibbough, John, 37
Birch Elijah, 72
Black basalt, 38, Pl.2
Bone china
   production of 49, 76-78
   body recipes, 76-78
Boston, export to, 45
Bottle oven, 34
   new drying, 102
Bradley-by-Stafford, 3
Brazil, agency established, 148
Brickkiln Field, 32
Britannic Works, Hanley, 135
British Standard,
   vitrified hotelware, for, 158
Broad Street, Shelton, 3, 7, 11
   factory closed, 11
   James at, 28
Broom Street, 62
BROUGH, James, 37
Brownhills Pottery Co. Ltd.
   liason with Dudson, 94
   as customer, 94
BUCKNALL, Robert, 30
Burgess & Leigh, 72, 141
BURGESS, Lizzie, 124
Burton Brothers, tailors, as customers, 81
BURTON, John and Sam,
   Burton/Keeling relationship, 8

Cafetaires,
   mosaic, 131
   design, 131
Canada, export to, 126, 151, 152
Caneware, 37
Cannon Street, 16, 17, 23
Captain's Lane, 16
Catering
   emphasis towards, 81
   exclusively vitrified stoneware 142 —
   jasperware, 143
   plain stoneware, 143
   bronze-green glaze, 143
   mosaic, 143

shapes, 144-148
Chamber of Commerce, 69
CHATTERLEY, Ephraim and Charles, 5
Cheddleton, Blakeley Lane farm, 103
China granite, 37
China opaque, 37
China tea services, 38
Clarence Street, 35, 62, 103
CLARK, Ann, 7
CLARKE, Richard, 102
CLOWES, William, 30, 32, 33
Coalport models for, 135
Cobridge School, James T. attends, 104
COLCLOUGH, Leah, later Dudson, 28
COLCLOUGH, Thomas, potter, 28

DANIEL, Alice, 32
DANIEL, John, 30, 32, 38
Davenport, W. & Co.,
    orders from 45, 72
    number of employees, 70
Defries & Sons, as customer, 121
Detergent proof glaze, adjustment to, 157
Dimmock & Co., as customer, 72, 121
DIMMOCK, Ann, 9
DIMMOCK, Hannah, 9
DIMMOCK, Hannah, (nee Keeling), 9
DIMMOCK, James, (born 1790), 9
DIMMOCK, James, (born 1823), 9
DIMMOCK, John, 9
DIMMOCK, Josiah, 9
DIMMOCK, Martha, 17
DIMMOCK, Mary, 9
DIMMOCK, Sarah, (later Keeling), 7
    Dudson/Keeling relationship 8
    Keeling/Dimmock relationship, 9
DIMMOCK, Sarah (born 1830), 9
DIMMOCK, Sarah, (nee Baddeley), 9
DIMMOCK, Thomas, (Snr.), 9
DIMMOCK, Thomas, (Jnr.), 9
DIMMOCK, Timothy, 9, 102
Dipped Ware, 37
    colours of, 53
Dogs, Staffordshire, 45
DUDSON
    potters family tree, opp. 1
    factory established 1800, 9-10
    as colour makers, 11, 15, 26, 28, 42,
        47-58, 71, 122

discovery of early factory documents, 24
early factory books, 37-44
as body makers, 47-58
articles produced, list of 1860-1880, 101
DUDSON, Ann, 4
DUDSON, Ann, (nee Clark), 7
DUDSON BROTHERS
    124 — ,
    Incorporated, 125
    production 1882-1917, 134
                1918-1939, 142-148
    as factor for others, 143
    purchased Albert Pottery, 151
    J.E. Heath formed, 151
    Grindley Hotelware Co. Ltd.
        purchased, 151
DUDSON, Charles, 8, 15, 26, 28, 68
    co. partner, 59
    marriages, 60
    as clerk and modeller, 60
    children, 60
    suicide, 60
DUDSON, Charles, (Richard's Son), 15
DUDSON, Charles Bruce,
    birth, 142
    joins company, 151
    joint managing director, 152
DUDSON, Constance, 104
DUDSON, Derek Hubert
    birth, 142
    joint managing director, 152
    death of, 159
DUDSON, Derek Max, works in group, 159
DUDSON, Edith, 109
DUDSON, Eliza, (nee Lees), 28, 60
DUDSON, Elizabeth, (died 1781), 4
DUDSON, Elizabeth, (nee Penny), 8, 26
DUDSON, Elizabeth, (nee Scrivener), 104
    works at factory, 109
DUDSON, Eric, 135
DUDSON, Evelyn, 104
Dudson Fine China, development of, 159
DUDSON, Florence, Irene, birth, 124
DUDSON, Hannah, (nee Mare), 13, 14, 16
DUDSON, Harry, 104, 109, 124, 125
DUDSON, Helen May, (nee Wilkes), 141
DUDSON, Helen Sylvia, birth, 142
DUDSON, Hubert Scrivener
    birth, 124

joins factory, 125, 141-152
director Ridgways, 142
resigns director Ridgways, 151
death of, 152
DUDSON, Ian James, joint
  managing director
working in group, 159
DUDSON, James, 10, 11, 26, 28, 62-103
Dudson/Keeling relationship, 8
co-partner, 59
purchases in Clarence St., 62
marriage, 62
takes over management, 68
number of employees, 70
exhibited, 70
death of, 95, 103
DUDSON, James Douglas, (Dudson,
  Wilcox, & Till), 109, 135-6
DUDSON, James Robert, 124-134
birth, 104
working at factory, 109
DUDSON, James Thomas, 10, 104-23
birth, 62
travelling, 76
takes over management, 95
out of retirement, 125
obituary, 123
DUDSON, Jane, 15, 103
DUDSON, Jane, (nee Keeling) 6, 7
Dudson/Keeling relationship, 8
DUDSON, Jane, (later King), 104
DUDSON Jane, (nee Spilsbury), 62, 103
DUDSON, Jane, (later Jane Yates), 8, 26
beneficiary under will, 60
DUDSON, Joan, (later Legge), 135-6
DUDSON, Joseph, 4
DUDSON, Leah, (nee Colclough), 28
DUDSON, Maria, (nee Williamson),
  67, 109
DUDSON, Mary Ann, 7
DUDSON, Mary, (nee Wardle), 60
DUDSON, May, 141-2
DUDSON, Rex, 124, 125, 142
DUDSON, Richard, 3-11
Dudson/Keeling relationship, 8
factory established 1800, 9-10
DUDSON, Richard (Jnr.), 7, 12-23
Dudson/Keeling relationship, 8
starts own business, 11

Dudson/Mare relationship, 12, 13
factory closed, 23
only marked pot, 23
Moved from Broad st., 28
DUDSON, Roy, 124, 125
DUDSON, Thomas, 6, 24-59
Dudson/Keeling relationship 8
as poet 25
will, 59
DUDSON, Thomas, (son of William), 28
beneficiary under will, 60
Dudson, Wilcox and Till, 109, 135-6
DUDSON, William, 8, 26, 59
as pottery printer, 28
DUDSON, William Henry
birth, 62
marriage, 67
recorded recipes, 71
inherits property, 103
death of, 109
Duraline Hotelware Co. Ltd.
change of name, 159
Dudson Fine China developed, 159

EARDLEY, Alfred, managed Brownhill's
  Pottery, 94
EARDLEY James
purchased Brownhill's pottery, 94
in Alsager, 95
Eastwood Mill, 36
Edge-sponging, oval, machine developed,
157
Edwards R. & Co., agreement with 148
Egyptian black, 37
ELKIN, George, 7 Ref. 9
Enamelling, 51, 85, 88, Pl.85
EVANS, William, Union leader and
  editor, 69-70
Exhibitions, James exhibited, 70

Figures & toys, Staffordshire, 23, 44, 56,
  71, 74-76
Flaxman moulds, 143
"Floral" and "Decorated", 132
FORSHAW, Guy, Rex partnership, 142
France, export to, 126
Furnival & Sons, as customer, 120

GARNER, George, 27
GERRARD, John of Hanley, order from, 46
Gilding, 88, 132, 133
GLASS, John, 6
Glassbrook, James, Birmingham,
    enamels from, 51
Gnosall, 3
Gold and gold colours, 53, 55
Great York Street, 31, 34, 35, 59, 60
Greece, export to, 152
Grindley Hotelware Co. Ltd.
    purchase of, 151
    expanded, 152
    vibro-energy mill, 157
    name changed to Duraline, 159

Hackwoods, milling by, 47
HACKWOOD, William, Jnr., 7
HAMILTON, Mr., cash from, 38, 43
Hammersley & Co. Ltd.
    Dudson as factor for, 143
Hanley Cemetry
    James buried, 103
    James T. buried, 123
Hanley Tabernacle, 18
Hanover Street, Lower, 29, 33, 34
Harrison W., as customer, 57
HAWTHORN, Thomas, 34
Heath, J.E. Ltd.
    formed, 151
    new Canadian market, 151
    expanded, 152
HEATH, J.E., London agent,
    Charterhouse St., 151
Henry Hall, metal mounter,
    bought part of New Hall factory, 72
Hicks & Meigh, 14
Hilditch and Hopwood
    order from, 46
HINDLE, Thomas, 34, 102
Holland, agency established, 148
HOLLINS, Catherine, 33
HOLLINS, Mary, (later Mare), 13
HOLLINS, Samuel, 5, 14, 30, 32, 33
HOLLINS, Sarah, (later Mare), 13
HOLLINS, Thomas, 14, 33, 62
Hollins, Warburton, Daniel & Co.,
    30, 32
    milling by, 47

Hollins, Warburton & Co., 10
Hope Street Works, 7, 11, 23
    factory 24 —
    production ceases, 159
Hope Street, 31, 59
HOPWOOD, William, 34

Incised numbers, 92-94
    in conjunction with B.P. Co., 94-95
India, export to, 132
Inskip, W. & R., builders, 102
Ireland, export to, 37, 45, 132, 152
Ironstone china, 78, 79
Italy, export to, 152

Jacobs & Co., Biscuit Mfrs. as customers, 81
Jasper dip
    phasing out of, 91
    re-introduced, 129
    badged, 129
    fully glazed, 146
Jasperware
    earliest records, 37, 55, 56
    sprigs as identification, 72, 73
    discovery of early sprig moulds, 74
    James Dudson jasperware, 91-97
    patterns, 95, 111-3
    new cheap, 111
    James T. Dudson jasperware, 111-113
    commemorative, 113
    1901-1920, 128-9
    drop in demand, 132
    for catering 143
    restarted after war, 150
    discontinued, 151
Jasperware manufacturers, 37
Johnson, Samuel, 59
Jug Inn, Bedford Row, 15

KEELING, Daniel
    Keeling/Dudson relationship, 8
KEELING, Enoch
    Keeling/Dudson relationship, 8
KEELING, Hannah, 9
KEELING, Isaac
    Keeling/Dudson relationship, 8
KEELING, James, 6, 7, 10, 16, 18
    Dudson/Keeling relationship, 8
    Keeling/Burton relationship, 8

Keeling/Dimmock relationship, 9
KEELING, Jane, 6
  Dudson/Keeling relationship, 8
KEELING, Martha, 18
KEELING, Moses, 16
KEELING, Ralph, 16
KEELING, Robert, 6, 7
  Dudson/Keeling relationship, 8
KEELING, Samuel, 6, 35, 36
  Dudson/Keeling relationship, 8
Keeling, Samuel & Co.,
  as customer, 46, 57
KEELING, Samuel the elder,
  Dudson/Keeling relationship, 8
KEELING, Sarah (nee Dimmock), 7, 23
  Dudson/Keeling relationship, 8
KEELING, Thomas
  Dudson/Keeling relationship, 8
  timber merchant, 9
  executor of Dudson will, 8, 59
  sells Bedson land, 102
KEELING Thomas father of Philip, 9
Keeling, Thomas, potter, as customer, 57
KEELING, Thomas, Samuel's grandson,
  Keeling/Dudson relationship, 8
KEELING TOFT Co., 7
Kilns, gas-fired intermittent, 157
KING, Henry Buckley, flour miller, 104

Lancaster, Duchy of, 18
LEES, Eliza, 28, 60
LEGGE, Isaac, 34
Limitation of Supply Act, 148
Litherland W., 72
Lithography underglaze, 157
Longsdon, Nr. Leek, 135
Lustre, 26, 85
Lyons, Joseph & Co. Kensington
  mosaic made for 119, 120, 130, 142

Maddock & Sons, as customer, 120
Majolica, 119
Malkin, C., as customer, 57
Malkin, E., as customer, 57
Maple & Co., as customer, 120
MARE, Daniel, 13
MARE, Hannah, (later Dudson), 11, 13
MARE, John, (born 1769),
  Mare/Dudson relationship, 13

bankrupt 1826, 14
MARE, John, (born 1745)
  Dudson/Mare relationship, 13
  factory, 10
MARE, Mary, (nee Hollins), 13
MARE, Mary (later Wilson), 13
MARE, Matthew, 13, 14, 15
MARE, Nancy, 13
MARE, Sarah, 13
MAYER, Elijah (born 1749), 13
  factory, 10
MAYER, Jane, (nee Mare), 13
MAYER, Joseph, 13, 62
Mayer & Keeling, Charles St.,
  Commission agents, 16
Mayer, Thomas
  as customer, 57
  number of employees, 70
Mayer & Son, 72
Meakin, J. & G., as customer, 121
Mecca Ltd., as customer, 120
MEIGH, Charles
  cash from, 38
  bought bone ash, 54
MELLOR, Samuel J. tutor, 104
Metal lids, 72, 90, 120
Midwinter, models for, 135
Mill field, the, 26, 27, 32
Mill Street, 27
Mintons
  as customer, 120
  railway ware for, 131
  models for, 135
MINTON, Mr., cash from 38, 43
Montague, S., tailors, as customers, 81
Morten, as customer, 57
Mosaicware
  technique, 97
  production, 98, 110, 119
  registered designs, 131
  badged, 130, 131
McFarlane, J. & A. as customer, 120

Nantgarw, china body recipe, 77
Necks, coloured, 120
  mosaic with, 131
New Hall Street, 30
New Hall Porcelain Co., 5, 30, 32, 34, 38
  indenture for new road, 31

sale of, 33
  Dudson production for, 38, 39, 40, 48
  Dudson purchases land from, 62
NEWLAND-Rev. R.W., 18, 23
Newton M.J., as customer, 121
New Zealand, agency established, 148
Norfolk Street Works, 62
Norton-le-Moors Parish Church, 6
North Staffs Technical College
  Derek trained at, 150
  Bruce trained at, 151
Norwood, ? retailer, 73

OUTRIM, William, 34, 102

PALMER, Humphrey, 5, 30
PALMER, Mary, 30
PALMER, Thomas, 5
Paraguay, agency established, 148
Parian, 85, 119
Parish registers
  early potteries, 3
  St. John's church Hanley, 6
  Norton-le-Moors, 6
Patent lock lid/cover
  interior marks, 95, 120
Paxton, retailer 73, Pl. 7
Pearlware, 37
PENNY, Charles, 26
Podmore & Sons, vibro-energy mill, 157
POINTON, William, 26, 32
Potters Union, 68-70
Pottery Trade Concentration Scheme, 148
POULSON, Edward, 43
POULSON, Joseph, 43
Powell & Bishop, 72
Pressed Ware, 128
Pure Coffee Co., as customer, 120
Purple of Cassius, 53

Railway companies
  badged ware, 131
  glazed jasperware for L.N.E.R., 146
  Southern Rhodesian, 148
RANDLES, Messrs, 37
  Registered designs, 86
Ridgways
  as customer, 10, 57, 72, 121
  number of employees, 70

jugs made for, 73
  Globe Pottery Co., agreement with, 142
  Dudson as factor for, 143
  sold to Lawleys, 150
  Hubert resigns directorship, 151
  similar shapes produced, 151
RIGBY, Elaine, Alsager, 124
Rivers, William & Co., 16
Rockingham glazes, 54
Royal Doulton, railway ware for, 131
RUSSELL, Elizabeth, 33

St. John's Church, Hanley, 6
Salisbury Crown China Co.
  Dudson as factor for, 143
Saracen's Head, 102
Sargeant, W.G., as customer, 57
Sand setter rings, 157
Scurvy, cure for, 56
SCRIVENER, Elizabeth, (later Dudson), 62,
  104
SCRIVENER, Sarah, (later Adams), 67
SCRIVENER, Robert, Architect, 62
  modernising works, 102
SCRIVENER, Robert George, potter, 62, 67
Seighford, 3
Shelton New Hall, 30
Shelton Old Hall, 30
Shippers, Liverpool, 37
SHIRLEY, John, 36
Shorter T., as customer, 121
Shorter, as customer, 72, 121
Silver, 55
Simpson, N., as customer, 57
Smear glaze, for coloured bodies, 53
Smith, James, as customer, 121
Soloman, Henry & Co., London, 45
South Africa, agency established, 148
SPILSBURY, Jane (later Dudson), 62
STEEL, S., 43
Staffordshire
  animals, 45
  figures, 23, 44, 71
STEPHENSON, James, 31
Stokes, Mr., London, 45
Stoneware bodies
  coloured 47, 132
  recipes for 55, 79
  firing, 79

gilded, 132
Stoneware, relief-moulded
  early master models, 74
  articles produced in, 87
  enamelled, 88
  registrations, 86
  market and designs, 126
Stubbs, William, as customer, 57
Sweden, export to, 152
Switzerland, export to, 126, 152

Taylor, Elijah, as customer, 57
Taylor, George, 14
Taylor, John, as customer, 121
Transfer printing, pink underglaze, 54
Turner, M. & Co., as customer, 57
Turton, as customer, 57
Twyford, Thomas, 72

United States of America
  export to, 126, 132
  agency established, 148
  special backstamp for, 150
Uraguay, agency established, 148

Victor Harber, Nr. Adelaide, Australia, 18

Wades, models for, 135
WARBURTON, Peter, 30
Wardle, James, as customer, 57

WARDLE, Mary of Leek, (later Dudson), 60
Wars, World
  First, effect of, 132
  Second, effect of, 148-9
Walley, J., as customer, 57
Wayte's boats, Worcester, 41
WEDGWOOD, Josiah, 5
Wheatsheaf Street, 15, 17
  Richard moves to, 28
Whispering Tubes Employee, 70
Wildblood, Heath & Sons Ltd.
  Dudson as factor for, 143
WILKES, Charles, modeller for Burgess &
  Leigh, 141
WILKES, Frank, Works manager/director,
  142
WILKES, Helen May, (later Dudson), 141
WILLIAMS, Hugh Henshall, 32
Williamson, as customer, 57
WILLIAMSON, Maria, (later Dudson), 67,
  109
WILSON, Robert, 13
Woolworths, as customer, 135
Worthington & Green, as customer, 57
Wright, as customer, 57

YATES, John, 5
York Tavern, the, 60

Zachary, the, 15

NOTES

NOTES

NOTES

NOTES

NOTES

NOTES